ALL ABOUT
TECHNICAL
ANALYSIS

ALL ABOUT TECHNICAL ANALYSIS

The Easy Way to Get Started

CONSTANCE BROWN

McGraw-Hill

New York   Chicago   San Francisco   Lisbon   London
Madrid   Mexico City   Milan   New Delhi   San Juan
Seoul   Singapore   Sydney   Toronto

4 5 6 7 8 9 0   FGR/FGR   0 9 8 7 6 5

ISBN 0-07-138511-8

All trademarked products mentioned in this book are used in an editorial fashion only, and to the benefit of the trademark owner, with no intention of infringement of the trademark. Where such designations appear in this book, they have been printed with initial caps.

McGraw-Hill books are available at special quantity discounts to use as premiums and sales promotions, or for use in corporate training programs. For more information, please write to the Director of Special Sales, Professional Publishing, McGraw-Hill, Two Penn Plaza, New York, NY 10121-2298. Or contact your local bookstore.

This publication is designed to provide accurate and authoritative information in regard to the subject matter covered. It is sold with the understanding that the publisher is not engaged in rendering legal, accounting, or other professional service. If legal advice or other expert assistance is required, the services of a competent professional person should be sought.

> —*From a declaration of principles jointly adopted by a committee of the American Bar Association and a committee of publishers.*

This book is printed on recycled, acid-free paper containing a minimum of 50% recycled de-inked paper.

Library of Congress Cataloging-in-Publication Data

Brown, Constance M.
   All about technical analysis : the easy way to get started / by Constance Brown.
     p. cm.
   ISBN 0-07-138511-8 (pbk. : alk. paper)
   1. Investment analysis. 2. Stock price forecasting. I. Title.
HG4529 .B76 2002
332.63'2042—dc21

                                  2002011404

*May you reach
the destination of your dreams
so that
they may fill the void of a
dream lost September 11.*

*Then
teach someone new
how to dream.*

CONTENTS

PART SIX

WHY DOES TECHNICAL ANALYSIS WORK?

Chapter 20

What Do Seashells, Hurricanes, and the Dow Jones Industrial Average All Have in Common?   254

Chapter 21

A Universal Higher Order and How All Things Are Indeed Connected   266

PART SEVEN

MARKET CYCLES AND LONG-TERM CYCLES OF IMPORTANCE

Chapter 22

Market Cycles and Long-Term Cycles of Importance   279

PART EIGHT

PUTTING IT ALL TOGETHER WITH RISK EXPOSURE IN MIND

Chapter 23

A Broker Has Just Recommended that You Buy a Stock. What Do You Do Next?   290

Chapter 24

The 27 Million Dollar Lunch   297

Appendix A

The Growth of Technical Analysis in Universities and Colleges   301

DISCLAIMER

It should not be assumed that the methods, techniques, or indicators presented in this book will be profitable or that they will not result in losses. Past results are not necessarily indicative of future results. Examples in this book are for educational purposes only. This is not a solicitation of any order to buy or sell.

The NFA requires us to state that, "HYPOTHETICAL OR SIMULATED PERFORMANCE RESULTS HAVE CERTAIN INHERENT LIMITATIONS. UNLIKE AN ACTUAL PERFORMANCE RECORD, SIMULATED RESULTS DO NOT REPRESENT ACTUAL TRADING. ALSO, SINCE THE TRADES HAVE NOT ACTUALLY BEEN EXECUTED, THE RESULTS MAY HAVE UNDER- OR OVERCOMPENSATED FOR THE IMPACT, IF ANY, OF CERTAIN MARKET FACTORS, SUCH AS LACK OF LIQUIDITY. SIMULATED TRADING PROGRAMS IN GENERAL ARE ALSO SUBJECT TO THE FACT THAT THEY ARE DESIGNED WITH THE BENEFIT OF HINDSIGHT. NO REPRESENTATION IS BEING MADE THAT ANY ACCOUNT WILL OR IS LIKELY TO ACHIEVE PROFITS OR LOSSES SIMILAR TO THOSE SHOWN."

ALL ABOUT TECHNICAL ANALYSIS

What Is Technical Analysis, and Who Can Benefit?

CHAPTER 1

Could Charts Have Called the Enron Collapse?

This is the book I wish I had had when everything about technical analysis was new to me. It is an introduction to how technical analysis is actually used; it gives descriptions of how markets work together around the world, without a bunch of confusing formulas and examples that are difficult to relate to when you are just getting started. It is different from most books about technical analysis. Why? It is a survival book with a focus on the reality of risk to your own personal dollars—not the risk to the millions of dollars that get moved in and out of a professional's account every day, but your own dollars.

What you may lack in market wisdom you must make up for immediately with solid risk management skills. That is the only way you can buy the time you need in order to learn. Introductory books on technical analysis are rarely written by traders. Trading or investing is entirely different from market analysis and making forecasts. Incorrect analysis may result in the loss of a client. Incorrect analysis that leads you to risk your own money hits your bank account. Most books on technical analysis give you the tools to begin market analysis without any consideration or discussion of drawdown or risk exposure. That is not the real world, and that is precisely why this book is very different.

"What is drawdown?" you may ask. That is the most important question in this book. No, I am not being flippant. There is no question of greater importance. If you paid $150 in 1999 for Microsoft (MSFT) with the intention of buying and holding for the "long term," you may eventually be right. But your drawdown was considerable, as the stock fell to $40 after your purchase. The stock swing would have reduced the value of your brokerage account substantially, along with your net worth. The capital erosion *before* you eventually get it right over "the long haul" is your *drawdown*. In fact, a drawdown does not mean a drop to less than your original investment. If you have a big gain, and the investment begins to decline, you are *not* giving back the "house's money." It was your money, and the drawdown begins as soon as the account begins to drop.

If you bought MSFT on margin with borrowed funds from your brokerage firm, the drawdown loss would have accelerated. As soon as the lending firm has risk it wants to transfer that risk back to you as fast as possible. So you would have come face-to-face with a *margin call*, an ugly notice demanding the immediate deposit of additional funds; the message is: "We don't care how you get it; just give us more cash or we liquidate you."

Should you meet their demands and deposit new capital into your account, you may think, if you're like most private investors, that you are wisely dollar-cost-averaging down. This is a slick little phrase to make you add more money to a current loss. When you buy at a lower price than your first purchase, your average price for the total shares you own becomes lower. However, you own more shares and have compounded your risk exposure. Professionals call this adding to a losing position, and it is one of the worse sins a novice trader can commit. So is it a sin for the rookie professional but a good idea for the private investor? I don't think so. What if you are contributing monthly to a fund? You would be better off contributing to your savings account and studying the correct time to move the cash into your fund. Market timing is everything.

Everything you do must take into consideration the drawdown exposure, or what we call risk exposure. Did you ever see drawdown listed in the prospectus or offering documents of an investment? No, you haven't, except for futures funds. The industry is governed by the Securities and Exchange Commission (SEC), the Commodities Futures Trading Commission (CFTC), and the National Futures Association (NFA). Professionals are licensed and regulated by one or all of these regulatory boards. Year-end returns are reported as a percentage, and stock investment funds are not required to disclose drawdown.

In 2001 there were futures funds with valuation swings greater than -70 percent. This means that at some point within a given month an investor's original investment had lost 70 percent of its value. But if the fund manager bet big during the last few days of that month and closed the month +0.41 percent, you would never know that the fund had had such a wild swing. People rarely think to ask the question, "What has been your maximum drawdown?" We are always asked for performance numbers. If you ask for performance numbers with a daily time horizon, you'll grow old before the data arrives in your mailbox. The question that you should ask once you have determined the maximum drawdown is, "And then how long did it take to recoup?" The speed at which recovery from a drawdown occurs is an important consideration. Less time is generally viewed as better.

I referred to futures a moment ago. I know that most people reading this book will have their expertise in other industries. It is common for people not to know what the futures markets are about. If I say, "Ever hear of those markets in Chicago for wheat, corn, and cattle?" that usually gets a nod of distant recognition. This may be news to you: Stocks are about to have futures markets. I don't mean options. Exchanges in Chicago and the Nasdaq in New York will soon launch Single Stock Futures, making futures available for individual stocks like MSFT. Volatility is likely to increase.

Now let's go back to the MSFT scenario. Consider an investor who bought MSFT at $150, knowing that if the stock fell below $120, she had been wrong. (We will go over ways to determine these levels.) When MSFT fell through $120, the investor took action and sold, executing the game plan she had devised when she first bought the stock: She sold. When the stock fell to $40 and everyone around her was in a total panic, believing that the end of the world was near, she decided to come out of her shell and buy MSFT again with the money she had received from the sale at $120. (This style of buying during extreme general public panics is what the Rockefellers and Kennedys were known for doing.) Now the investor owns three times as much stock at $40 as she used to have at $120. That's what we call *leverage*. (There has to be a specific technical reason why that price level was the one at which to buy. Hearing it as a tip on television is not a reason!)

Now this savvy investor decides she will be wrong once again if Microsoft falls below $30. She holds three times as much stock as she did at $150, but she has the same risk exposure as when the stock fell from $150 to $120. Since she believes that MSFT will not fall below $30 and will in fact return to $150, she has a potential loss of $30 (a drop from $40 to $30 is a $10 loss times three times as much stock) and a potential gain of $110 times three. We then turn that into a ratio: $330 to $30. That's a win/loss ratio of 11 to 1. For every dollar the investor is willing to risk, she now has the potential of making 11 dollars in return with this scenario. The buy-and-hold investor, if he is lucky, will get his money back. Personally I look for trades or investments that have a minimum win/loss ratio of 3 to 1. It is the only way I know of to survive the periods of drought that everyone eventually experiences.

If you had a buy-and-hold strategy, while MSFT was nosediving toward $40, your account statements would describe this rapid capital depreciation as *an unrealized loss*. True, as long as you own the stock, it has the potential to climb out of this nasty hole. Your original investment is recovered when MSFT crawls back to $150. But your brokerage statement does not show a line for *opportunity loss* while your funds were trapped in the swing downward, not earning interest, and held hostage until they return to their original value. The fact that your brokerage account went down the tubes during the bear market means that you cannot buy additional stocks when the opportunity presents itself near a bottom. But you may ask, "How can anyone know when a market is near a bottom?" We will go over that problem as well within this book. You have to know where a stock or market should not be trading as well as where the market will go when you are right *so you can exit*.

Technical analysis without regard to drawdown and leverage is just another forecast. Ultimately the forecast could be right, but if the timing is wrong, you won't care. It's kind of like rain on your wedding day.

Anyone who has been a professional trader on the Street for more than 12 years is viewed by most professionals as one of the "old dogs." I don't consider myself old, but to survive long enough to become one of the old dogs, you have to learn a bunch along the way.

You may be a fundamentalist who has become interested in charting after a rough period filled with deceptive earnings reports or who has found that fundamentals cannot keep up with market volatility. You may be an investor who has found that your broker cannot protect you from the ravages of a true bear market. You may be a trader who needs tools to increase market probability and timing. Whatever your reason, it is clear that you have decided to take a more active role. In a sense, you have come to a critical fork in the road. Turn right and keep diving into technical analysis. In hindsight you will be very glad you made this decision.

I generally have breakfast in a small diner near the beach. Our community is a resort area and golfing Mecca, with visitors outnumbering locals much of the year. People from all corners of the world pull up to the counter of this diner to have breakfast. You literally rub elbows with the guy beside you, so it is no surprise that a few conversations erupt between total strangers. I rarely say anything to a stranger, but I have found myself engrossed in conversation with European exporters interested in international currency trends, with a Japanese banker on vacation whose homeland is teetering on the brink of a 1930s style depression, or with local business owners who are struggling to construct a business plan with interest rates at historic lows, but knowing their home construction business will surely stagnate when interest rates begin to climb again and kill real estate prices. While these people's levels of expertise and points of views vary, there is a common question being asked by all: "How can an individual keep up with today's volatile market environment?"

We are going to stay with real-world scenarios instead of covering lots of hypothetical situations. For example, consider Enron. A lot of people were hurt when Enron Corporation imploded. The Wall Street analysts who were called before the Senate committee read carefully prepared statements about how the corporate disclosure documents prepared by Arthur Andersen gave them a bum steer. The truth is that they were all analysts who relied on fundamentals. I found it interesting that the Senate did not ask to have any analysts who utilized technicals called on the carpet. We knew there was a problem with Enron. We didn't know the magnitude of the problem. But it was clear that you would not want anyone to have their lifelong earnings in that stock. The stock at its highs was due for a 50 percent retracement. This means that the value of the stock was due to retrace at least half of the entire gain it had accumulated since the inception of the rally.

Here is your first technical chart. We call this way of displaying stock prices a bar chart. Each vertical bar represents the range
within which prices have traded during a given period of time. In
Figure 1-1 the period of time is a month. Each new month begins a
new vertical bar. At some point during the month, the stock traded
at the price high at the top of the bar, and the bottom of the bar was
the price low for that month. Each bar in a bar chart can represent
minutes or years. We will go over how to create these charts in Part
2. What you want to observe now is the historic price highs in this
chart top directly under the 45° line running through the chart.
That line is resistance on the scale of the Great Wall of China. In
longer-horizon charts, like this monthly chart, prices hitting a 45°
line of resistance will produce a reaction down. When additional
technical indicators are added later, you will see that the stock was
ready to head south within a period of weeks after this line of resistance was touched. Where is there support in this monthly time
horizon? At the next line under the price high. That is, there is a little more than a 50 percent retracement to the next area of major
support. This chart does not give any warning that the major support area after a 50 percent retracement will be broken, but if the
support area were broken, you would know that something very
serious was amiss. You wouldn't want to be there. The whys always
come after the event.

Here is another example. It will also introduce you to your
first "squiggles" that can be added to any market's price data.

I trade for a living. But part of my discipline to ensure that I
do my homework each night is to write a report for other professionals. A portion of the March 3, 2002, evening report is shown in
Figure 1-2.

A countertrend rally means that the market is about to move
in a direction opposite to that in which it has been moving in the
bigger picture. If you have an investment or trade in place, what
we call a position, you are probably tracking the bigger-picture
direction of the market. A countertrend move is therefore detri-
mental to the majority of people holding positions in the market.

The target offered in the report shown in Figure 1-2 was 7845,
and the report would be read miles away from where the $/Yen
was trading at the time the report was put online. The report was
online Sunday, and Monday generated a news report from
Bloomberg.com with the headline displayed in Figure 1-3.

F i g u r e   1-1

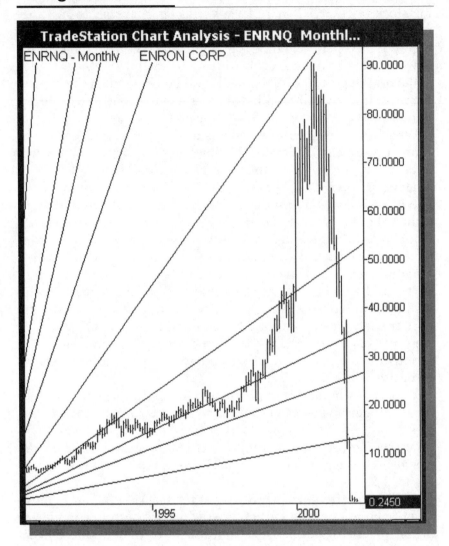

By Tuesday the currency world was getting really excited, and Bloomberg.com reported the events in the manner shown in Figure 1-4.

All this news hype and excitement is about the price move seen in the last two bars of the daily chart displayed in Figure 1-5. It means that *billions* have changed hands rapidly. In addition, take a look at the daily chart and determine the current trading price

F i g u r e   1-2

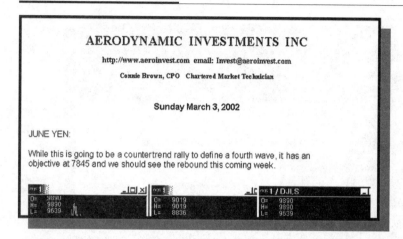

F i g u r e   1-3

at the time the screen capture was made. The market level is in reverse white text in a black box on the right-hand side of the chart. The report had given 7845 as the target, and the chart shows that a couple of days later the market was trading at 7848. Such a move had not been seen in 9 months.

So which came first, the fundamentals or the technicals? The truth is, the yen was ripe for a move for *any* fundamental reason. We don't care what reason finally surfaced. However, there comes a point in time when a few reasons "why" will increase your comfort

F i g u r e   1-4

level, and we will discuss this at a much later time when we start looking at specific situations.

The chart in Figure 1-5 is a daily chart, and clearly the data is predominantly heading in a southerly direction. The decline means that the yen is falling and the U.S. dollar is strengthening because this is really an exchange rate. One currency's loss is always another currency's gain.

When you see a chart with the label JY or EU, it is reflecting the trading prices of futures for the Japanese Yen or the new European Currency that replaced the German Mark futures contract. Futures are contracts to receive or deliver a predetermined amount of a commodity, in this case foreign currency, on a specific day in a given year (in the case of foreign currency, there are four such days). You can buy or sell your "future" intention to receive or deliver the foreign currency. Futures have delivery dates, a date when you must arrange a huge cash wire to meet your end of the contract. Most people do not want any part of that mess, as they are just speculating. When you trade these instruments, you ante up only about 9 percent of the instrument's total value. If you really had to meet your obligation on the delivery date, you would have to be a bank, corporation, or subtantial network investor.

Figure 1-5

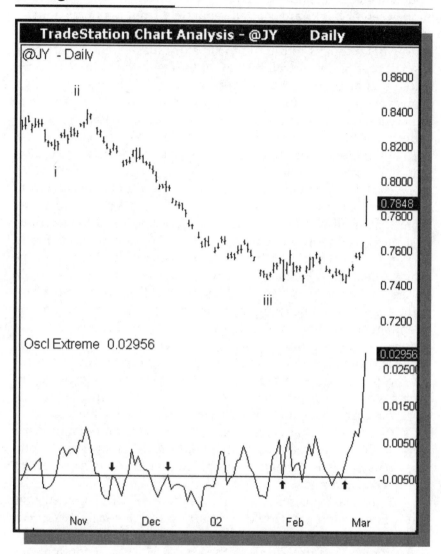

If you go to a commercial bank to exchange the U.S. dollars in your pocket for foreign currency, you are really selling dollars and buying foreign currency. The foreign currency transactions conducted around the globe through huge wire transfers constitute the largest financial markets in the world. If a bank can conduct a cash transaction, it is known as a money center bank. This is something you will need to know when we look at stock sectors because money center banks are charted separately from regional banks.

Currency trading is the largest market in the world, and it dictates what happens to the American stock market. Stocks are only a small part of the overall scheme of things in the financial world. Thus a change in direction for the yen is always big news. However, if I give an analogy now, it will help. Most private American investors and their brokers (known in the financial community as the retail market) think the New York markets are the core of the global financial apple. This is a very serious misunderstanding within the retail market.

At 5:03 P.M. on October 17, 1989, the third game of the World Series was about to begin in the San Francisco Bay area. As Americans pulled up their chairs with beers in hand to watch the first pitch, suddenly the game ended before it ever began. Earthquake! As the world watched, the focus suddenly changed to the major 7.1 earthquake shaking the field and stadium. Like the World Series, the stock market is a big event. But the currency markets form a silent fault line running under the stock market. They are an even bigger influence than interest rates. When the currency markets rumble, suddenly everything else seems to have a different focus and urgency. Retail investors and their brokers mostly focus on the players who make it to the World Series. However, the world is becoming too small for the retail sector to remain ignorant of global cash flows and how markets interact with one another.

You are probably beginning to sense that I am not a broker. I am not. But I will help you understand the different types of professionals in the financial industry at another time. Let's move back to my yen example.

If my chart was reflecting the cash market for yen rather than the futures market, it would be charting the *spot market*. You can think of that as the price demanded on the spot. But transactions actually take a couple of days to clear. A U.S. chart for spot Yen would be written $/Yen because we put our currency first. If you were in Europe or Japan, the chart would be inverted so that it would be read Yen/$ because the other currency comes first, which can be confusing.

In Figure 1-5 we see that prices are declining throughout most of the period covered by the chart. This means that more people have been selling Japanese Yen and buying U.S. Dollars. All the news and excitement is about the fact that the yen has begun to strengthen. That means that people have begun to *buy* yen and *sell* dollars. Should this continue, it would start a long chain of events that would have a direct impact on your wallet. For example, that home theater system from Sony that you wanted to buy just went up in price, as you will have to fork over more U.S. dollars to get it. In these 2 days you lost a little buying power. On an imaginary financial Richter scale, the 2-day move in the yen described by Bloomberg would not even register except as a deep and silent rumble.

OK, so how did I know that the yen would begin to strengthen when it did? This gives us the opportunity to look at our first technical indicator.

Let me begin by explaining how to look at an indicator that has been added below market prices. The chart in Figure 1-5 also includes the simplest of the oscillators you will meet. How to create it will be discussed later. When the market goes up, the oscillator goes up; when the market is falling, so is this indicator. If prices are not tracking the oscillator, this also tells us something about the market. But the first step is to learn how to study a chart and how to really see what is in it. This skill is not programmable into some automatic search-and-find black box system that will do all the work for you.

In Figure 1-5 I have drawn a horizontal line through the oscillator. This particular oscillator is free to travel to any extreme it can. It is able to swing in either direction. The reason I drew a line through the oscillator at this particular level is that the market itself respected this level. These are not big signals. If you follow the horizontal line slowly, you will find two upward-pointing arrows as your eye moves from *right to left*. Keep going. Along the same line you will find two more arrows that point down. The market had sharp reversals when the oscillator failed at the same level. That's important. There is not a market, a stock, or a chart for which I do not first want to ask, "OK, so how does this particular market want to work with this indicator?" No two markets are alike. If you are taught to always look for a specific pattern, it will be the only pattern you will ever see. Sometimes a market likes to make "W" patterns on one of these horizontal lines before it reverses, and sometimes you will see a single sharp V defining a bottom. Let the market tell you how to read its own chart.

We are still referring to the horizontal line running across the oscillator that I added. When the recent data touched this line a second time, it was time to look at a chart with a longer time horizon. Figure 1-5 is a daily chart, so I then study weekly and monthly charts. A monthly chart showed that the same indicator was touching its extreme low where a major bottom had formed in the past; this chart is shown in Figure 1-6. Again move from right to left and you will find that the current price rebound has the oscillator on the same level that produced a rebound in 1998. As you move toward the left, you will see other reactions to the same horizontal level as well. In essence, all I have done is draw a horizontal line connecting the dots. The dots are the pivot points at the oscillator turns.

Both the daily and monthly chart indicators were in sync, so the odds were pretty good that a reaction would occur. The price objective method that I used will be detailed in this book. I didn't know the fundamental reason why, days before the move occurred. There wasn't time to do the research. In fact, there is never enough time to collect and sift through all the raw fundamental data. Markets move too quickly. There is one other small problem: The raw fundamental data would be in Japanese.

That was a lot for a start, so I'd better begin to backtrack more slowly. We will come back to this when you learn how to make and read your own charts.

F i g u r e   1-6

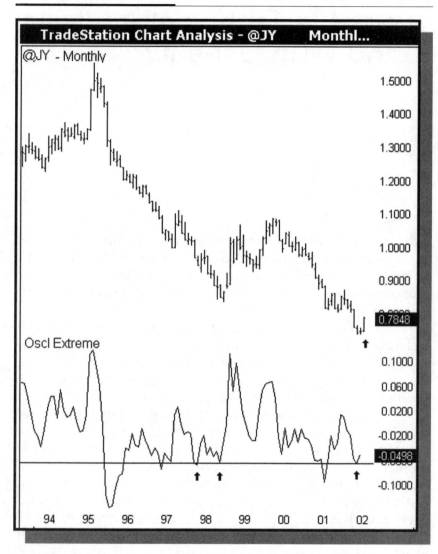

CHAPTER 2

What Is Technical Analysis, and Who Uses It?

One does not have to look back more than 10 years to find a time when technical analysis was looked at as being like reading tea leaves to generate market opinions. The perception has changed dramatically over those 10 years. I'll give the reasons why in a few moments.

One recent story told in the newsletter for the Market Technicians Association (our industry's governing board for professional conduct and accreditation in the United States, www.mta.org) involves a technical analyst who saw the portfolio managers in his firm quietly disappear one by one.

The portfolio manager is one of the types of financial professionals whose function is least understood by the general public. Before I can continue, it is important to clarify what some of the key positions in our industry are. Not everyone is a broker or an investment banker. If you invest in a mutual fund, the fund is made up of a number of stocks that collectively are known as the portfolio. Every fund has a single person who is ultimately responsible for what goes into the portfolio and how much is going to be bought or sold and when. That person is called the portfolio manager or fund manager. Brokers aggressively go after the business created by portfolio managers, as they want some of the commissions that are generated when the fund buys and sells to adjust the large positions within the portfolio.

But there are many different kinds of brokers. There are pit and floor brokers, retail and institutional brokers, to name a few. A retail broker, the type that you may be most familiar with, does not conduct business with fund managers. Funds work with institutional brokers, who shop around—*rapidly*—to find the best *offering* price from among numerous offering firms. They directly "work" the order that is given to them. Because of the size of these orders, working them requires special skills. Institutional brokers do not give their clients market opinions unless the client expressly asks for them or the trader requests news on specific stocks. Institutional brokers do not make decisions on what should be bought or sold or when.

Fund managers who use technical analysis as the basis for their decision criteria use charts primarily. This school of thought assumes that everything you need to know is already factored into the market price. Therefore, portfolio managers who use technical analysis do not want to hear day-to-day news from a broker. The broker earns their business by being exceptionally good at working the orders given to him or her. If the final order fill price is different from the price level when you placed the order, that difference is called slippage. Slippage is many times more costly than commissions. Therefore, the need for speed is paramount.

The retail market has slippage because of the number of steps involved. Retail brokers take smaller investors' orders and pass them on to an order entry department, which is responsible for bundling individual orders from several retail brokers' clients; the entire bundle will then be filled, or executed, at one time. The order entry department then passes the bundle on to the firm's floor broker, who actually does the trading on behalf of the individuals. The floor broker reports back to the order entry department the final transaction price for the bundle. The bundle will contain split fills as the transaction likely did not occur at one price. The bundle must then be unbundled by the order entry department. Split fills are assigned based on the time stamp of the order, which in turn is passed back to your broker, who ultimately reports back to you. Orders coming into a retail brokerage firm are executed at the best price the firm can offer. Other firms are not involved if your firm can help it. (As soon as you need to add someone else to fill your order, you have to pay for the extra service. That fee is called a "give-up" transaction fee.)

The institutional market has slippage because of liquidity issues. It takes time to work a large order to buy or sell in an effort not to move the market itself with the transaction. Plus, large orders have to enter the market quietly and with some strategy involved so the buyer or seller can retain some anonymity. The common bond between both the retail and the institutional client is the impossible wish to have an order filled 5 minutes before the order was entered! You can see that the activities and services performed by institutional brokers are very different from those performed by the retail brokers whom the general public must contact for their business.

The opposite of a liquid stock is a thin stock. One day I entered an order to buy 15,000 shares of a software stock. The only problem was that I was the market for the first 7 minutes after the stock opened the new trading day. That's a very small order, so the total number of shares traded each day was incredibly thin. Volume is a technical variable that we will examine closely. Liquidity and volume must both be considered when you trade stocks or futures. Changes in these variables can tell you something about the market direction and timing. These are elements that a fundamentalist would have no interest in knowing.

What about orders that a retail trader may enter directly into his computer? You still have an order desk involved. Just try to short something that cannot be found and you will get a personal phone call. (I'll explain short selling at another time.) But orders that are considered business as usual can be filled electronically. I could write a book just on the mechanics of electronic order filling and the differences between the retail and institutional markets, so I won't go down that road.

Retail brokers may elect to change over to the institutional side of the house in order to become more intimately involved in the process of working or executing orders. As you can see, the retail broker is some distance away from the people who actually work the order.

Some retail brokers find that they are good market timers in their own right and become traders. The incentive for a broker to switch over to a trading desk is tremendous if the broker is skillful at market timing. The different pay scales of brokers and traders are the motivation for the change. A trader is normally paid 20 percent of the profits accumulated over a calendar quarter. This is called the incentive fee. The key word here is *profit*—no profit, no pay. However, traders also earn 2 percent per year in maintenance fees, as there are overhead costs associated with the position. Thus, when a trader is hot, the pay can be substantial, far exceeding that of a broker. Brokers make their living through cumulative commissions. Win or lose, they get paid a very small commission for each transaction they pass on to be executed. It does not matter if they are right or wrong. It does matter if they can grow their client base, however.

Therefore, it is essential that you do your own technical work and do not listen to your broker, or your neighbor, or your business colleague who has a big tip. You can also toss your *Wall Street Journal* away as you learn technical analysis. Newspapers explain what happened after the fact. By the time something is in print, it is too late to act on it. The time it takes to read a paper could be spent determining what will be in tomorrow's papers.

When new retail brokers are hired, they must develop their own book, or client list, and continually make cold calls to find the business to grow their book. If your broker is talking about earnings and using phrases like "solid investment for the long term," he is probably tracking the fundamental research within his firm. If your broker is talking about momentum, using terms like overbought and oversold, and referring to support and resistance areas within the markets, she is following the technical analysts within her firm.

Should a retail broker change firms, the client book usually goes with the broker. Retail brokers enjoy working closely with the public, and over time the good ones develop very large books. They begin to have minimum requirements regarding the size of a client's investment account. The reason for these minimums is time management limitations. An individual, even with support staff, can serve only so many clients well. So as the demand for their services grows, they can become more picky about whom they serve. As they make a living from commissions, they need to strive to serve higher-networth investors who submit larger orders. By then they have gained a fair amount of market wisdom on their own and do their own research to supplement their firm's.

The institutional side of the railway tracks is far less personal as a result of geographic limitations, but not less intimate. The network of professional traders specializing in a specific market is actually fairly small. We are closely networked by telephone lines and through the Internet. We know some of the people we deal with by phone better than we know members of our immediate family, as we are always talking. It takes a career to build such a closely linked network of people who form an inner circle and support structure. Those with any longevity in the industry discover that they cross paths with the same individuals over and over again, although job descriptions, locations, and firms may change.

The general public cannot comprehend the devastation to the closely knit professional networks in the financial industry caused by the events of September 11. The bond market traders were perhaps hit the hardest, as the largest firm specializing in bonds had all but vanished. Cantor Fitzgerald had the top five floors of the North Tower—including the 104th, a floor I once worked on before I decided to move so that I didn't have to spend 3 hours round-trip each day commuting from Darien, Connecticut. (It is scary that we can only comprehend later just how important a particular decision may have been.) The business Cantor Fitzgerald used to conduct in a year approached nearly a trillion dollars. I have retired one of my speed-dial phones, as I cannot come to grips with having to overwrite and reprogram the numbers. Instead I bought a new phone and programmed it from scratch.

The U.S. Treasury actually feared that the bond market would not be able to open on schedule without Cantor Fitzgerald, and those remaining in the firm who were located at other sites were asked if they could pull together to help reconnect the broken threads throughout that segment of the industry. The general public did not know what was involved to open the bond market. Bonds opened before any other market, as there *could be no other market* opened without the bond market being able to conduct business. The bond futures pit was open for business because the Cash Fixed Income market was in place. No one tried to take advantage of the horrific situation by starting a frantic trading frenzy for speculative gains the first few days. The essential transactions needed to keep the economy going were completed eloquently. Everyone else stayed out of the market, holding their breath, so that the market could find its footing again. I had never been more proud of the people in my industry. The bond market set the standard for the rest of us. Business was being conducted with dignity and professionalism, though Fixed Income had suffered the greatest personal loss.

Institutional traders do not often interact with the general public. You will soon find yourself in the same position, as you will find that people in general do not want to do their own work. They want someone else to tell them what to do; that way they do not have to be accountable for the outcome. However, the good ideas will be theirs and the trades that turn out poorly will be all yours, even if you had not been part of the stock selection. So over time good private traders finds themselves in isolation from the general public as well.

It takes work to become a successful trader. It takes discipline. There is no Holy Grail formula or magic system. The answer is to put hard effort into learning how markets work, as you are doing now. It is the hours we spend in learning that provide the payback. There are no fast-track substitutes. I sincerely respect and congratulate you for being proactive and making the effort to learn.

So good traders become isolated from the public, and this is even more true when a trader or analyst moves on to become a fund manager. The payment for fund managers is 1 to 2 percent management fee and 20 percent incentive fee, which means 20 percent of the profits. Good traders on desks with smaller asset allocations have a strong incentive to become fund managers because a fund provides a larger capital base from which to grow their 20 percent share of profits for their efforts.

I'm a fund or portfolio manager. My clients are often other institutions. The type of fund I manage does not let me accept assets from the general public. Institutions invest in funds just as you would. But regulations are very strict about who participates and how information is distributed. As an example, documents must be sent by registered mail only after prequalifications have been confirmed.

That is enough background on some of the individuals that make markets along with you. It may also give you a better understanding of why a retail broker may not have discussed some of the market situations we will cover in these pages. Retail brokers in general have little exposure to some of the things we see on the institutional side of the business.

OK, back to my opening story. I was sharing with you a story involving a technical analyst who saw the portfolio managers in his firm quietly disappear one by one throughout the first half of 2001. Most portfolio managers use fundamentals to decide what will be bought or sold in their portfolio. In this story, the last remaining portfolio manager in a particular firm who used fundamental analysis exclusively stopped by the technical analyst's office to ask the analyst to recommend a book on technical analysis. Here was a man who had built a career on statistics and financial reports. Now he wanted to know how to chart to help him define market direction and timing. He saw the writing on the wall: Fundamentals alone are insufficient in today's markets.

Why the change? What are the differences between technical and fundamental analysis? Why has there been a major shift in the recognition and acceptance of technical analysis within the financial industry? In fact, accredited courses in technical analysis utilizing course curriculum guidelines prepared with help from the Market Technicians Association have begun to be offered at major colleges and universities. (See Appendix A.)

For equities, fundamentals include the underlying data for the specific stock, such as corporate earnings, price-earnings ratios, and corporate breakup valuations. The fundamentalist has to knock on the door of the corporation to get a stream of business statistics from which to make a decision on the future price potential of the stock. Fundamentalists are not accountants. Their expertise begins with the interpretation of the data given to them, not its preparation. Fundamentalists also work within a framework that assumes that investors act in a rational manner at all times. (Fear and greed is never rational.)The technical analyst assumes that market prices already contain all the fundamentals that could be relevant, but we also use tools to monitor the mass psychology of the marketplace. Markets are made up of people's opinions and expectations. The economic equation that defines the laws of supply and demand does not have an exponential variable to quantify fear or greed.

This element of human nature is called market sentiment or behavioral analysis, and fundamentalists give it no consideration. Fundamentalists without question offer checks and balances on valuation. But they can provide only big-picture, long-horizon outlooks. Therein lies the problem: If you can provide projections only on a long-horizon macro scale, it is impossible to manage the risk that slips in under your radar screen.

If a company has experienced strong earnings over the past 4 years, fundamentalists will extrapolate those results to future years. They cannot see broken railway tracks ahead that could derail their earnings forecast unless the insiders tell them that the railway tracks are damaged.

As markets become more volatile, meaning that there are larger market swings both up and down in shorter periods of time, timing becomes more and more important. Technical analysis is better for market timing and is extremely flexible, as the same methods apply to 1-minute charts and time horizons comprising months or years.

One of the reasons technical analysis is growing rapidly in acceptance is the change in technology. For example, a change in business conditions in Japan now ripples through all the global markets in hours. In order to keep up with these global ripples, fundamentalists would have to obtain, read, and understand reports written in a number of languages. Markets today react instantly, whereas only a decade ago they would have taken weeks to react. When I am in sync with a market, I go into total isolation. No television, no magazines, no newspapers—in fact, I want a period of total blackout. The reason is that technical analysis is not only a mechanical way of creating charts, but also an art. Charts will speak to you, but you have to filter out all the chatter and noise around you in order to hear them. I am known on the Street as an independent thinker, and I think outside the box. The reason I elected to stay independent is isolation. If I hear that all the big-name firms think X and my view is that Y will happen, suddenly I have to work like crazy to make sure I did not overlook something. Simply knowing about other opinions forces me to spend additional time verifying my own. So I left the Wall Street mainstream in order to be more isolated from all the chatter. This is one of your truly great strengths as well. Recognize independence for what it gives us: the freedom to step away from the chatter any time we want so that we can focus on what is important, our charts. The best analysts all develop an inner voice that they learn to trust. The only way to develop this inner voice is by working intimately with charts on your own.

The best chartists frequently have an eye for art or an ear for music, and they bring a sense of balance, symmetry, and harmonics into their chart work. Much later I'll show you reasons why the sense of rhythm and harmonics are in fact variables.

Don't chartists ever want to know the fundamentals? Sure we do. I'll give you an example. One indicator you have not yet been introduced to is called Stochastics. It is widely used. Its founding father is Dr. George Lane. George lives in a very small town in Illinois that is surrounded by huge commercial cornfields. One day when I was visiting him, I asked him why he lived in the middle of intersecting cornfields. He said, "See those grain elevators?"

"Yes," I replied.

"Well, I own them." (He used to be a huge corn trader.) He then asked, "Want to know how I price the cash corn crop during the 2-week frenzy to bring in the harvest? I draw a line across the road at various distances away from the grain elevators. The farther back your truck sits behind my lines waiting to deliver your harvest; the lower your price will be!"

If you think about it, that's the world of supply and demand in a nutshell. A technical analyst who specializes in agriculture markets will always have both the cash market for corn and the corn futures market charted. Futures reflect the changing prices in the cash crop. There is one exception: During harvest season, the cash charts always head south, with declining prices. When the harvest is over, the cash market rebounds rapidly to the prices prior to the harvest. The futures prices during this same time period don't budge when the cash market falls. It is the only time during the year that the futures seem to totally ignore what is happening to the underlying cash market prices, and it happens the same way every year.

While the technical analyst doesn't need to know why this differential spread between the cash and futures markets for corn occurs, it sure is nice when someone gives you an explanation—any explanation—of why your charts look so weird. Then we chartists say, "Oh, OK, that's why." It's enough to know that it makes sense to somebody out there with a fundamental bias and that it is likely to be repeated the same way next year.

There is a huge trend reversal approaching in the U.S. dollar as this is written early March 2002. Major market turns are very rare. When I began discussing this market change on the horizon in my evening report a few months ago, it was reassuring to find that subscribing money center banks in Switzerland and Germany said that their work had yielded similar warnings. As they were fundamentalists, I did not fully understand the reasons they gave me. But it was useful to me to know that institutions that are leaders in their field could provide reasons for the major global shift that I was detecting through chart work alone. The important thing here is that this is *noncorrelated* and *independent* research. On opposite sides of the Atlantic we are each doing our own thing with entirely different methods. We are very good at what we do. Fundamentals and technicals can provide that element of increased probability because they are noncorrelated. But this is true only in the big picture or for longer time horizons.

Before we move on, let me just say a word about the title of this book, *All About Technical Analysis*. The most common error that people trying to learn technical analysis make is to get the idea that more indicators are better. This is not true. As soon as these people experience a loss, they switch to another indicator in a never-ending quest to find the perfect squiggle. Such an interpretation of *All About Technical Analysis* would lead to an encyclopedia. You can't make money with an encyclopedia.

All About Technical Analysis is in fact all about developing your own inner voice and developing your skills as a technician with risk management as the principal partner. Therefore, in the time we have together, we will focus first on how to put together a proven foundation and then on how to go about experimenting and exploring some of the many methods that can enhance and develop your basic analysis.

Work toward developing two noncorrelated methods. Then a third approach, very different from the two primary ones, can be used as an experimental technique that is kept in isolation from the first two. That way potential changes you might introduce into your analysis can be monitored separately as a side-by-side comparison. As you grow and develop, always ask yourself a series of questions about a new technical formula or method that is said to be a better approach.

First, does the new method tell you something that your two principal methods could not detect?

If it appears to add information, ask yourself, "Does it tell me the same thing as one of my existing methods, but in a way that lets

me read the signals more easily and accurately?" Continually filter and refine your methods. If a new method is easier to read, it
may replace or modify one of your current methods. *Your goal is to
develop three noncorrelated methods.* Make changes one at a time so
that when you make adjustments, you know what you are tweaking. If the new method provides the same signal as your existing
methods and is not considerably easier to read, dump it. Changes
should be introduced only after considerable evaluation in a real-
time market environment. Avoid the temptation to make changes
based on historical back-testing alone.

If the new method is in conflict with your existing methods,
ask the following: "If it tells me something different, is it noncorrelated with the methods I am using now?"

If the answer is yes, keep it for further evaluation to learn
more about how it works. Of the three noncorrelated methods you
want to develop, the first two are anchors and the third is more
experimental. If you already have a third method, the new method
must either be better than or modify one of your existing methods.
This is an evolution, and it means that you do not go back to the
old method when you get befuddled. There are four market signals, not three. They are buy, sell, hold, and I don't know. If your
charts say "I don't know," this is a valid option, and you will do
nothing but watch from the sidelines.

There will come a point in time when you feel as if you have
seen and considered every chart method in the universe, and that
none of them add much to your favorite three. At that point, the
only way to improve your market entry and exit timing will be to
know time itself. To know that a bear market may occur from
January 2000 to December 2002 and then rally into August 2003
before potentially falling again is invaluable. The ability to tell time
will become the fourth branch in your technical arsenal. It is the
toughest, and it will force you to accept methods that are considered to be outside the financial industry. You need experience in
developing the three noncorrelated methods first. Then you can
tackle time itself. Maybe that will be the topic of my fourth book,
which is the one my peers keep pushing me to write.

Are you ready? Let's take a look at a chart with just price data
to start.

CHAPTER 3

Can Mutual Fund Investors Use Technical Analysis?

When you first become aware of technical analysis, you will find that there is a perception that only active traders can use charts. So let me share a chart application right from the start that may unexpectedly broaden your thinking. This application uses price data alone and will prove invaluable.

Two friends of mine promised themselves that this was the year they would become more proactive in the way they invested and saved their earnings. For years they had made monthly contributions to a mutual fund that was recommended for government employees. Like many people, they did not look at their monthly statement on a regular basis. In 1999, when technology stocks were skyrocketing, they were understandably perplexed, as their fund was not keeping pace. They went to the trouble of studying the fund's annual report one evening, and they saw that the fund had technology stocks as part of the total portfolio. So why were they losing when it seemed that everyone around them was caught up in the great bull market with no end in sight?

When I was asked to help, it became immediately clear to me just from looking at their statement returns that their fund had dumped the technology stocks that made the annual report look *marketable* and then invested in bond-correlated stocks for the rest of the year.

End of quarter window dressing occurs when funds that are marketed to the general public sell the stocks that people may not like and buy stock winners that they know the public will want to see in the fund. An annual report for a fund is just a photograph of a single day. Changing the stocks in the portfolio is fairly routine, so the annual report can be made to look perfect based on public sentiment at the time. Say "cheese." Snap! The day after the "family photo" is captured, the added stocks are dumped and the portfolio manager goes back into what he or she liked before the photo.

The annual report stated that the fund owned some technology stocks, but its returns did not show it. Had my friends moved into another fund at the end of 1999 when they became disheartened with their current investment in order to join the technology party, they would have stepped in just as the Nasdaq was at its high. In fact, their fund was really a bond fund, and I could see this in only a few minutes even though it was not clearly documented in the fund's literature.

A picture may be worth a thousand words, but a chart can be worth thousands of dollars.

The chart in Figure 3-1 displays a price comparison between the Nasdaq Index (NASDQ) on the top and the Pioneer Value Fund (PIOTX) on the bottom for the same period of time. This chart and all fund price data are free additions to Omega's TradeStation.

My hunch that this was really a bond fund was correct. In the last quarter of 1999, the bond market was falling rapidly. Any gains from technology stocks held by this fund were lost by the stocks in the financial sector. Financial stocks track with bonds, as they are interest rate sensitive. You learn this by charting both the stocks and various market indices. It does not take long to see that when the bond market goes down, so do interest-rate-sensitive stocks. So this particular fund went nowhere during the stellar technology rally into the end of 1999. But it didn't go anywhere in 2000 either when the Nasdaq imploded because bonds began to rise. If you need a little more proof of this fund's market bias, consider the information in Figure 3-2.

The column on the left gives information for the Pioneer Value Fund. On the right is information on another fund within the same family of funds, Pioneer Independence. As of January 31, 2002, the value fund was weighted toward financial stocks, which

F i g u r e   3-1

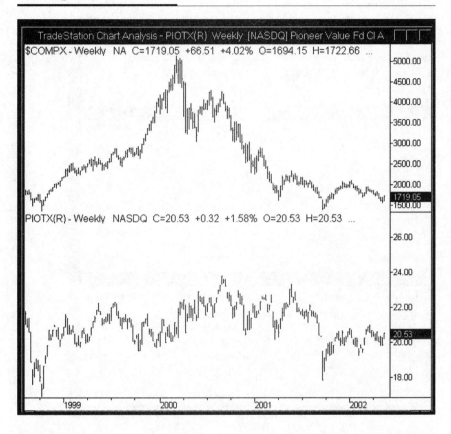

are correlated with bonds. (The word "value" in the name usually indicates a bias toward slow-growth investment instruments.) This information can be obtained from the fund or from services like Morningstar that reprint the information the funds provide. Pioneer Independence had one financial stock in its top five during the comparable period of time. (These examples do not constitute a recommendation of either fund.) Charts allow transparency for information the fund documents had not disclosed clearly. An additional benefit is that you can time your purchases and withdrawals using technical indicators. All the methods illustrated in this book can be applied to fund net asset value (NAV) data for weekly and monthly time periods.

F i g u r e   3-2

PIONEER VALUE FD CL A			PIONEER INDEPENDENCE FD		
Total Number of stock holdings 99			Total Number of stock holdings 90		
Total Number of bond holdings 0			Total Number of bond holdings 0		
% Net Assets in Top 10 Holdings 27.37			% Net Assets in Top 10 Holdings 18.39		
Turnover 12 %			Turnover 106 %		

Sector Weightings			Sector Weightings		
Data through 01-31-02		% of Stocks	Data through 01-31-02		% of Stocks
Utilities		4.7	Utilities		1.4
Energy		14.1	Energy		7.8
Financials		22.2	Financials		18.0
Industrials		15.4	Industrials		14.2
Durables		3.9	Durables		1.9
Staples		3.9	Staples		4.9
Services		12.8	Services		14.1
Retail		1.9	Retail		6.1
Health		11.4	Health		13.9
Technology		9.9	Technology		17.7

Top 5 Holdings			Top 5 Holdings		
Name of Holding	Sector	% Net Assets	Name of Holding	Sector	% Net Assets
Dominion Resources	Utility	3.49	Microsoft		2.26 %
Ambac Finl Grp	Financial	3.19	Citigroup	Financial	2.08 %
Charter One Finl	Financial	3.08	ExxonMobil		2.01 %
Washington Mutual	Financial	2.85	Intel		1.95 %
Citigroup	Financial	2.81	Pfizer		1.90 %

www.BigCharts.com

One small line that you might miss is the fourth line under the fund names in Figure 3-2. It gives turnover. You might notice that the Pioneer Value Fund has a 12 percent turnover, meaning that it doesn't change the holdings in its portfolio often. However, the Pioneer Independence Fund shows a turnover of 106 percent! This is more than just window dressing, but further research revealed that a new portfolio manager had taken the reins only a couple of months earlier. That would explain such a high turnover.

In the chart for the Pioneer Independence Fund in Figure 3-3, you can see that when a comparison is made between the Nasdaq Index and Pioneer Independence in the first half of 2000, the fund had insulated itself from the technology crash. You would not

F i g u r e 3-3

know that the fund had shifted its risk exposure away from technology without a price chart. But the fund returned to technology too soon, as so many funds were enticed to do. It was caught eventually. What can a mutual fund investor do to develop his or her own opinions about the decisions being made by a fund?

Most mutual fund investors make a decision based on past performance. This is the same approach that economists use, and it leads to horrible market timing. You can chart the fund itself and chart an index that the fund has to be compared or benchmarked to for performance.

The first thing you need is an understanding of what you want to chart. I'll stay with these two Pioneer funds to develop an explanation of market indices and what you need to monitor through

F i g u r e   3-4

Pioneer Value A PIOTX		Pioneer Independence PINDX	
Size Median Mkt Cap $Mil	19,315	Size Median Mkt Cap $Mil	28,513
Market Capitalization	% of Portfolio	Market Capitalization	% of Portfolio
Giant	32.17	Giant	36.26
Large	29.72	Large	39.47
Medium	28.22	Medium	22.41
Small	9.21	Small	1.86
Micro	0.68	Micro	0.00

www.BigCharts.com

charts. Most Internet resources will help you identify a fund's or a stock's market capitalization. The market capitalization, also known as market cap, is found by multiplying the share price by the number of shares outstanding. (The number of shares outstanding is the total number of shares of stock held by the general public that could be actively traded.) It is actually a fundamental variable. For example, a company whose stock is trading at $10 with 20 million shares outstanding has a market cap of $200 million. As a guideline, a small-cap stock would be one with a market cap of under $500 million. A mid-cap stock would have a market cap of over $500 million but under $1 billion, and large cap usually means having a market cap of over $1 billion. A stock like Exxon Mobil Corporation fits in the large-cap category. A stock like Symantec, a small company that writes virus protection software, is in the small-cap category.

Once you have the general idea that there are different ways to bundle stocks together, you no longer have to make any calculations involving fundamentals. You have the concept in mind, and that is all that is needed.

In Figure 3-4, the data is presented with a few more categories of "caps." As in this case, your fund might use other classifications, but you should combine them so that you have three caps only. Giant and large are companies with market caps of over $1 billion and can be combined, mid-cap remains unchanged, and then we would include micro in the small-cap group.

When you look at these two funds, you can see that the Pioneer Value Fund was more willing to buy small-cap stocks than was the Pioneer Independence Fund. Is that consistent with your own investment goals? Does that mean that an investor has to determine what stocks fit into which market cap category and analyze hundreds of stocks? Of course not. You don't have to figure this out at all. It has all been done for you. You only have to know that there are small-cap and large-cap stocks and that different funds have different weightings to these market caps. What you need to learn is how to use market indices other than the Dow Jones Industrial Average. The general public is not at all well informed about indices. I know this from the blank stares I get when I am asked what market is my specialty. (The answer is the S&P500.) So here's my chance to clear the fog.

The Dow Jones Industrial Average (DJIA) is *not* the most important stock index. It is just the oldest and most famous. On July 3, 1884, Charles H. Dow added together the closing prices of 11 actively traded stocks and then divided the total of their price closes by 11. (This became known as the divisor and has since evolved into something more complex.) The average for the daily close was printed in the *Customer's Afternoon Letter* daily. On October 7, 1896, the *Wall Street Journal* first printed the average trading price over the last 30 days for 20 railroad stocks and 12 industrials. Since that time, the DJIA has had substitutions and changes to the divisor many times. When stocks started moving around a little more as people became better informed, the daily open and close and the trading high and low for the day were added as well.

Now the DJIA has 30 stocks and is an indication of what is happening to large-cap stocks only. When people talk about the historical price changes of the DJIA, they are actually talking about an index that is continually tweaked so that it keeps its market appeal for the general public. It is rare for stocks in the index to be bumped out and other companies' stocks brought into the index. It will be of interest to you to know that when substitutions are made, this generally happens near a major market top or bottom for the index being tweaked. Take, for example, the last substitutions made by Dow Jones & Company to the DJIA. On November 1, 1999, Microsoft

Corp. and Intel Corp. were added to the DJIA, along with Home Depot and SBC. Microsoft and Intel were the first Nasdaq stocks ever to be added to the DJIA. That was only a few weeks prior to the historic high in the Nasdaq Index before it crashed.

Why did Dow Jones & Company make the change? The Nasdaq was receiving all the media air time, as it was weighted toward Internet and technology stocks. The DJIA was moving little and was the same story day after day. So to spice up the index, Dow Jones & Company tossed out Union Carbide, Chevron, Goodyear Tire & Rubber, and Sears and replaced them with stocks with a little more marketing pizzazz. The company said the change was needed because of the ascendance of computers in the U.S. economy and financial markets. If you would like to know more about the DJIA, visit http://www.djindexes.com.

While the Nasdaq dot com stocks are now dot gones, keep in mind that these indices are marketing tools. This is true of exchanges as well. Whether it be the New York Stock Exchange (where only large-cap stocks are listed), the Nasdaq, or the American Stock Exchange, it will make changes as needed to ensure its survival. Not

F i g u r e 3-5

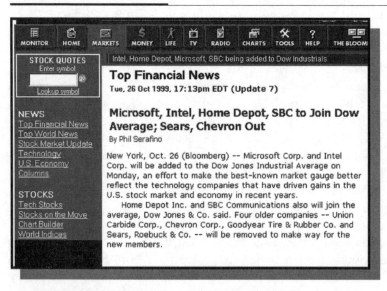

only do the exchanges have rules that allow them to drop companies that are in serious trouble, but they have the ability to change the rules on how to become listed. They can thus have more clout than any government regulation. The exchanges and indices will do whatever it takes to retain or regain market and media appeal. Therefore, forecasting the direction of an index using fundamentals is nearly impossible.

Dow Jones & Company likes having its corporate name attached to the index that the media report on the nightly news— "the market closed at 10000," etc. "The market," is not just the 30 stocks within the Dow Jones Industrial Average, but the general public identifies with it that way, so the media will continue to call the DJIA "the market." However, if the DJIA is not the principal equity index in America, what is?

Mutual funds have to outperform a benchmark index, or a stock index to which they are compared. You do either better or worse than the index you are judged against. A small handful of funds are benchmarked to the DJIA. More than $1 trillion is benchmarked to the Standard & Poor's index called the S&P500. Instead of 30 stocks, it has 500. But these stocks are not all given equal weighting, so the name is somewhat misleading. Later we will go over the construction of these indices in detail, along with some very recent and important changes. The S&P500 Index has been my career specialization. If you tracked the S&P500 and Nasdaq, you would have a much better idea of the equities market in the United States than if you tracked the DJIA alone. If you then added indices that reflect mid-cap and small-cap stocks, you would have access to the most important benchmarks.

Dow Jones & Company and Standard & Poor's Corporation both have other indices. For example, the S&P600 is an index that is more weighted toward small-cap stocks. Dow Jones also has a large-cap and a small-cap index. There are many other indices as well because companies love to have their name in front of an index. To learn more about the Standard & Poor's indices, visit http://www.spglobal.com. The S&P indices are defined in the following ways.

S&P500 Index. Widely regarded as the standard for measuring large-cap U.S. stock market performance, this popular index includes a representative sample of leading companies in leading industries. The S&P500 is used by 97 percent of U.S. money managers and pension plan sponsors. More than $1 trillion is indexed to the S&P500.

S&P Mid-Cap 400 Index. This index, which measures the performance of the mid-size company segment of the U.S. market, is used by over 95 percent of U.S. managers and pension plan sponsors. More than $25 billion is indexed to the S&P Mid-Cap 400.

S&P Small-Cap 600 Index. The small-company segment of the U.S. market continues to attract investors. Approximately $8 billion is indexed to the S&P Small-Cap 600.

S&P SuperComposite 1500 Index. Combined, the S&P 500, Mid-Cap 400, and Small-Cap 600 indices make up the S&P SuperComposite 1500, representing 87 percent of the total U.S. equity market capitalization.

S&P100 Index. The Standard & Poor's 100 Stock Index, known by its ticker symbol OEX, measures large-company U.S. stock market performance. This market capitalization–weighted index is made up of 100 major (translate that as large-cap) blue chip stocks across diverse industry groups.

Now that you realize that people other than just market traders can use technical analysis, the next step is to get your computer set up so that you can begin charting.

PART 2

How to Create Charts

How to Get the Data into Your Computer

A good place to start is to review a shopping list so that you know that the data vendor you select can meet your needs. You will need market data and software that will let you display and analyze the data. Sometimes a vendor offers a complete package. However, it is common for people to buy data and then find they need a different set of features in a different data format, and so end up buying the data all over again. There are many compatibility issues, so let's cover the basics so you can avoid the more common pitfalls.

Market prices are packaged in various ways. Here is a list of things to consider.

Can you get by with end-of-day data, or do you need intraday data as well? The first consideration is the time horizon your data covers. Some data vendors sell only end-of-day data. That means that your data are updated when the market closes and you get only daily data that reflects the trading prices for that day. End-of-day data doesn't limit you to just viewing charts created in a daily time horizon (that means bar charts in which one bar reflects the trading range for one day). Once you have daily data, your analysis and charting software can compress that data to show the range in weekly and monthly time intervals as well. However, you will not be able to view the data in periods smaller than one bar for the day's trading range.

How much historical data do you need? Does the supplier charge for historical data? So far we have considered only the collection of data as of today going forward. However, you need historical data to create a chart. Many people do not realize that they have to ask, "How much historical data do you provide?" If the data supplier you are considering displays only a few years of weekly data, it is useless. One professional vendor is Commodity Quote Graphics, known as CQG. It provides both the data and the ability to chart and analyze the data. CQG's basic service is very expensive, and the firm then charges an extra monthly fee if you want to see a wider window of historical data. Another professional data vendor with charting capabilities is Omega's TradeStation. It gives you enough stock data for good basic analysis, but it doesn't offer enough data to let you see long periods of history. (CQG has data for the DJIA from 1900.)

Then you also want to ask, "How clean is your historical data?" I use several different data vendors, as each has its own set of strengths and weaknesses. One vendor rattled off all the markets it covered, and I was sold, as it sounded as if the vendor had everything I needed. After I bought the data, I discovered that much of the international data was useless, as it was full of bullet holes. The charts literally had missing prices for weeks at a time and displayed wrong data.

Does your Internet data vendor have to be based in North America? Market data is either right or flawed. Data vendors in Australia supply data through the Internet just as easily as a computer service based in Chicago or New York. If the data is clean the only difference to you is the exhange rate. At the moment all Aussie invoices have a 50 percent discount because of a favorable exchange rate when the Aussie invoice is paid in U.S. dollars. Just keep in mind an Internet product has no geographic boundaries. The world of data vendors is a frustrating one. The more questions you know to ask up front, the better off you will be.

Do you want to chart stocks and/or futures? If so, what exchanges do you need? The New York Stock Exchange, the American Stock Exchange, Nasdaq—you probably need all of them if you trade stocks. Stocks trade on different exchanges, and each exchange is in the business of obtaining commissions in the form of exchange fees for supplying you with data. Some vendors give some data for free, as they pay the exchange fees for you. However, most vendors charge you for their basic package, and then you have to pay exchange fees on top of that. You also want to know if the exchange fees are part of the vendor's billing or if the exchanges will each send you a separate invoice. The latter is very irritating, but this is entirely controlled by the vendor's agreement with the exchanges.

Then you need to consider futures exchanges. You can probably see the cash S&P500, but will have to pay $60 a month to see the futures data. Ask your vendor what indices it provides and whether there are extra fees. If you trade futures there is another important consideration. Several vendors offer a continuous futures contract. When the front month rolls over to the next contract some vendors subtract the differential from the entire historical database. As an example, TradeStation 6.0 has back adjusted their bond futures in this manner so that the historical data actually plots on the screen below zero! CSI, an end-of-day data vendor, offers different back-adjusted continuous contracts. They believe this adjustment retains the trend of the market. In reality it is technically wrong, as you cannot make price projections, use historical price pivots for key calculations, or read historical patterns within the data, and your long horizon work is limited in many ways. What you need is continuous contracts that have not been adjusted. Vendors will tell you otherwise and will not change until people understand the differences and ask. Both CQG and FutureSource have excellent data, but their software has significant limitations. The world of data suppliers and how they bundle data can only be described as very screwball. Do your homework carefully.

Do you need real-time data, or can you work just as well with delayed data? If you can work with delayed data, the exchanges will give you the data for free or for a minimal cost, as they want you to have access to their markets so that you can trade with them. Every trade or order that passes through any exchange will have an exchange fee attached for doing business on that exchange. So if the data was never free, it could hurt the other side of the exchange's revenue stream. Some international markets still have minor token fees for viewing their data—$6 a month for German markets, for example. But this changes all the time. You just need to know that you do have options about exchange fees. Data suppliers rarely advise you of this.

Now you have to consider data format. What does your charting software support or require? To know what format you need, you have to know up front how you want to massage your data. Don't worry about the format, just worry about the charting abilities you want. Then see what data format is required by the analysis package. There are a few snags if you step into this blindly.

What do you want your charting software to do? You want intraday data for anything you are going to trade regardless of whether you are planning to carry positions for weeks or just for a few days. Why? You need this data for analysis and market timing. The better your timing, the lower your capital drawdown. You can also see faster when you are getting into trouble. A mutual fund investor doesn't need intraday data. Someone who is making his or her own investment decisions on what to buy and sell needs intraday data. Period. (I'll show you why at another time.)

If you need intraday data, you must have the ability to pick the time interval you want to use. Some analysis packages force you to view intraday data in one of the intervals they have predefined. They pick intervals like 5-minute, 10-minute, 15-minute, 30-minute, and 60-minute bar chart options. Weed those guys out by asking them a simple question: "Can you display an 88-minute chart? How about 360 minutes or 120 minutes?" Most of them will choke and say no. Then they will try to put you on the defensive by asking why any crazy person would want those. Just hang up and move on. Lots of people look at the predefined intervals because they don't know any better. If you are coming out of my school, you don't want to be part of that majority.

Then you need to ask the vendor a simple question about analysis capabilities: "Do you support the ability to create my own studies?" This does not mean that you can modify the studies the software vendor offers. You need to know whether you can actually define your own formula and have the program display the custom indicator in the manner in which you want to see it. That will filter out a bunch of packages on the market as well.

Can you pick the color you want for your indicators, Fibonacci grids, and data foreground and background? If you set a Fibonacci grid to have a default color of red, when you change it, does it change every Fibonacci ratio on your screen or just the one set of Fibonacci ratios you want to change? You need to see a demo to answer this one. Omega TradeStation is one of the best for this, but it has other limitations, like no international data and incorrect continuous futures contracts. No vendor does everything well. You have to pick through the minefield with your eyes wide open. FutureSource offers Fibonacci ratios, but they only display them after you have defined a price pivot start and end point. That means you cannot make any judgment about their placement until after you select the price pivots. This is technically incorrect as you should use internal references in the data to select these important pivots. So the vendor does not understand the correct application of the technique. CQG does not allow changes once the grids are on the screen. That means you have to redraw all the grids on your screen when just a simple adjustment is needed to one pivot point.

If the package is just black-and-white, it is not even up for consideration.

We have not discussed Fibonacci grids yet, but by the time you have finished reading this book, you will be well informed about them. A lot of the people I teach toss their software out when they go back home or to their office, as they cannot use it to do what our seminars cover. How a vendor displays Fibonacci grids is usually one of the primary reasons for this. You will quickly see this as well when we discuss the basic methods in later chapters.

Can I skip all this and just look at a chart on the Internet? I use the Internet freebies all the time. The chart showing the two Pioneer funds is a perfect example. But when I want an informed decision, I have to massage the price data by adding specific indicators that are not available in any of the basic services. To do this, the data has to be in my computer or I have to have a package that allows this capability through the Internet.

Once someone has picked a software vendor and data, it is not uncommon for that person to hunt elsewhere for additional data that the primary supplier doesn't offer. For example, you may have stocks, but you usually have to shop around to find stock sector indices.

There are no vendors who do everything well. You will always be juggling one problem against another as you pick and choose. The four different vendors you will see throughout this book are Bloomberg (http://www.bloomberg.com), CQG (Commodity Quote Graphics; http://www.cqg.com), FutureSource (http://www.FutureSource), and Omega Research (TradeStation 6.0 and SuperCharts; http://www.omegaresearch.com).

Once you have selected a source for your data and software to display the data, you will be ready to start charting.

CHAPTER 5

Weekly, Monthly, and Intraday Time Intervals: How to Display the Data

Once you have data and software, the next question will be; "How do I display the data?" When I teach a trading seminar, I begin the program by asking each member to give his or her observations on charts that were sent to the participants before their arrival. It is clear that a great many people consider charts to be independent, stand-alone entities. But a decision made on the basis of a single chart on its own has a lower probability of being right. So let's get you started on the right foot from the very beginning.

Charts need to be displayed in such a way that you can always cross-compare two different time horizons. For example, you can display a monthly chart beside a weekly chart, or display a weekly chart with a daily chart. Then we move down to the intraday time horizons. A 240-minute chart works well beside a 60-minute chart, and a 60-minute chart beside a 15-minute chart is a good ratio to set up.

When you want to view a larger chart, all you need to do is maximize your window using the Microsoft conventions that all our Windows-based software packages use; they are located on the top right of your screen. Then minimize the chart or use the restore button for your software. All the vendors have this ability. At the moment, TradeStation has an irritating quirk: It does not expand the chart with more data when you maximize the view, it just gives you the same data spaced out across a larger window. You have to change a default setting so that the x-axis retains the same spacing as you see in the smaller window. To change the default within TradeStation, select from the top menu VIEW. From that menu select Chart Analysis Preferences. You will be offered a pop-up menu with the default settings. The first tab is named General and this is the one you will need. Move your mouse pointer into the box beside the option; Auto space bars when chart resizes. Then uncheck the default selection. Be sure to save the change by selecting OK on the bottom. Now your have the same ability to easily expand a chart window to view more data as others vendors provide.

The S&P 500 Cash Index is displayed in Figure 5-1. On the left is a monthly chart, and on the right is a chart showing a weekly

F i g u r e   5-1

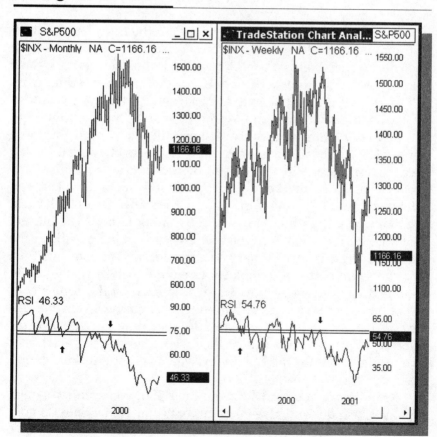

time horizon. Below the data is what we call a momentum indicator. This particular one will be available in any charting package you choose because it is widely used. It is called the RSI or Relative Strength Index. Most momentum indicators are just variations on a similar theme, so don't worry about the formula at the moment. Here's why you always want to have at least two charts with different time horizons in view at all times. (I use three.) The chart on the left in Figure 5-1 is the monthly view. In the first chapter, I discussed looking at charts from right to left. In this chart, the 1999 high has the RSI stalling at a high-risk zone in the indicator. I drew horizontal lines across the RSI to make it easier for you to see this. If you look from right to left, you will see that the same horizontal zone was used in previous years as the launching pad for rallies. Therefore, this zone on the RSI is a high-risk zone for potential market turns.

In addition, do you remember that in the first chapter I told you that you should let the market teach you how it works with each indicator? Well, this is extremely important, as this chart tells you what to expect. This zone that the RSI bounced up from in October 1998 is called an area of *support*, as the zone was tested by the indicator from above and the market then continued to rally. In later years, the indicator has failed to exceed the same zone. As the indicator has stalled under the level, we call this an area of *resistance*, and the failure of the indicator at this same level warns of the market decline that followed. So how can you tell which test of the line is the more significant? If you look back, the line was tested three times as the market rallied. The market took three (or, if you count the one little test in the middle at the line, four) tests before it changed direction in earnest. This time horizon told you what to look for when the market was going to change direction. It told you that it wants to test the zone a couple of times before it pays attention to it. The zone levels that this market respects are different for different time horizons. In the monthly chart, the zone is near the 75 level when your eye tracks over to the y axis for the RSI. In the weekly chart, this key level is near 60.

Oh, I know, you read all about the RSI in your vendor's manual. Every vendor will give you automatic horizontal lines on your RSI at predefined levels of 20 and 80 or 30 and 70. Well, I remove those lines. If you cannot remove them, change their color so that they match your chart's background color and disappear. That's what I had to do for these charts, recorded from TradeStation. The vendor and most books will tell you to buy at 20 and sell at 80. If you do this, you will assuredly lose a lot of money. They call these levels oversold and overbought. They are wrong. In bear markets RSI will fail to move through 60 to 65 and will then find a bottom range near 20 to 30. In bull markets the RSI will find a bottom near 40 to 45 and then top near 80 to 90. So the overbought and oversold ranges will change based on the market environment. For this reason a 14-period RSI is used to retain this consistency within ranges. There is much more about this in my advanced book, *Technical Analysis for the Trading Professional*, when you are ready to explore these ranges in more detail.

What do I look for when I draw these horizontal lines on the indicator? In both charts, there was a level at which the indicator was respecting a horizontal line. We call this situation where the indicator first is above the line and then later tests the underside of the line as "support becoming resistance," and it naturally can work in the other direction as well. The point is that the tests occur at the same horizontal level in the chart.

Now let's compare the weekly chart signals to the monthly chart. There is only one spot where the weekly chart fails to exceed a horizontal line drawn on the RSI at the same time a signal forms in the monthly chart. The time horizons I gave you will produce a domino effect. You will first see a signal in the monthly chart. When you see this signal by itself, it will be too soon to take action. When you are early the drawdown exposure is excessive, so we wait for the same signal to develop in the weekly chart.

If you are comparing the monthly and the weekly charts, would it not be useful to know whether or not the signal in the monthly chart was extremely important? Unfortunately, Trade-Station displays data only up to a monthly time horizon. So now I have to switch to CQG because it can compress the data further. This also means that I am paying exchange fees for both systems along with the expense of the basic services. The charts in Figure 5-2 show a comparison of the Cash S&P 500 in quarterly and monthly time horizons.

The quarterly chart (with one bar created for every 3 months or calendar quarter) on the left shows that an extreme momentum high was made in 1998. This indicator can only go to a maximum

F i g u r e   5-2

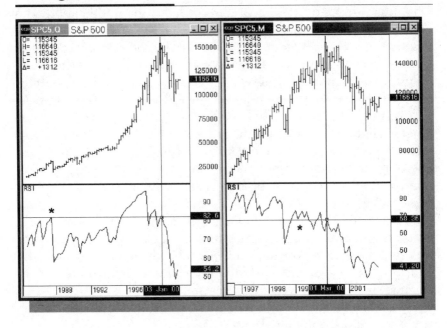

displacement of 100, so a quarterly chart rolling over at 97 is a rare event indeed. But if you thought that because this indicator was so high, the bull market was over, your timing would have been horrible. As you look from right to left, you will find that the January 2000 high in the RSI was at *the same level at which the indicator topped in 1987.* Now that is significant. A high-risk level in the past is a high-risk level in the present. You would never have seen this if you had access to only monthly charts.

Now we look at the monthly chart, and you will see that I have drawn a horizontal line slightly lower than the one I drew in Figure 5-1. It warns you that the indicator is failing once again at a *lower* level at which support once held the market; this level is now resistance, as the market has failed to push the indicator above the line. This one is more subtle. But in fact, as your experience grows, you will find that subtle is deadly. These are the final warnings.

If the quarterly chart is forming resistance at a level that was also a resistance level in October 1987, and if a correction occurs, as it in fact did, it would be of interest to gain a sense of where the present bear market fits within the bigger scheme of things. To find this perspective, we need to compare the quarterly chart with a chart with an annual time horizon. That's right, one bar equals the range traded within one entire year. This is shown in Figure 5-3.

The annual chart for the Cash S&P 500 was off the map! But the decline into March 2002, when it was captured for this book, shows that the indicator has fallen back to a level that defined momentum highs through 1960. Resistance has become support and the strength of the U.S. dollar, not economics, will be one of the principal factors for determining what lies ahead. We will be looking at this critical relationship between the U.S. dollar and the DJIA in Chapter 7 because support will be broken.

Did the DJIA tell the same story? Figure 5-4 gives the annual and quarterly charts for the DJIA. The charts show momentum extremes in both time intervals in 1998. But when indicators are at such extremes, it takes time for the "domino" effect to occur. Momentum extreme signals will pass down from long-term to intermediate-term charts. As the various time horizons come into alignment, the

F i g u r e   5-3

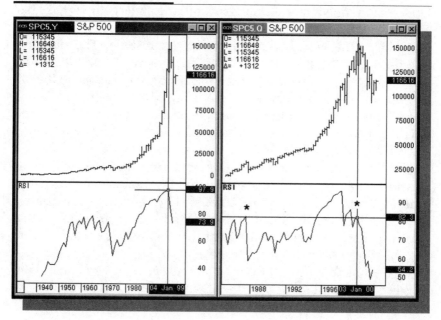

Figure 5-4

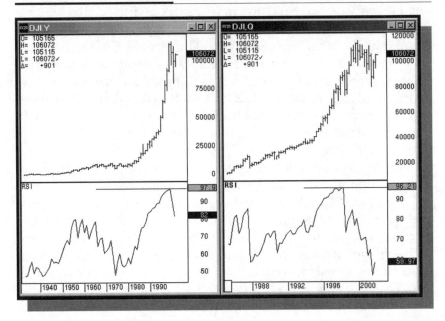

DJIA may define a market pattern similar to a large inverted "N." The first leg will set the stage for a multiyear down-up-down pattern before the very big-picture rally can resume. The potential down-leg could fall until late 2002. The potential "up" leg could then end late in August 2003. Then the last down-leg back to the old lows would follow to complete the inverted "N" pattern. We will spend time developing the skills to create market scenarios like this one. But your skills to develop associated target dates will follow years later.

In Figure 5-5 the broken horizontal line that I added in the quarterly chart on the right also matches the momentum high prior to the 1987 market high. In the annual chart, I added a line to help you visualize how this decline is in fact falling toward the line that was resistance through the 1950s and 1960s. Both the S&P500 and the DJIA are telling the same story.

So what about the Nasdaq? You will see plenty of charts later in this book, but if you cannot wait, add it to your screen now. We will discuss it when we have covered the basics.

Figure 5-5

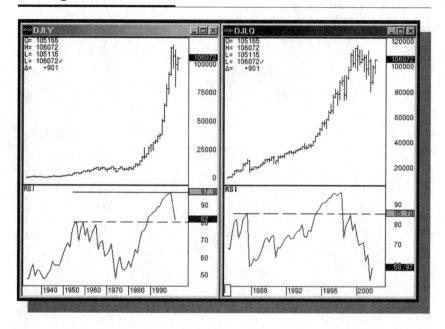

A final example of ways to display charts is to switch from a really long horizon chart to a short horizon for intraday perspectives. The Cash S&P500 is again offered in Figure 5-6. The left-hand chart is a 240-minute view, and the right-hand chart is a 15-minute view. In this case, the indicator is showing that the rally is incomplete, as both time horizons are using a zone within RSI that was once resistance as a level for support. That means underlying short-term strength, and so the market still has strength to advance in this time horizon.

In all these examples showing the S&P500, you may have noticed that TradeStation uses the symbol $INX and CQG uses SPC5. You will find that every vendor uses a different symbol. You will learn your vendor's symbols quickly enough.

Do you realize how much you have learned? You have begun to look for support and resistance within an indicator. You know how to display your charts. We introduced the use of multiple time horizons to increase the accuracy of your market timing. We discussed the really big picture in American stocks. This is great progress. Let's move on to the next step.

Figure 5-6

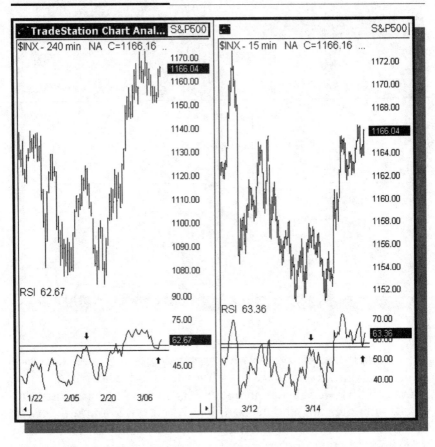

CHAPTER 6

How Asian Traders Prefer to Display Data

So far, we have set up your computer using bar charts. In addition, we looked at the use of an indicator to define support and resistance levels within the price data. Most books will begin by stepping you through a series of price patterns. The truth is that with what you have in your computer right now, you are miles ahead of someone who is just looking for recognizable patterns within prices alone in a single chart. But you probably do not want to wait until signals align in a domino effect through long- to short-horizon chart windows before you trade. So you need to build on these principles.

There are other ways you can chart your price data. As we take a look at some of these other methods, however, don't forget your original game plan, which is to develop three independent methods that are noncorrelated so that you can increase the probability that you are right in your market opinion. One way to develop noncorrelated methods is to cross-compare Western analytics with Asian techniques.

Asian market traders don't use bar charts as their first preference for displaying data. They use a charting method called *candlestick charts*. Candlestick charts display the opening, high, low, and closing prices in a manner that visually enhances the relationship between the open and closing prices.

F i g u r e   6-1

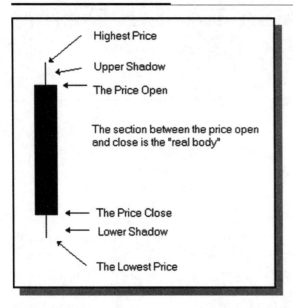

Highest Price

Upper Shadow

The Price Open

The section between the price open
and close is the "real body"

The Price Close

Lower Shadow

The Lowest Price

Figure 6-1 is a candlestick chart with its components labeled. Like the bars in bar charts, one candlestick displays the trading range for a single unit of time. This candlestick could represent the price range over one year, one quarter, one month, one minute, or maybe 60 minutes. You can use whatever time interval you want, just as with a bar chart. What is different about this Asian charting method is the way it displays the trading range between the opening and closing prices for the time interval you select. This range between the opening and closing prices is called the *real body*.

The trading ranges above or below the real body are called the shadows. (I think they look more like wicks than shadows.) When the closing price is below the opening price, the real body is filled in, as in Figure 6-1. If the closing price is above the opening price, the candlestick is left white or empty. Technicians study the appearance of a specific individual candlestick and read market directional signals from the specific patterns formed by groups of candlesticks. You will run into names like Long White Line, Hammer, Piercing Lines, and Bullish Engulfing Pattern. The candlesticks corresponding to these names are shown in Figure 6-2.

F i g u r e   6-2

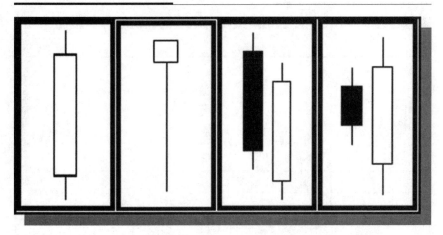

It is the ever-changing relationships between the opening and closing prices relative to the trading range that makes these different candlesticks. Many of the patterns identified within a group of candlesticks have names that sound like Japanese armies advancing and retreating: three white soldiers, river bottoms, mountain tops, dark cloud covers, counterattack lines, and gravestone dojis.

Names relating to armies and battles may seem odd at first, but candlesticks came into existence in Japan during the 1600s to aid rice traders. Rice traders were samurai warriors, and it didn't pay to do well if you were not a samurai. One particular fellow got so good at rice trading that the samurai warriors thought he had exceeded his social level, as he was a commoner. This commoner was so good, in fact, that his backyard became the exchange where rice was traded for all of Japan. But he had stepped out of the feudal social order for his time, and this crime was intolerable. What was his punishment? His family and children were murdered and all his belongings were taken.

While I will let you explore the hundreds of candlestick patterns on your own through the Internet or from books on the subject, I will now lead you in a direction that you will not find as easily in the books you study. What we will use candlesticks for is to find market support and resistance.

F i g u r e   6-3

Figure 6-3 shows a weekly S&P500 chart. One candlestick is the range for a full trading week. The filled-in or black real bodies tell us that the market's closing price for that week was lower than the opening price. The white real bodies show weekly closing prices that were higher than where the market opened. Take a look at the lower horizontal line drawn in this chart. You will see asterisks directly above several real bodies. The shadows may exceed the horizontal line, but the real body for each of these candlesticks is on or directly below the horizontal line.

In the candlestick chart in Figure 6-3 there is a higher horizontal line drawn near 1227. If this market should exceed 1185, we could suggest that the next price objective for the Cash S&P500 is 1227. That is a big rally. But we never use price objectives alone. We add technical indicators. The indicators are under the levels of resistance, so we know that there is far greater risk of the market breaking down than the chance of seeing it make further gains. I have placed an asterisk above a few key candles in this time horizon that respect this line. Areas of support or resistance drawn from charts of longer time horizons are of much greater importance than those derived from time horizons of less than a day.

Some investors may not know what a stop loss order is or may have an incorrect view of why such orders exist. A stop loss order is an order to cover a position at the market if the market trades at the level at which you placed your stop loss. If the market should jump right over your stop level, the order will not be entered on your behalf. Since the order is entered as a market order, your filled or executed price will rarely be the same as your stop level. In addition, a lot of retail traders and investors do not use stop loss orders because they think this is a sure way to lose money. Such a view simply shows how inexperienced and misinformed they are.

There are several different kinds of orders available. Do the work before you take the risk.

You can connect the real bodies of candlesticks with an imaginary horizontal line to define levels of market support (when the line is under the current trading price) or resistance (when it is above the current price).

Through these lines, you control your drawdown and your win/loss ratio. For example, if you buy a market, you know you are wrong if the market falls through the second support line under the market level at which you are buying, but if you have learned how to determine that if you are right, the market is likely to run through four resistance lines above your entry price level, you suddenly have a quantifiable risk-to-reward ratio. We will be looking for ratios of at least 1 to 3. That's just an introduction. We will add indicators and directional signals so that we can get "permission" to take action by buying or selling at specific lines or tight cluster of lines forming zones of support or resistance. If you are new at this, do you feel that you are struggling? Don't worry. I have lots of examples ahead to help you put this together in small steps. However, this paragraph is the larger game plan and summarizes where we are heading. The depth of your understanding will grow as we continue.

Let's take another look at candlesticks using a different market. The chart in Figure 6-4 shows weekly U.S. Treasury Bonds. The long black candlestick that is third from the right shows a market

Figure 6-4

move that we could describe as a meltdown. But take a close look at the top of the real body of this candlestick and track the horizontal line across the chart from right to left. Very big, and hence important, moves originated in the past at this same horizontal level within this chart. The asterisks show how the real bodies are used to create the line defining support or resistance. But I have also added a symbol (@) under some candlesticks where the shadows showed respect for this same line. When the market failed under this line, the term we use is a market failure under major resistance. The third candlestick from the right was a doozy of a failure. What was once support for the market has become the price that began a meltdown. This price zone will always have significance in the future, as strong market moves up and down have originated from this area.

Asian traders chart their prices in other ways as well. Someday you may wish to explore the methods called Kagi, Renko, and

Three-Line Break charts. These charts ignore the passage of time and display only changes in prices.

Western analysts have their own methods for plotting prices without taking time into consideration. The most popular is called Point-and-Figure (P&F) charting. You will end up with a window full of small o's and x's on your computer screen. Rather than having price on the y axis and time on the x axis, P&F charts display price changes on both axes. There are several books specializing in Point-and-Figure charting techniques that you may want to explore. All these different ways of displaying data have their place, and all have different strengths and weaknesses.

CHAPTER 7

Why the U.S. Dollar Dictates the Longevity of an American Equity Bull Market

To understand what fueled the bull market of the 1990s and what lies ahead, it is necessary to think like a global chess player. The international game is called "collecting basis points," and the world is your chessboard. This does not imply that you have to invest globally in order to win the game, but it means that you do have to think like a global player to do well.

Because the game board involves different markets, such as currencies, bonds, and stocks, across all continents and cultures, the global player has to find a common denominator or similar means of comparison for all these different markets. Every professional defines the potential of any given market, derivative, or specialized custom investment by its potential to make basis points.

You probably already know what basis points are, although you may not realize it. When the Federal Reserve announces that it has raised the Discount Rate by a quarter point, it has in fact increased short-term rates by 25 basis points. So 1 percent or 1.00 percent is the same thing as 100 basis points.

If your stock portfolio lost 10 percent in the course of a year, you in fact lost 1000 basis points. You are not winning the basis point game. The global chessboard is the race to collect as many basis points as you can in any given year. All the savvy global investors are playing on a three-dimensional board, as different countries and different markets are no limitation when a common denominator for measurement is used.

So here is why the currency markets dictate the direction of all the other markets in the world. Let's say you are a very rich investor in Japan. Your wealth would naturally be tied up in the currency of your homeland. All your expenses and bills and bank accounts are denominated in yen. The problem in the 1990s was that the yen was losing buying power, as it was becoming weaker against other nations' currencies. Your homeland currency becomes weak when your economy and confidence in the government backing your currency falters. The Japanese economy was in a tailspin, and confidence in the banking system was declining as well.

If you are this Japanese investor, you are losing the basis points game if you simply sit there and do nothing. Everything you need to buy is becoming more expensive because it takes more yen to purchase all the products you depend on that have to be brought into Japan and paid for in a foreign country's currency.

You also have another problem: The yen savings that you have sitting in the bank are not earning any interest. The Japanese government had tried so hard to stimulate the Japanese economy by reducing interest rates that rates are nearly at zero. So banks are paying you almost nothing on your cash. On the other hand, it does not cost you much to borrow cash. As the problems in Japan became worse and the Japanese government continued to lower the prime lending rate, you could have borrowed yen for less than 2 percent or 200 basis points. With borrowed yen in hand that cost very little to obtain, you and other Japanese investors only had to find something with a higher return than 200 basis points.

Japan's problems are about to get worse because the money you just borrowed will not be staying in Japan to help stimulate the Japanese economy out of its slump.

On the other side of the world, the American government was raising interest rates because the American economy was overheating, leading to inflation. In the United States there was an employment boom, as there was a shortage of people who could fill the open jobs. People are getting the pay they asked for, and everything else costs a little more as a result. That is, *normally* it costs more. In the 1990s, however, the rising costs for labor were offset by declining energy costs. So companies found that they could handle the extra labor cost without passing it on to their products and services. On the surface it looked as if the Federal Reserve was crying wolf.

Inflation? Where? But the Federal Reserve knew that the American economy was overheating, so it continued to raise short-term rates. While it cost American businesses more to borrow money, they earned more on their existing cash.

Let's return to the Japanese investor with cash yen in hand. You look over at America, and you see three things. The strongest currency in the world at the time is the American dollar. That means that if you switch your yen for U.S. dollars, you have just solved the problem of your buying power declining on a daily basis. If you just put your U.S. dollars into an American bank, you make basis points with your borrowed yen, since the interest rates on short-term bank deposits in the United States are higher than those in Japan. In fact, you make out like a bandit. You borrowed yen for, let's say, 200 basis points or less, and you convert them into U.S. dollars and leave them in an American bank. The banks in the 1990s will pay you about 3 percent for doing nothing. That means it pays you 300 basis points on money that cost you 200 basis points, for a net gain of 100 basis points.

It gets even better. The game is to accumulate as many basis points as possible over the year. So you look at the American stock market. If you buy a stock and its price doesn't change, you will still earn more than you would if you just left the cash in the bank if the stock pays dividends. The catch here is that U.S. stocks pay dividends in U.S. dollars. Excellent! The dividends are potentially higher than what the bank pays for just a simple deposit. So suddenly a lot of people in Japan want large-cap U.S. stocks, as these are the ones that pay highest dividends. The DJIA starts to rise.

Now, not only are you making money on borrowed money, but your underlying principal is beginning to increase in value, as the market is beginning to advance. Your dividends start to decline, but the number of basis points you can gain from the increase in your principal as the stock marches up is much greater. This is getting so good that you want to borrow more yen back in Japan so that you can put more money to work and increase your leverage in the United States.

While the market expands and your principal grows, there is a third factor to consider: The U.S. dollar itself is strengthening against other world currencies. This means that anytime you bring your original investment home with all those new basis points you gained, you get another basis-point bonus from the exchange rate when you sell U.S. dollars to buy back yen. In essence, the 1990s provided a Japanese version of financial Camelot if you had money to invest overseas.

When does Camelot implode? Assuming that Japan does not enter a depression because there is no cash left in Japan to rebuild from the devastating economic collapse, it will be when the yen begins to strengthen. When the yen starts to strengthen, Japanese investors caught in overseas markets will be losing basis points on all three fronts. The leverage that compounded their borrowed funds so well will turn very sour because the losses will be compounded incredibly fast. Because the 1990s experienced a scramble of Asian investors into the U.S. stock market, it is paramount to monitor when a mass exit away from the American markets could occur. *We have not seen this yet as of April 2002.*

The crash in the Nasdaq did not truly have an impact on the DJIA, as Japanese investors rotated out of technology stocks and purchased large-cap basic industry stocks on the New York Stock Exchange. During the 2000 and 2001 Nasdaq implosion, the underlying relationship between currencies did not change. In fact, the U.S. dollar continued to strengthen rapidly against a weakening yen. If Japanese investors got out of technology stocks, they still did better than investing at home if they held stocks that were in the DJIA. They just didn't win as much. This also explains why charts of the decline in the Nasdaq and the same period in the DJIA are extremely different.

In Figure 7-1 we see charts with a monthly time horizon showing the Nasdaq on the left and the DJIA on the right. Relatively speaking, you can see that the DJIA is holding up fairly well in comparison to the Nasdaq.

In the first chapter of the book, I showed you charts of the Japanese yen. It should now be easier for you to understand why a big move in the yen that may suggest that the larger trend may be reversing is so important to the U.S. stock market. The strength of the U.S. dollar will in fact dictate whether the DJIA will rally in the near future or will rapidly fall and shadow the recent path of the Nasdaq decline.

Will the culprit be the new common currency in Europe, called the *European Currency* (Euro), gaining in appeal? Will it be the yen

F i g u r e   7-1

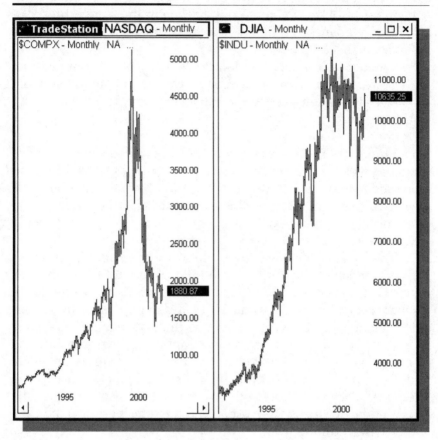

strengthening in Japan as that economy recovers? Or might world opinion about the United States being a safe haven change after the events of September 2001? We may not have all the answers, but as technicians we will be able to see the flash point through our charts. We may not know why, but the trend change in the Japanese yen that was early in the book must be monitored closely.

One of the easiest charts to monitor is the Dollar Index. The decline that may have just started could move toward 100, or *parity*. By the time the Dollar Index realized 100 the technical indicators would be at extreme lows in weekly charts. We refer to rebounds from extreme indicator lows as a technical bounce. The Dollar Index would likely attempt to recover for several months if 100 was real-ized in 2002. Then after two or three quarters the dollar may resume the decline toward the 1995 lows where very long-term support is located. Such a decline in the U.S. dollar would be horrific for the DJIA. The long-term health of the DJIA is in the hands of the global investor. Myopic American investors who focus only on American markets will be hit by a truck and never know what hit them. Even, worse, the major news outlets will focus on whatever national issue is present and fail to see how their focus on a new scandal or corpo-rate business failure will serve only to contribute to negative per-ceptions about America overseas.

Now suppose the U.S. dollar is weaker and the overseas market favors the euro. Which equity market would investors favor? The German stock market would benefit by allowing the German Dax to bottom *before* the American stock market bot-tomed. This is an example of Intermarket analysis that will be dis-cussed in Chapter 9. However, before we can look at global stock indices, we need to discuss how interest rates fit into this multi-layered puzzle.

CHAPTER 8

Help! Short- and Long-Term Interest Rates Are Really Confusing

When it comes to the basis-point game, the master gunslingers are the fixed-income security professionals. They have a language all their own, and the tuition fees to step into their arena are in the millions of dollars. It is therefore understandable that the general public is a little unclear about this investment segment beyond how it affects the interest rates we pay on our credit cards, car loans, and mortgages. Even then the interest rates charged for consumer loans do not always mirror the directional bias of the Federal Reserve, adding further confusion.

In the financial food chain, currencies come first, fixed-income securities come second, and stocks are at the tail end. Everything rolls downhill to hit stocks. Unlike equities, where there is no maturity date or guaranteed rate of return, an investor holding a fixed-income security until its maturity will earn a fixed rate of return. The promised interest rate is called the *coupon rate*. Periodically the security issuer will send a coupon payment to each investor. This usually occurs every 6 months. The final payment is made on the *maturity date* and will include the last coupon payment and the principal or face amount of the issue.

In the United States and other industrialized countries, there are five issuers of fixed-income securities: Governments, Federal agencies, Municipalities, Corporations, and Banks. These five issuers segregate their markets into two segments: *Money markets* and *Capital markets*. Money market securities are investment products that mature in 1 year or less. In the money market segment, we measure returns using *money market* yields. Capital markets have maturities greater than 1 year. In the capital markets, the correct way to measure returns is *yield to maturity*.

For fixed-income securities, the most important word is *yield*. Yield is the rate of return to an investor that is being paid by the borrower or security issuer. The calculation of yield can be complex because it is a function of creditworthiness, maturity horizon, and liquidity. The liquidity is the ease at which you may find a willing buyer or seller on the market for your particular security. The most liquid securities are the U.S. Treasury securities.

MONEY MARKET SECURITIES OR SHORT-TERM INTEREST RATE MARKETS

You already have the most important building block in place, as you have an understanding of basis points. Let's start from this point. If you have a cash savings account (we are back in the United States now), you know that your bank sends you lots of flyers trying to entice you to buy *Certificates of Deposit* (CDs). CDs have a maturity of 1 year or less, so they are within the category of money market securities. All money market securities are short-term interest rate investments. The banks know that when you lock up your funds in one of their CDs for 3 months to 1 year, they have the use of your funds for a fixed period of time. As a result, they are willing to pay you a slightly higher interest rate than you would receive on an interest-bearing savings account, where the cash always has to be available in case you decide to withdraw your funds. In reality, the bank is borrowing your cash to play the global basis-point game. Like the Japanese investors in the last chapter, the bank needs to find a way to make more basis points on your money than it is paying out to you. You see how the basis-point game never goes away?

Suppose you decide to buy a 6-month CD with a promised return of 3%, or 300 basis points. Your promised return is always annualized, so after 6 months you really get paid only 1½%, or 150 basis points. To make 300 basis points, you have to buy another CD that promises to pay at least 300 basis points on an annualized basis. You can see an immediate problem: What if the Federal Reserve is lowering short-term interest rates? You will make less in this case, as similar investments will have lowered their payout by the time you are ready to *roll* your funds into a new CD.

If you don't like the idea of making only 3% or less on your money, there are also short-term securities other than bank CDs that you can consider. Treasury Bills (T-Bills) are short-term obligations of the U.S. Government with maturities of 13 weeks, 26 weeks, and 52 weeks. The minimum denomination is $10,000, then in increments of $1000. While they are unsecured, they are guaranteed by the full faith and credit of the government, the taxpayer. They have less risk than bank CDs and so will pay less.

We might then consider agency securities. Money market securities of federal agencies are issued in maturities from overnight to 360 days. There are two kinds of agency securities. One, called mortgage-backed securities, is collateralized by different kinds of home mortgages, and the other is noncollateralized debt issued by the Student Loan Marketing Association, the Federal Farm Credit Bank, and housing agencies. The minimum denomination is also $10,000, and then in increments of $1000. Commercial Paper is short-term unsecured debt issued by corporations with maturities from overnight to 270 days. The credit rating of the corporation will affect the return associated with the security. The minimum is usually no less than $25,000, but even these short-term securities will not pay much more than bank CDs, as the borrower selling you the investment will have your money for 1 year or less.

INTERMEDIATE- AND LONG-TERM FIXED INCOME MARKETS

In order to obtain a better interest rate, you have to agree to lock up your money for longer than 1 year. Someone who is able to use your money in the basis-point game for a longer period of time will agree to pay you more basis points. You also demand a higher interest rate because of the greater risk you have with a longer maturity date. The instruments with the lowest risk in the intermediate-term horizon will be those issued by the U.S. Government. U.S. *Treasury Notes* have maturity dates of 2, 5, and 10 years out. Other federal agencies and corporations also issue notes; these are slightly more risky, so they pay slightly more than government notes with similar maturities. Their returns as a group will generally move up or down when government notes with similar maturities fluctuate.

The *long bond* is the 30-year U.S. Treasury Bond. There's just one small problem: The bond market is all in a tizzy in 2002 because the government has announced that it is not going to issue any more 30-year Treasury Bonds (T-Bonds). That means that when the last 30-year T-Bond issue reaches maturity, 30-year bonds will disappear. So the bond market is in turmoil because there are many complex factors working together at the same time. After September 11, 2001, the United States entered into a war against terrorism. Wars produce a rush into bonds to protect assets. Such a rush to buy bonds is called a *flight-to-safety*. However, since the government has announced that it will discontinue the 30-year T-Bond, every professional trader knows that at some point there will be a rush to sell the retiring bonds in favor of the 10-year notes, which will be far more liquid, as there will be a current market willing to buy and sell. With such a battle of fundamentals at work in the bond market, it is best not to try and sort this out by using logic. Here you see another reason why charts are of great value: They can demystify a very complex environment. While T-Bond futures are only trading near 98/00 as this is written, you may see the 30-year T-Bond spike toward 114/00 or 117/00 before it begins a free fall toward 84/00. The 117/00 price objective is purely a technical target where major resistance is located. We will look at how to make such a price projection later and then look at how momentum indicators can help you identify the market timing when a market may reverse.

The correct way to write prices for the 30-year T-Bond is the format "117/02," where the numbers after the "/" refer to 32nds. (Some quote vendors use 117^02 as well.) Therefore, 117/02 is the same as 117.0625, but we use decimals only when conversions are required for analysis purposes. Notes, on the other hand, are traded in 64ths, and they are traded using decimals.

PRICE-TO-YIELD RELATIONSHIP

You can chart notes and bonds using either market price or yield. This is a concept that you must understand before you chart fixed-income markets. There is always an inverse relationship between price and yield for a security. As the price for an issue rises, the yield *must* fall, and vice versa. This has nothing to do with Fed action; it is the pricing dynamics of the security itself. A fixed-income security is just that: fixed. An easy way to think this through is from the perspective of the bond issuer trying to raise capital by selling you the security. You are the lender, and the issuer is the borrower. When the price of the security is offered for sale at 100 percent of its face value, it is said to be trading at *par*. When a bond is trading at its face value, the coupon rate and the yield to maturity are equal. This means that an 8% bond would also have a yield to maturity of 8%. However, if the market value of the bond should fall, the current yield must go up *or the bond issuer would be underpaying the promised rate* because the principal has declined in value. A higher current yield is the only way to make up for the price decline.

If the face value should rise as a result of market demand, the current yield *must* decline because the issuer promised to pay only 8%. You cannot have it both ways: receive a gain in the face value and receive a current yield at the original 8% coupon rate. Therefore, we can chart the market price for a fixed-income security or we can chart the yield for the same security, but the two charts will always be inverted because of this price-to-yield relationship.

YIELD TO MATURITY VERSUS REALIZED YIELD

You now know some of the different kinds of fixed-income securities and that they can be charted in two ways. We have not begun to look at charts, as there are still some basic concepts that you need in order to understand why you will want to set up your computer in a particular way.

However, you could chart and invest in fixed-income securities without knowing the following: *The coupon rate that the issuer sets is the fixed cost that the issuer must pay in order to borrow funds from you; the issuer is not promising you a realized return.* You are being paid *x*%, but you are not necessarily earning that percentage rate. What you do with the coupon payments over the life of the note or bond is not the issuer's concern.

If you buy a note, your money is locked up longer than if you purchase a money market investment. Let's say that instead of 300 basis points, you are promised 5½% or 550 basis points. If you are like most investors, you are probably unaware that when the issuer promises a 5½% return, there is a hidden flaw in the formula for the purchaser. The series of coupon payments is called the cash flow from the interest-bearing security, and the yield-to-maturity formula requires reinvestment of all these coupon payments. Each payment *has to be reinvested at the same rate as the calculated rate on the purchase date and remain invested at that rate for the life of the issue.* In other words, if you purchase a 5-year Treasury Note at a yield of 5½%, the reinvestment rate for every coupon payment received over the life of the note is presumed to be 5½%. As soon as you start spending the interest payments or cannot find another 5½% investment to buy with your coupon payment, you are not making 5½% or anything near it on your investment.

Some readers will want proof that they must reinvest the coupon payments. You will need to read a book dealing with fixed-income securities. It will give tables of cash flows from a non-callable coupon-bearing security and show how they are part of the total valuation at maturity. Each book is the same, as the formula does not change. The math proves that each coupon must be reinvested at the coupon rate or better, and most books will show you just how rapidly your *realized yield* declines when the coupons are reinvested at lower rates in declining interest rate economies. One book, though very advanced, was written by a friend of mine who trained many professional traders on fixed-income desks. The book is named *Investment Mathematics for Finance and Treasury Professionals: A Practical Approach*, by Gregory Kitter.

YIELD CURVES

A yield curve is a way to study interest rates as a series of securities with equal creditworthiness but with different maturities. The most common yield curve is one that displays the securities offered by the U.S. Government, as displayed in Figure 8-1. The curve visually shows us short-term interest rates on the left (T-Bills), intermediate-term interest rates in the middle (T-Notes), and the current 30-year Treasury Bond (T-Bonds) on the far right. There are other maturities in the middle, allowing the curve to be connected from left to right. On the bottom you will find the numbers, from left to right, 3, 6, 2, 5, 10, 30. These numbers correspond to the 3-

F i g u r e   8-1

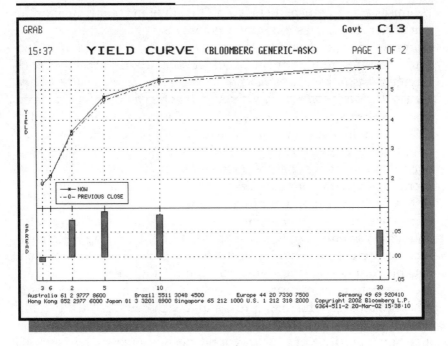

and 6-month T-Bills; 2, 5, and 10-year T-Notes; and 30-year T-Bonds. The solid-line curve displays current market yields at the moment the screen was captured. The dotted line is where the yield curve was when the market closed the previous day. In order to see visually which maturities along the yield curve have changed most versus yesterday, look at the spread, or difference, shown under the yield curve as a histogram. There are no surprises in some of these changes today (on March 20, 2002). The previous day the Federal Reserve had announced that it would make no changes in current interest rates, and had also proclaimed a change in bias to a position that it is unlikely to lower rates in the future. As a result, there was a lot happening in the world of fixed-income securities.

Because of the Federal Reserve's (the Fed's) comments, the middle of the curve is actively trading. When a change in the interest-rate environment appears on the horizon, the holders of very-long-term bonds *shift down the yield curve* by selling T-Bonds and buying Treasury Notes with intermediate-term maturities. People tend to take refuge or huddle together in the middle of the curve during times of confusion. There is also concern about what lies ahead for the U.S. dollar. Lowering interest rates in a weak economy hurts the dollar. Therefore, the government will find it difficult to lower rates because this reduces the return for overseas investors. As we learned in the previous chapter, the health of the DJIA is linked to the strength of the U.S. dollar, so lowering rates further will be complex.

When the Federal Reserve lowers or raises Fed Funds and/or the Discount Rate, this usually has an impact along the entire yield curve. You would think that if the Federal Reserve lowered the short-term benchmark by 25 basis points, the same would apply for all the maturities along the yield curve. But things do not work so slickly and cleanly in the real world, where you have to factor in people. In 2001 the Fed kept tweaking rates lower. The short-term interest rates declined immediately. As a direct result, the banks were quick to lower their short-term rates, as this meant that they would pay less interest on the interest-bearing savings accounts and CDs that they offer. The long-term rates generally adjusted as well, but more slowly. However, in 2002, when the Fed tweaked short-term rates again early in the year, long-term rates and mortgage rates actually went up and then stalled. Why? For one thing, long-term rates had dropped to levels the baby boomers' parents once paid for their mortgages. Thus, demand for fixed-rate mortgages was high, and banks were not required to lower their mortgage rates any further. Therefore, there came a point in time when the Fed was lowering short-term rates, but the slope of the yield curve became steeper because the bond market was no longer paying attention.

Yield curves are important. Consider this: If you decide to lock away your cash for 30 years in a bond at a time when interest rates are low, what happens to you if rates begin to climb? You are being underpaid, as you could be making more basis points elsewhere. In that case you would rather be in maturities further down the yield curve, and so you would buy instruments with short-term maturities. That way, when you get your money back, you can roll the money into something that takes advantage of the rising interest rates without penalty. This shifting back and forth between the ends of the yield curve is what causes the teeter-totter effect within the curve. The 5-Year Note, being in the middle, is least affected, so the extreme ends shift up and down, leaving the middle with little movement and the most stable. In Figure 8-1 the 5-Year Note is getting a lot of attention because people want to own something that will sit in the middle and be less affected than the outer-maturity extremes when the Fed starts to hike rates (the extremes being the 3-month T-Bill and the 30-Year T-Bond).

Figure 8-1 cannot be drawn on either CQG or TradeStation. In fact, most technical analysis software packages do not offer yield curves. (They would be nice to have, though, guys!) This chart is from a company called Bloomberg, which is the biggest provider of information in the fixed-income securities arena. Professionals get all excited if they can find a way to pick up just 10 extra basis points. For example, if they can get paid 5.10% instead of 5% or 510 basis points versus 500, they will do cartwheels to make it happen if the risk is the same. So Bloomberg has a slew of fast calculating formulas to answer a host of what-if scenarios. That is trading using fundamentals, and that is what Bloomberg does best. If you are trading $90 million, finding a couple more basis points makes a huge difference. But it doesn't pay to shop for 10 more basis points if you are holding $1000 and buying a single bond.

The yield curve is not something you actually put technical analysis indicators on, so technical analysis packages don't include it. But we do use technical analysis for the spreads between these different maturities and to analyze the individual maturities by charting T-Bills, T-Notes, and T-Bonds.

If you have no idea that a yield curve exists, you have no idea what you are really looking at if you just analyze a single chart within the fixed-income market. The interaction between short-term rates, intermediate, and long-term rates is important. Figure 8-2 shows how I display the yield curve indirectly on my computer by arranging my charts in a manner that allows me to see futures markets for short-, intermediate-, and long-term government securities at the same time.

On the left is the chart for Treasury Bills. In the middle is the 10-Year Treasury Note. On the far right I still display the 30-Year Treasury Bond. These charts all show the prices for futures on the top from the Chicago Board of Trade. The display in Figure 8-2 is the actual screen I work from, so it is full of indicators that we

Figure 8-2

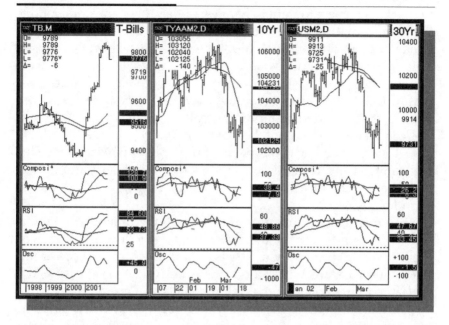

have not yet begun to discuss. As long as the 30-Year Treasury Bond remains in the market, professionals will trade and analyze it. As time goes on it will become thinner and thinner, as the volume traded will become smaller and smaller. But when I look at these three charts, I am essentially obtaining a view of the yield curve and watching the teeter-totter shift around the center fulcrum point, which is the 5-Year Note.

How will I change my computer screen once the 30-Year Bond is not around or is of limited value? I will continue to use three charts showing T-Bills on the left, 5-Year T-Notes in the middle, and 10-Year T-Notes on the far right. Keep in mind that this is just one extra screen, as I also have screens set up for each individual Treasury market to cross-compare different time horizons, as we covered in Chapter 5.

In some ways, dropping the 30-Year T-Bond solves a problem for us. The long bond for England is roughly a 12-year maturity (London's bonds are called Gilts). In Germany the long bond is a 10-year maturity (German bonds are called Bunds), and in Japan it is the 10-year maturity that is to the far right on the yield curve (we call these bonds JGBs, for Japanese Government Bonds). The exact maturity is subject to minor changes, but all three are similar. Soon the longest maturity in the United States will be closer to the long bonds in these other industrialized countries. I suspect there was a little international arm twisting to get us to conform, as we were making the global basis-point game harder to play. Of course, the reason the U.S. Government gave was that it was paying down debt, as that sounded better for the voting public. In any event, the 30-Year Treasury Bond will become extinct.

Then September 11 happened. Suddenly billions were needed to clean up New York, to prop up the airline industry, and to help heal the psyche of a nation. The goal of paying down debt was abandoned.

To pay for such huge promises, the government will have to issue new bonds to raise the cash. If you issue lots of bonds, you are increasing the supply of bonds, and that means that prices fall. And what happens when bond prices fall? Yields go up, which is the same thing as saying that interest rates will go up.

What happens when short-term rates are extremely low and the economy is weak or becomes weaker? That is a deflationary environment and is exactly what the Japanese experienced in the late 1990s. The Japanese government tried to lower short-term rates to stimulate investments and business in order to rejuvenate the Japanese economy. Instead, the money was borrowed and the yen was sold for dollars to invest in a higher-interest-rate environment. That lesson should not be forgotten. If our economy weakens as a result of a falling dollar, the Fed will be all too aware of what could follow if it were to lower rates further. I would suspect that it will do all it can to stall its decision to lower rates further. On the surface lower rates will look like an economic boost, but by hurting the dollar this action will trigger a fall in the DJIA. The Fed will be well aware of this, but the media are not likely to see it and will cry out that the Fed is not taking the necessary action.

The final chart in this chapter, Figure 8-3, is your first introduction to spreads. We can analyze the spread between maturities within the yield curve. If I want to compare 10-Year T-Notes with the 30-Year T-Bond, all I need is the current price or yield at which each is trading. Then I subtract one from the other to find the difference. It is the difference that is plotted. When you plot a spread, you normally use a line chart instead of a bar chart. This line chart is placed at the top of your screen. Then you can add any indicator that you would use for normal price data.

We technicians are very flexible. Later on you will see that we will analyze anything we can get our hands on that has a set of data. Real estate prices, economic numbers, you name it—if we can chart it, someone out there is applying technical analysis to improve market timing. In the case of spreads, if the indicators tell us to buy or sell, it means that the spread relationship is about to invert or change direction. One of the maturities will fall and the other will rise. As a result, you sell the one you think will fall, and you buy the one you think is about to rise. That is a spread trade. Figure 8-3 shows the spread between the 10-Year and 30-Year Treasuries with a monthly view on the left and a daily time horizon on the right. The same principles for displaying multiple time horizons that we covered in Chapter 5 apply. In addition, the same RSI described in earlier chapters has been added to help identify support and resistance levels for potential turns of the spread. This chart alone is a wonderful tool to have just for business purposes as an early warning that interest rates are about to change.

F i g u r e   8-3

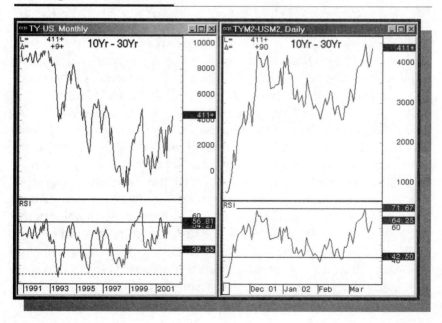

CHAPTER 9

Why a North American Needs International Market Data

Wouldn't our lives be a whole lot easier if we could just see tomorrow's prices on our computer screens today? Where can I subscribe to that data?

In fact, this is not such a crazy idea, because markets do not move in perfect unison. If you find the market that is leading the others, you will have a couple of days' advance warning of what is to come.

In Figure 9-1 we see an overlay of two markets. On the top is the German stock market (called the DAX), and on the bottom is the stock market in Switzerland. This is not a chart display offered by most vendors, but here is how to produce it.

When you do not have an overlay feature in your analysis software, you can still create this chart by making a picture of each market when the time axis is set to the same scale. For Figure 9-1 the pictures were made from Internet charts. Go to the Web site for FutureSource (http://www.futuresource.com) and visit the chart section. When the chart you want is displayed on the screen, use a software utility that takes a quick snapshot of the chart. Then switch to a different market, being careful that the *x*-axis scale does not change, and take another snapshot of the second chart. You then go into Microsoft Paint, which is shipped with every Microsoft operating system. To go into Paint, use the task bar at the bottom of your screen and go to Start > Programs > Accessories > Paint. If you have an older Windows version and Paint is not there, you can add it, as it is part of the original Windows software. Go to your Control

Figure 9-1

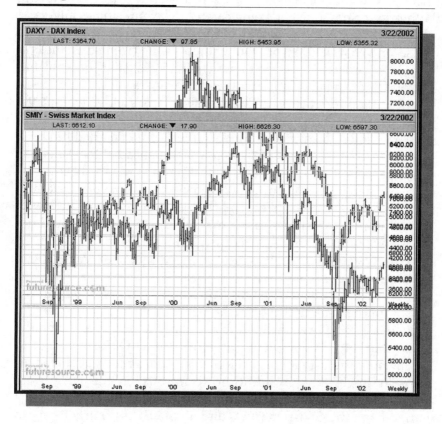

Panel and select Add/Remove Programs. Then go to the Windows Setup tab. Now click on Accessories, open the details, and put a check mark beside Paint to add the software. Have your Windows operating diskette handy, as you will be asked to put it in the drive. Now you have Paint.

Once you are in Paint, at the top of the menus, go to Image and uncheck the menu line that says "Draw Opaque." This ensures that you copy the chart with a transparent background. Now you are ready to open the first chart you took a picture of and copy it. The easy way to do this is to use "Select All" from the Edit menu and then use Copy from the Edit menu. Now open the second chart and plop it on top of the first one you copied by returning to the Edit menu and using Paste. Drag the chart to a spot where you can see both price charts together, being careful to keep the dates aligned. I always add space to the bottom of the underlying chart first so that the second chart has lots of room without being cropped on the bottom. Most professionals don't know how to use Paint software, but it is one of the most creative tools in my arsenal.

OK, why do you want to do this? Take a close look at the German DAX. It broke out of a trading "funk" in 1999 much earlier than any other global market. In fact, the German market has been ahead of all the European stock markets and ahead of the American stock markets at major junctures. It was about 8 weeks ahead of the huge Nasdaq rally. OK, but why compare it to the Swiss stock market? Because the Swiss stock market is strongly correlated with American mid-cap stocks, and a major bull market run would not be in force until the mid-cap stocks got out of their funk. And the nice thing was that the Swiss market was a couple of weeks ahead of the American market.

Now let's consider the decline from the market high in the DAX. You can see that the Swiss market rallied into September 2000, while the DAX declined from its high. However, when the Swiss market was completing its rally, the DAX formed a dead giveaway pattern that we will look at when we look at chart patterns in price data. In addition, technicals on the DAX were screaming SELL! So we knew that there was a black cloud on the horizon for the Swiss market, and if the Swiss market was in trouble, the U.S. markets were going to see major trouble in all the indices.

As a short-horizon trader, I watch German markets before the American markets open. Frequently I get a hint of what is about to happen, as we are behind Europe. Why? I don't know; you have to ask the fundamentalists. I do know that Germany has completed technical buy/sell signals in its charts, from monthly to daily, ahead of the development of the same signals in North American stock indices. I do hear answers to the question why through my large overseas clients. So I tend to be aware that a comment like "Germany is leading the global equity markets" is not far-fetched. OK, let's take a look at a few more examples.

In Figure 9-2 I have the Toronto stock market on the top and the Dow Jones Industrial Average on the bottom. Because the DJIA chart label covered some data I want you to see, I used the eraser

Figure 9-2

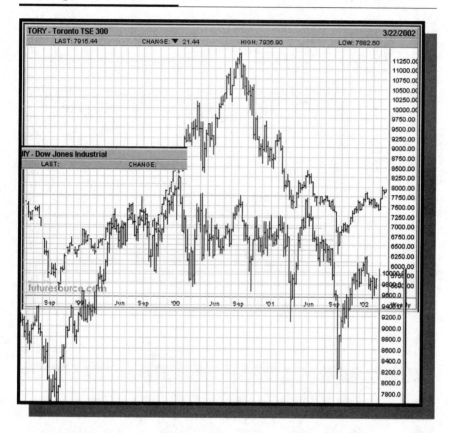

tool in Paint before I copied the DJIA, so the title bar is shorter. From April to September 2000, the DJIA chopped around in a directionless manner. Toronto, however, was forming very distinct and clean price patterns. Therefore I switched to the Toronto market to read its sell or buy signals along with the German DAX signals. Toronto is correlated with German markets because the country's culture is more in tune with Europeans. But Toronto is also strongly affected by what happens to American markets, so it is an interesting way to back into what the American market will do next.

Figure 9-3 is a comparison between gold prices and the Nikkei stock market. This chart shows a fairly high correlation, with one huge exception: In 1988 and 1989 gold moved south as the Nikkei steamed north. You cannot tell when a market bubble will burst; no one can. But you can recognize when a bubble is unfolding, as with

Figure 9-3

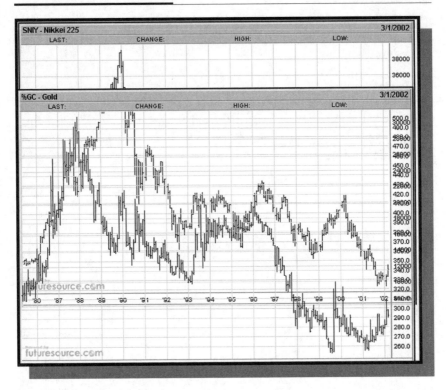

the Nikkei, and with the Nasdaq years later. You also know what happens when the bubble bursts. We will look at the Nasdaq market bubble in more detail in a later chapter.

What could the Asian markets have told us in 2000 about our own equity markets? In Figure 9-4 I have the Toronto stock market on the bottom and the Hang Seng index of Hong Kong, which was the strongest Asian stock market at that time, on the top.

The Hang Seng index displays a price pattern that we call a double top. I drew a black arc over the double peaks to highlight them for you. An old high was tested a second time, and the market used the old high as resistance. When the market reached the old high for the second time, it failed. This is an extremely bearish pattern. If you look at the Toronto index, it was forming an inverted V top while the Hang Seng's bearish pattern was forming. If both Toronto and Asia are about to experience serious declines, do you think American equities will be immune? In fact, both Toronto and

Figure 9-4

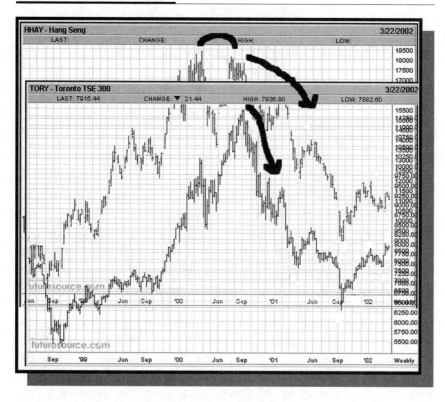

Asia fell continuously from that point for the entire following year, and so did the American economy. All you had to do was look at the charts together—and we haven't even begun to talk about indicators.

FutureSource's Web site also has all the currencies and global bond markets. You can mix and match to your heart's content, and you will be surprised at some of the intermarket relationships that exist. If you would like to know more about intermarket analysis, you may find John Murphy's book *Intermarket Technical Analysis* to be of interest. Keep in mind that this is big-picture analysis, not something you can trade directly from, as relationships just tell you when something is way out of line. When the relationships are seriously wrong, you know that something big is going to happen to bring them back to normal. You know it will be coming, but you need to use indicators to tell you when that trigger point will happen. That's why we need to move on to build your skills.

Wait a Minute! Isn't That Real Estate Data?

While we are on the subject of creating charts, you may want to think about charting more than just market data. Figure 10-1 displays the Housing Market Index on the top as a line chart. Below the index data is the indicator you have seen me use before, the RSI or Relative Strength Index. Just as on the charts that showed market data, I have drawn zones on the indicator where the indicator has defined support and resistance.

The end of 1998 was a very high-risk market high for the housing market, as the RSI had failed at this same level in 1993. The market low in 1990 was an extreme that is likely to define a future market bottom. In the middle I have drawn a support/resistance zone on the RSI. As before, trace back from right to left to see what has happened in the past at this line. At the point where the RSI bounded away from this zone, cross-compare it with the market data itself.

How did I create a chart from economic data? I used another charting package called SuperCharts, which is a cheap version of TradeStation. (I like keeping some of my more esoteric data charts in a separate computer.) However, you could do the same thing in any analysis software that accepts third-party data. I created a custom data series and called it Housing Market Index. I then typed in the data that had been reported by the government. My computer does not know the difference between Microsoft exchange stock, and my own custom market. The computer will display custom market data, letting me analyze it. The data itself was real easy to obtain.

F i g u r e   10-1

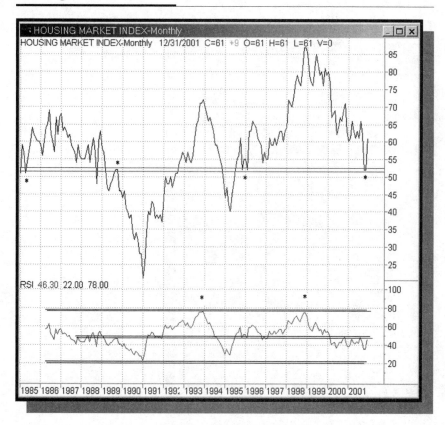

Figure 10-2 shows a copy of the Internet page I used to build this data series.

Many Web pages offer economic data in an Excel format. If the data you are looking for is offered this way, your life is even easier: You create a Microsoft Excel file, being sure to save it as a text file or ASCII format file. Your software vendor will have to help you the first time, as every package is a little different. But once you have imported the data into your software for analysis, you are ready to set up a chart.

I would suggest using the mean selling prices for your specific geographic area. Contact a real estate agent's office to find out where to obtain this information or surf the Internet.

F i g u r e   10-2

NAHB: Housing Market Index History - Microsoft Internet

File   Edit   View   Favorites   Tools   Help

Address http://www.nahb.com/facts/hmi_history.htm

Housing Market Index (Historical data)
Single-Family Sales
(Seasonally Adjusted)

	Jan	Feb	Mar	Apr	May	Jun	Jul	Aug	Sep	Oct	Nov	Dec
1985	51	59	57	51	54	57	60	64	62	61	60	60
1986	59	56	60	64	65	69	62	60	57	67	62	67
1987	68	63	64	63	61	62	59	58	57	54	59	56
1988	55	55	55	57	59	54	58	61	57	48	60	63
1989	58	57	52	47	46	48	49	51	52	52	46	46
1990	44	46	41	40	38	39	34	32	34	32	28	28
1991	21	25	34	40	39	43	42	38	39	38	39	37
1992	44	50	48	48	50	47	49	51	51	54	55	57
1993	56	54	57	55	54	56	61	55	66	71	71	72
1994	70	68	66	67	65	63	59	59	57	55	53	49
1995	44	47	42	40	45	48	52	55	56	61	52	55
1996	55	52	63	63	66	65	64	61	60	59	54	57
1997	55	55	61	59	59	61	59	61	63	63	60	63
1998	64	72	71	70	73	77	79	77	76	81	87	87
1999	85	79	77	76	81	85	82	79	80	76	81	79
2000	80	77	67	68	69	62	64	67	66	60	71	63
2001	60	61	66	63	61	63	61	66	62	52	52	61
2002	64	62	65									

In addition, Chapter 9 showed you a charting method using overlays. We know that interest rates play a big part in the housing market. So why not overlay average mortgage rates on top of housing data? Is the correlation tracking, or is there an inverse relationship? I'll let you explore this. (By the way, in Microsoft Paint, when you use Select All, there is a tool that lets you flip the chart upside down before you copy it. That way, when you do an overlay, you are always looking at data that is correlated. That makes it easier to see when the two markets separate.)

Now let's return to the housing market data and add another chart, a chart of potential buyers, from data obtained from the same Internet Web site. This chart is shown on the right in Figure 10-3.

I do not need to make an overlay of the data in these two charts in order for you to see an important signal that we discussed in the

F i g u r e   10-3

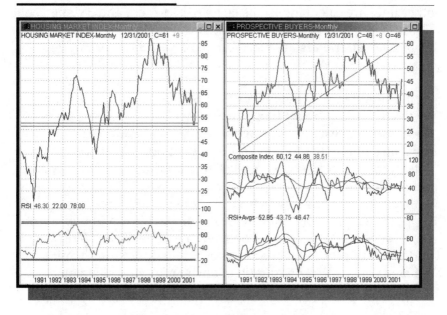

last chapter. Remember the double top that was present in the Hang Seng index? Take a look at the prospective buyers data on the right. You will see a double top in the highs established in 1999 and in 1993. The Housing Market Index on the left topped in 1998. But potential buyers did not reach the danger level of chart resistance until 1999. When the housing market data stalled after 1998, you had a clear indicator that a sell-off was ahead. Currently a rebound is being experienced in the housing market because of extremely low interest rates for mortgages. We now know that when bond prices begin to fall, interest rates will have to go up because of the price to yield dynamics for fixed income markets. Therefore, the astute real estate investor would be wise to chart the 30-year T-Bond in an overlay chart comparing this same housing market data.

I am going to use the chart of prospective buyers to introduce you to another way of calculating support and resistance. Do you see the large Z drawn on the right-hand line chart? The Z identifies the top and bottom I picked, and the computer then used these values to make three calculations. In the middle of the big Z is a line that will be at the dead center of this range. It is a calculation of 50 percent of the range contained within the boundaries of the Z.

You will also see lines above and below the halfway divider. These other lines are calculations of exactly 61.8 percent and 38.2 percent. The numbers or ratios 0.618, 0.500, and 0.382 are about to become your dearest friends in life. You have just been introduced to Fibonacci ratios. All markets expand and contract in these ratios.

Many market professionals would be astonished at the chart on the right because the prospective buyers data bounced directly off the 61.8 retracement line. It was exact. Professional traders use these ratios constantly on market data to identify support and resistance in any market and for any time horizon. But I just used data from the real estate market to introduce you to Fibonacci ratios, and they still work the same way. Why? Because anything with an expansion/contraction or growth and decay cycle will support the application of Fibonacci ratios. This is a universal constant, and we will spend considerable time developing a full understanding of it. Fibonacci ratios will help you to identify and manage your risk/reward ratio in any market in which you decide to invest or trade.

How to Read the Data to Make a Decision

A Big-Picture Summary of the Different Approaches within Technical Analysis

Before we look at various methods of obtaining market signals, we should step back and develop an overview or summary of technical analysis. Up to this point, we have been looking at ways to display market data. We have covered a few simple methods for defining market support, which may hold the market during a pullback, and market resistance, which may stall the market's progress at an invisible wall. We have also looked at how to study a chart in order to let the market teach us how the chart works for any method we may apply. So far we have looked at only one style of technical analysis, which fits into a category that is best labeled market geometry. But there are other approaches.

When I was learning technical analysis, it was hard to tell when methods just did the exact same thing over and over again in different ways. My probability of being right had not increased just because five oscillators all said the same thing. In hindsight, if there had been a clear way to know which methods were similar to one another and which were truly different, it would have been a whole lot easier. So let me provide you with a big-picture summary that gives a general outline of the different disciplines technical analysis has to offer.

In the old school of thought, technical analysis techniques were divided into two primary groups. The first group focused on trending tools and patterns, and the second group used oscillators to identify market extremes, when the market had overextended its course for the time being. Just because momentum was at an extreme that warned that the market was overbought or oversold it did not indicate that the market's larger trend had reversed.

Dividing techniques into two categories is now outdated. The new idea is that there are probably four categories, and these will assuredly evolve as well. But recognizing groups of techniques with similar approaches will help you when you encounter a new indicator or technical method. I suggest a simple method that will help you prioritize the methods you may study. Just ask yourself, "Does this method tell me the same thing as the method that I now use, but in a better way?" If the method is no better and is redundant, toss it out. The great risk is that you will develop such a large library of signals that you will become trapped in analysis paralysis, like so many people who view too many signals. These four categories will give you a guide.

CATEGORY ONE: DOES THE METHOD OR TECHNIQUE DEPEND ON PATTERN RECOGNITION?

We looked at one charting technique, called candlesticks, that Asian traders prefer. This approach seeks to identify specific candlestick formations or styles of candlesticks in order to obtain a market outlook. There are other methods that generally fit into this category, because the data in bar charts or Point-and-Figure charts also form shapes that develop in ways that lead to a predictable outcome. We will see patterns, such as triangles, and know that the resolution is often in the direction that was dominant prior to the formation of the triangle. We will look at these directional patterns that form within price data in the next chapter. Any method that involves pattern recognition can fit into this category nicely, with the single exception of the Elliott Wave Principle, because it is associated with market psychology or behavioral analysis of participants.

CATEGORY TWO: DOES THE METHOD FOCUS ON THE GEOMETRIC MATHEMATICAL RELATIONSHIPS WITHIN THE MARKET'S PRICE DATA OR INDICATORS?

This second category, market geometry, primarily uses linear Euclidian geometry. The standard conventions of geometry that we learned when we were in school lead to various methods of uncovering mathematical relationships within data.

Geometry can be used with both market data and indicators. By recognizing that the mathematical relationships of the past repeat themselves, we can infer that future mathematical relationships with geometric similarities will also occur. As the patterns are not random, they serve to guide our expectations of future market patterns.

In the more advanced techniques of market geometry, the methods focus on the mathematical relationships of both price and time. You must learn to walk before you run, however. When you are first learning, you must master price before you can tackle time. Some of the analytic methods that fall into this category are trending tools, cycle analysis, Fibonacci ratios, and a method known as Gann analysis that studies both price and time.

CATEGORY THREE: DOES THE METHOD STRIVE TO IDENTIFY BEHAVIORAL TRAITS AND STUDY EXTREMES OF MARKET PARTICIPANTS?

This third category is better identified as market momentum and sentiment analysis. It measures the psychology and behavioral actions of market participants in any time horizon. Most oscillators fall into this category, as they serve to identify when the emotions of the market participants have pushed the market to an extreme. However, there is much more to oscillators than just a bunch of rigid formulas that produce wavelike squiggles that fit under your data. While oscillators are a way to monitor market extremes, we also have methods to measure behaviors of market participant opinions, such as commitment of traders analysis, market profile, put/call option analysis, and the Elliott Wave Principle under this same umbrella.

The Elliott Wave Principle is a method that recognizes 13 repeatable price patterns within the data itself because mass market psychology and human behavior are themselves repeatable. You are perhaps more familiar with business marketing models that demonstrate consumer buying behaviors. Categories of consumers that indicate how quickly buyers adapt to a new widget have been identified. The same categories are seen in stocks and other markets. These categories are the Innovators (the quick rabbits who are first to recognize the potential of something new and brave enough to jump to buy), followed by the Early and Late Majority (who believe that letting the first year of a new car pass is wise so that the innovative buyers can work out the bugs), and then the Laggards (the group that hates new things, but dislikes even more being left out of saving or making a dollar when the majority are cashing in). As a result, there are always three distinctive rally phases as a bull market evolves with two corrective pauses or setbacks separating each phase. In fact, in the consumer buying models used in business, the Early and Late Majority generally represent over 64 percent of the general population. Therefore, it is no surprise that the middle phase of a bull market campaign is also the strongest.

This predictable wave of human behavior produces patterns in prices that tell an analyst, "You are here" in the cycle of predictable human behaviors. The Elliott Wave Principle is not a method that beginners are likely to dive into, but there are a host of sentiment indicators that strive to monitor and study market sentiment in different ways. The bottom line here is, any way you slice it, you are using market data to look at the behavior of people, and you are using prices and indicators as a way to predict what people will do next.

CATEGORY FOUR: DOES THE METHOD STRIVE TO DETECT CORRELATIONS BETWEEN DIFFERENT MARKETS TO DETERMINE IF ONE MARKET IS PROVIDING A LEADING SIGNAL FOR ANOTHER?

This is a category you have seen demonstrated earlier. Chapter 9, which used chart overlays of various markets to compare intermarket relationships, fits well in this category. We have other methods as well to help us evaluate the relative strength of one market compared to another, or one sector compared to another. When you study comparisons between different markets or markets in different countries, you are developing *intermarket* analysis techniques. If you are comparing the relative performance of semiconductor stocks and software stocks, both of which fit within the technology sector comprised of American stocks, you are focusing on *intramarket* analysis.

Now that we have an idea of the general approaches to evaluating markets, we are ready to look at some of the specific techniques. Let's begin

CHAPTER 12

Directional Patterns and Signals within the Data

A good place for us to start looking at technical analysis in more detail is pattern recognition. The patterns that form in price data warn us that a market could be defining an important bottom or top or indicate that the market is just resting in preparation for another move in the direction in which it had previously been going. Any book you pick up that covers the basics of technical analysis will display these patterns for you and then provide ways to project price targets for some of these patterns.

This is where I depart from the other books offering basics. I promised to give you the straight scoop about the methods we use. You want to be able to recognize these patterns because so many people know them. But patterns have no time limits, they often have boundaries that can extend, and as a result they are useful tools *for analysis purposes only.* As a rule, they are dreadful for someone who is concerned about market timing and risk. The majority of people act on the basis of what they expect will happen. However, these patterns can stretch and deplete trading accounts before the expected outcome occurs. Therefore, what is far more valuable is being able to recognize when a pattern has failed and the majority of people have just been caught in a trap.

What is a pattern failure? If you are risking dollars, market timing is paramount. Traders watch these patterns because they know that everyone knows about them and that the majority of the market participants will therefore act in accordance with their common expectations. A failure occurs when the market suddenly destroys the pattern that it tricked the majority of people into believing was being formed. As a result, a lot of people are suddenly on the wrong side of the market. Pattern failures provide better timing information and better risk management. You act on the pattern failure to establish positions. But there are always much better ways to decide when to act that mean less risk and less capital drawdown exposure. If you missed the discussion about drawdown, please go back to the first chapter for a review. Everything we do depends on drawdown, which is the decline that your account may have to sustain before the market moves in a direction that proves you were right all along.

In Figure 12-1 we are looking at a weekly bar chart for Rational Software. First, focus on formation A. The stock bottomed in April and then began to rally toward the July high. Every time a market rallies and defines a pivot top within the data series we call it a high. The extreme price high that you may find in a monthly chart is the historic high. In Figure 12-1 each of the price highs within this time

F i g u r e   12-1

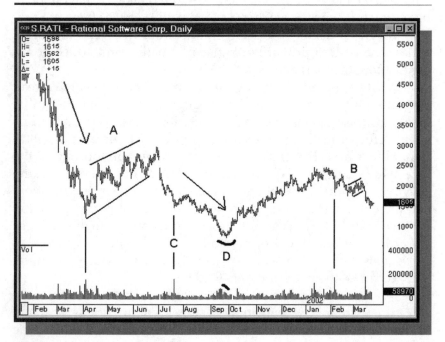

period are higher than the last one, and each of the lows are also a little higher. I have drawn lines above and below these price extremes. It is these lines that form the patterns. This one is called a *Flag*. If you shift to formation B in this same chart, you will see another, much smaller flag. Both flags ultimately lead to a continuation in price movement that fits the market direction prior to the formation of the flag. OK, here's the catch. Let's go back to formation A. Do you see the last move up from the line before the market actually breaks down through the lower line to continue the decline? That last move up is from about $20 to near $30. If you thought the pattern had ended near the $20 level, your drawdown as the market advanced to $30 would be painful. Yes, this is a flag all right, but we both know the stock is not going to fall to zero unless a bankruptcy occurs, so if you had sold the stock, a $10 drawdown versus the potential gain does not meet the guideline you want to keep in mind, which is a risk/reward ratio of 1 to 3. In addition, you would not have known you were wrong until the market blew above the top line of the flag pattern. The angle of the top line for the pattern is so steep that the line extends to $40 and keeps rising. So now you know what a flag looks like and what it means. But do not trade with them, because when we look at Chapter 15, we will see that there are precise ways to measure risk versus return from more specific target zones. The pattern primarily offers confirmation and added confidence about the market direction.

What happens if this price pattern fails? The market will break out through the upper line of the pattern. Often, after the initial breakout, the market falls back to test the top of this upper line again before it really takes off to the upside with greater acceleration. However, if Rational Sofware falls below the top line of the flag, astute traders will cover their position, as this is a new failure. There is an exact level where you should get out of the position, and there is a market entry point that is not far from the signal that allowed you to buy. That is how to use technical analysis. Work toward the development of methods that help you find the entry point that offers the lowest risk. Don't act just because you think you recognize the pattern that is forming.

Below the price data is information displayed in a manner we call a histogram. The information shows volume, or how many trades (both buyers and sellers) have changed hands during the time interval that matches the bar chart. Therefore, in this chart, one histogram bar shows the volume of trading for a single week, as it is a weekly bar chart.

If you look closely in Figure 12-1, you will find a few spikes that far exceed the histogram bars that define the normal background noise or activity for this stock. These spikes are important, as they are important clues to what is happening. At point C I have drawn a vertical line to help your eye trace up to the price bar that fits. This is a price bottom that lasted several weeks. If you look to the left and right, there are also volume spikes in April 2001 and February 2002 where I have drawn additional vertical lines to allow comparisons with price. The price bars above these dates show sharp declines that mark bottoms that lasted for several weeks. When volume forms an extreme spike, it tells us that the majority of people in the market are on the same side. Those who thought the market would go up are dumping their stock and accepting a realized loss. The traders who expect the stock to continue to sell off are selling the stock short. (To sell short means that you are selling something you do not own. Selling short is like selling your neighbor's car when they are away! It is not your car and you know you must buy another that is exactly like theirs before they return. However, you want to pay less for the replacement than you received when you sold it. Ideally you want to sell the stock for more than you will have to pay when you buy it back, so that you can keep the price differential. It is called short selling because you have this wee problem: You have sold somebody else's stock, and eventually you will have to replace it.)

So when these spikes in volume occur, everyone is on the same side of the market. In this case, they are all selling. It is a panic situation, and the spike in volume is called *capitulation*. If everyone is on the same side, the market exhausts the number of people remaining who are inclined to sell. So capitulation often marks a bottom, and then the market begins to rise simply because of the absence of sellers. As the market sneaks up, the traders who sold short start to lose money. These sellers have to buy back the stock to stop their capital drawdown. If enough traders get into trouble, that can lead to what we call a *short squeeze*. As the traders start to buy, the pain gets greater for those who decided to hang in there and are still short. But soon they too cover their short sales by buying the stock back, and before you know it the people who sold to stop their pain on the way down now feel that they made a big mistake and start to buy back their stock. *But if the market is not ready to reverse, no new buyers will step in.* Without new money stepping in the stock will start to slide back down again. That is what happened in these charts.

How do you know when new money is coming into the market? You look at the volume under the price data. The background noise will start to pick up and the histogram bars that give the average background noise reading will be higher.

What about the price bottom at D? Compare the prices near the arc that I drew with the volume. Volume is drying up, as we say, or declining, as the market tries to make a new low. You read this as a market that just ran out of sellers. It means a major bottom. Books will call this a pattern and use the name *double bottom*. Traders do not call this a pattern. It is a market signal, and market signals are very different from patterns. A market signal has no option of changing how long it takes to complete. The stock made a new low only slightly below the previous one or tested the exact same low and then reversed. It has no chance to do something different. If the lows at the double bottom are broken, the formation failed, so you know exactly where you are wrong with limited capital drawdown. Market signals are trading signals that demand immediate action. The faster you are to take action when a signal appears, the closer you will enter the market to the actual signal. The reason this is good is that it minimizes your drawdown, and defines precisely where you are proven wrong should it fail.

In Figure 12-2 we are looking at a weekly chart of Japanese yen futures. Let's start at the bottom, where another double bottom market signal has formed. You also have spikes in volume forming market capitulation. The second spike is lower than the first. I drew a declining line above the two volume spikes because they mark divergence with the double bottom in prices. Experienced traders know that they should buy on a retest or pullback to a significant low when the retest is accompanied with lower volume. We know that there are fewer people out there to shake us out of the position we want. So this particular double bottom is very important.

The chart in Figure 12-2 also has three triangles identified. Just drawing lines over the coiling price ranges makes it easier to highlight the triangles for you. This chart demonstrates that triangles can develop in small to large proportions. Analysts teaching you pattern recognition will call this a pennant. There's just one problem: In some countries, pennants are called flags and flags are called

F i g u r e   12-2

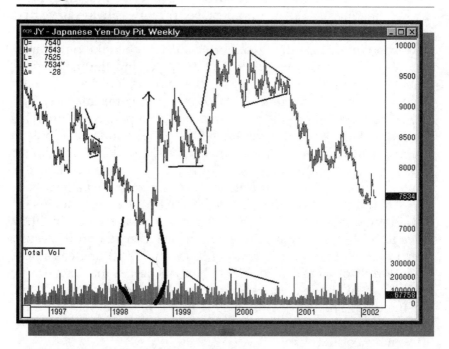

pennants. So when price data is coiling, I'll call it a converging triangle, which is what it really is, as the lines defining the coiling action ultimately converge by coming to a point. In the Elliott Wave Principle, this consolidating pattern is also called a triangle.

Regardless of the name, the same expectations for a resolution should follow: The market is coiling to explode in the direction it was going before the triangle formed. Another useful thing to know about triangles is that the lines connecting the coiling price highs and lows come to a point and mark where the triangle must end. If the data is still futzing around and going nowhere past the apex of the triangle, you know it is not a triangle.

Let's look at the middle triangle around 1999. This is a textbook triangle that provides an expected outcome when the prior rally continues. The lower-risk place to buy is when the triangle is breaking above the upper line in this bullish pattern.

What about the triangle that formed in 2000? This one is tricky. It is a coiling triangle pattern, but is it a triangle coming from the prior rally that will lead to new highs, or is it a triangle that formed after the market declined from the high the first time? I can pass on one more clue: the number five. Triangles always have five swings. If you count to six, your triangle has inverted. If you are uncomfortable, trade the breakout or failure when the outer lines are exceeded. So this was a bearish triangle, and the majority of people would have traded it with the expectation that it would have the same resolution as in 1999. Instead, the majority got trapped on the wrong side when this became a pattern failure. The market broke below the lower line of the pattern and never looked back. If you sold yen (in exchange for U.S. dollars), you knew exactly where the market could not go, which was back into the range defined by the outer dimensions of the triangle pattern.

This same chart offers a tremendous opportunity for us. If you look closely, there is a smaller triangle that formed in 1997. If we looked at this triangle in a daily chart instead of this weekly time horizon, it would be very large as well. This triangle is a perfect example of what can go wrong. First, recognize that I am drawing lines well above the price highs and lows so that you can still see the data. The upper line in 1997 easily fits across all the bars defining the coiling pattern with one exception: There is a single spike in prices in the middle.

When I look at data, I see and hear the market. The volume serves as my ears, and the price is akin to recalling movie segments. I have submitted my S&P orders directly to the floor for such a long time that I hear signals. That single spike is read first as a pattern failure, as it broke above the upper line. The people selling with expectations that the market will resume its prior decline bail out in fear, as these patterns take no prisoners when they begin to move. The traders who know that this is a pattern failure buy and then discover that they too have been trapped as the market falls back into the old range of the triangle. Now everyone is afraid to touch this triangle, as with just this chart we don't know which way the triangle will explode. We are confident that prices will explode, but we don't know the direction. Then the market breaks down through the lower line of the coil, and that is where you discover whether you have the guts to trade it or not. There was blood in the Street for everyone the last time it happened. Yet you have to have the guts to step up and sell the same signal. The only way you can have the guts to do this over and over again is if your drawdown was an accepted risk when you failed the last time.

Before we move on, I would like to be sure you noticed that the larger triangles are accompanied by declining volume as the pattern develops. This is an essential characteristic that should be present if the pattern under construction is a triangle. The first triangle, which is much smaller in this chart, should be viewed in a daily chart, where you can see that volume was also declining in the daily time horizon.

When the triangle in 2000 was being discussed, did you detect the market signal in the chart? If you look at Figure 12-3, you will see that there is a double top present. *Look for market signals first and then study market patterns second.*

In Figure 12-4 the monthly IBM chart is forming a huge triangle. This pattern in IBM also has huge ramifications for the DJIA. But, as we saw in the charts for yen, IBM also has a double top in place. Though we have not seen the outcome, I would suspect the double top will be proven correct, as it is very similar to the 2000 triangle we discussed for yen. Ultimately this triangle in IBM will lead to a breakdown before it ever makes new highs.

Figure   12-3

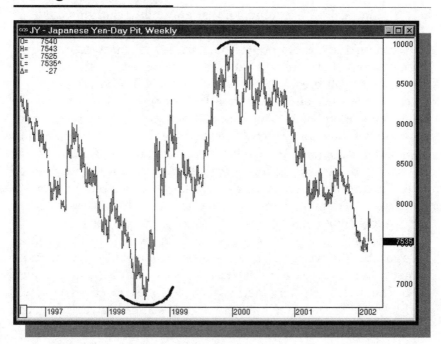

F i g u r e   12-4

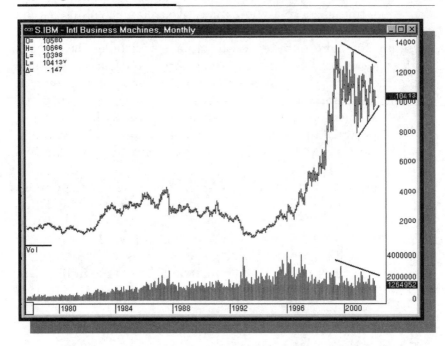

In Figure 12-5 we are looking at a monthly chart for the DJIA when a triangle developed in 1996. But triangles do not always have to be coiling into an apex point. They can also coil outward in a megaphone pattern. Each swing up makes a new price high and then fails. The lows are all breaking prior lows as well. The last leg down is incredibly emotional, as everyone lost money in the prior swings when the market failed to have any follow-through after beginning a new market direction. When you recognize a megaphone pattern or expanding triangle, there will be lots of evidence in the underlying stocks about the last leg down if the pattern is forming within an index. In addition, to survive this pattern, you need more sophisticated ways of defining support and resistance, which we will discuss later in this book when we look at using Fibonacci ratios.

Another price pattern you should know is a rising or falling wedge. We like wedges. They are termination patterns that end a larger move, as we see in the chart for Newmont Mining in Figure 12-6. The price highs for a declining wedge are consecutively lower and lower, and the price lows are also lower and lower. However, the range between the price highs and lows is narrowing, so the

F i g u r e   12-5

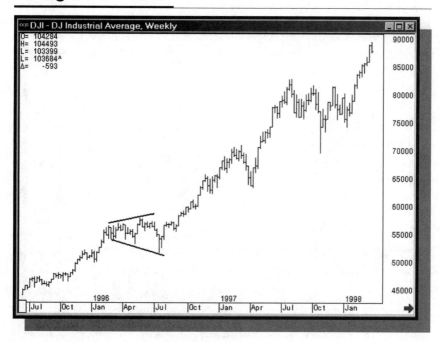

outer dimensions form a wedge pattern. There is a very specific mathematical way to know when a wedge will end. Within a falling wedge there will be three principal swing highs and lows. Draw a line from each high to low swing in a downtrend or from lows to highs in a rising wedge. Then study the slope of the three lines. You have the right three swings if the slope of each swing becomes increasingly more flat toward the end of the pattern. In a wedge defining a market top, the slope of the three coiling swings will fall forward. If the swings have parallel lines connecting highs and lows, the pattern is incomplete and will become a larger wedge.

The problem with wedges is knowing when they will end. The method just described is a big help, but it is fairly advanced for most people. Wedges tend to take on second lives and rip traders to shreds if they step in too early. But why do traders want to go after these patterns so aggressively? Because when they are complete, the market moves like a hot knife through butter back to the start of the wedge as a minimum objective. In the Newmont Mining gold stock chart, the wedge ended with a bottom that allowed prices to rip right past the origin of the wedge. That's why we like wedges. Therefore,

F i g u r e   12-6

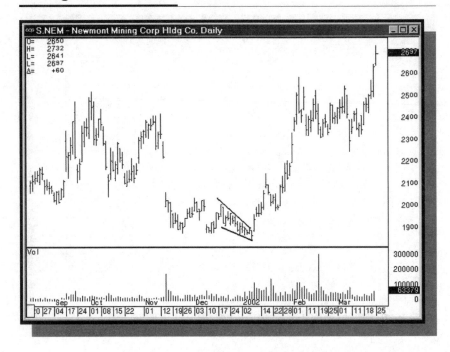

when a wedge starts to form, a lot of people take notice and get impatient for it to end. It may take until the first quarter of 2003, but several software stocks are forming falling wedges. Wedges, once satisfied, often mark the end of a market move and the fast retracement of the wedge is just the start of a new trend.

There is a particularly menacing wedge forming in Figure 12-7, which shows the long-term data for U.S. 30-year Treasury Bonds. "This is a wedge?" you may ask. If you think the wedge is hard to see in Figure 12-7, study Figure 12-8.

The wedge shape is much more apparent in Figure 12-8. Wedges can form huge spikes right near the end of the pattern. The lower boundary could be drawn to fit the lower breaks, but I draw boundaries where they will contain the majority of the trading range. This gives me an early warning to pay attention. This chart for the 30-year T-Bond futures warns that the big-picture outlook will soon change, bringing higher mortgage rates, credit card rates, and so forth.

We could not see this wedge forming without access to a semiannual chart. It is not as clear in a monthly chart because the data is too spread out.

F i g u r e   12-7

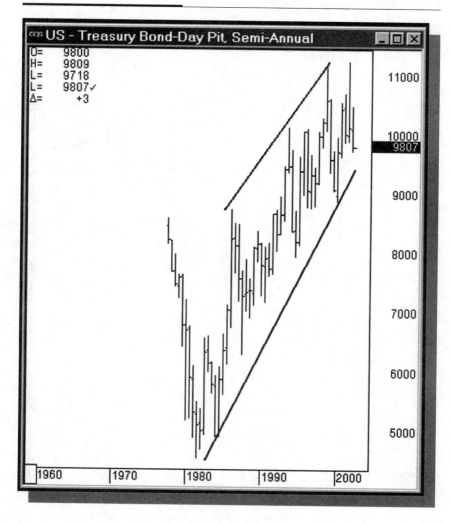

As if the wedge pattern were not enough warning, each of the twin spikes that form the double top is itself a market signal. Notice that the closing price on each of these spikes is well below the high of the bar's range. These spikes with lower closes are called key reversals. The word *key* is an understatement, to be blunt. It is a directional signal that the market is at a major turning point. So in this chart there are two key reversals, a double top, and a termination wedge! The problem is that most people know these signals but don't have access to them because most data vendors

F i g u r e   12-8

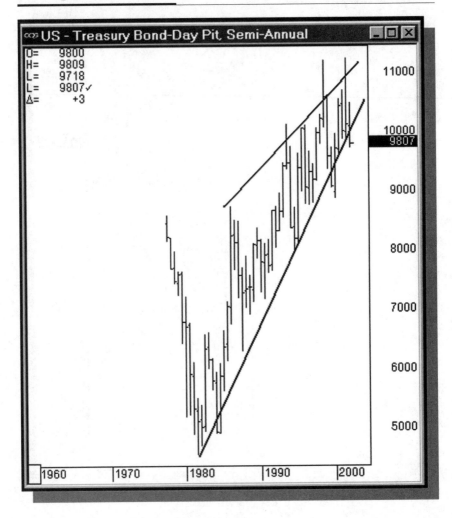

provide monthly data as their longest time horizon. Ask your quote vendor to provide longer time horizons. You need this big-picture view for technical signals as well, especially if this wedge ends with a characteristic spike up through the pattern as a termi-nal blow-off and then reverses back down to start a major new trend. Without the data in this time horizon it will be hard to see.

Let us move on to Figure 12-9, which displays the monthly Commodity Research Bureau Futures Price Index (CRB Index). Since we were just discussing bonds, it makes sense to look at the

F i g u r e   12-9

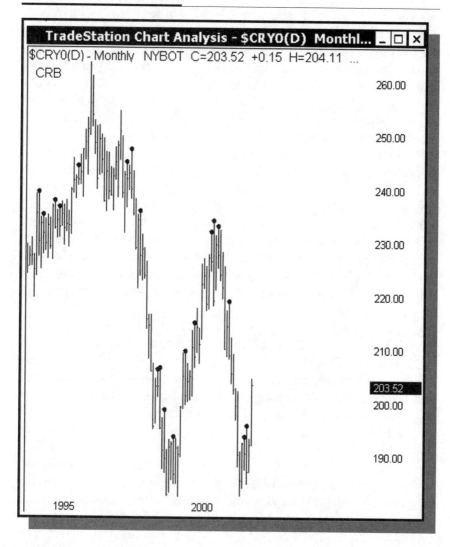

CRB at the same time. If you chart only two markets with an overlay, let them be the CRB Index and the 10-year Treasury Note yields.
They track with a positive correlation. (If you tracked T-Note prices,
there would be a negative correlation, which is harder to visualize.)
The reason the CRB is important is that it is a direct barometer of
inflation. Bond yields rise when inflation is present.

The chart in Figure 12-9 suggests inflation is moving up from
a double bottom market signal. The signal is correct, but we are in a

deflationary environment. The way to learn the interaction between markets is to study historical charts carefully. Changes or movements in the dollar are seen first in commodity prices. Commodity prices provide clear information about inflation, to which the bond market responds. If bonds are in an inflationary environment, that will roll downhill to the stock market. So add the CRB index to your watch list. As I like to know what is brewing under the surface of an index, I also monitor the primary components of the CRB index, which are precious metals, energy, and the grain markets.

The CRB was displayed to introduce this index to you and to demonstrate a software problem. In Figure 12-9 there are dots over several bars. Some charting services offer features that automate your search for market signals. *Don't use them.* Learn to study charts without automated scanning. This chart was created through TradeStation, and the dots are the program's automated detection of key reversals using the "ShowMe" feature. In this chart, notice that the program missed the high. In addition, there are many bars that are marked that I would not call key reversals. So please don't learn analysis through the definitions of computer programmers' algorithms.

If the CRB Index can warn when bond prices will fall, (don't forget there is an inverse relationship between bond prices and yield) is there a chart to warn us when the economy will fail or begin to recover? You may think this is a trick question as this squarely targets fundamentals. However, if we can chart real estate government statistics to track the housing market, we can find a data series and add technical indicators to help us track the health of the economy. The data series most professional traders do not know to watch is the tonnage rates charged by ocean freight liners. Freight rates rise sharply in periods of robust economic growth due to trade activity between countries. When demand begins to fall, so too do shipping costs. *There is a 6- to 9-month lead time in ocean freight rates before an economic recovery or slowdown that can be detected by the stock market.* The Baltic Dry Index (formerly called the Baltic Freight Index) is the data series you want to monitor. It is a composite of three other indices tracking major ocean freight routes: The Baltic Capesize, Baltic Panamax, and the Baltic Handy indices. Just be aware higher bunker fuel prices also contribute to rates. This intermarket relationship was taught to me by the man who reportedly hired Michael Milken into Drexel. While the Baltic Freight Index has changed its name, it con-

F i g u r e   12-10

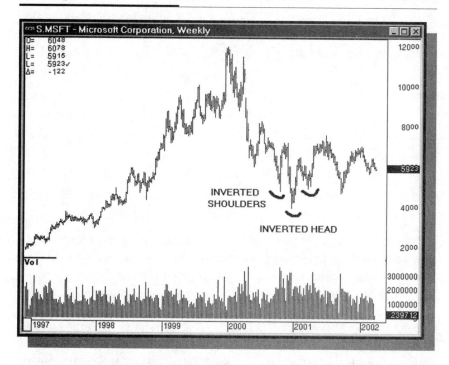

tinues to have value as a bellwether indicator for business that later affects the stock market.

Figure 12-10 displays another directional pattern. When this pattern appears, it is a warning that a market reversal is developing. The weekly Microsoft (MSFT) chart allows us to look at an Inverted Head-and-Shoulders pattern. Later in the book you will find a perfect Head-and-Shoulders pattern in General Electric (GE). Such a pattern warns of a top. The price high forms the head, with a major shoulder on either side. In the MSFT chart in Figure 12-10, two shoulders formed around a new low. Both the Head-and-Shoulders pattern and the Inverted Head-and-Shoulders pattern can be thought of as a double top or bottom with a market fake-out or trap in the middle.

We have looked at some of the more common patterns recognized by the majority of analysts and traders, but remember that price patterns are used to confirm other methods, and should not be used alone.

CHAPTER 13

Why Are There Holes in My Data?

Everyone will at some time have holes or intermittent price breaks in their data for various reasons. In this chapter we will take a look at the different reasons price gaps can occur.

You may chuckle at the break we see in Figure 13-1, which shows the weekly DJIA. At first glance it looks as if my data vendor had several weeks of missing data. This is confusing at first, but the price break represents the start of World War I, as markets did not open for several months when that war began. Sadly, another break will be present for evermore in our historical data as a result of the September 11, 2001, attack. Such large gaps are rare, however, and you should always have an identifiable reason why the information is missing.

Single-day price breaks will appear when markets close for national holidays. Technical indicators are not affected by such brief closings. (One exception, be aware that for Elliotticians, holidays can be important missing puzzle pieces in short horizon data. You may in hindsight discover that a single-day holiday is the missing fourth wave in intraday time horizons. For example, I have often seen the closed session become the missing leg in a triangle.)

The two charts in Figure 13-2 show futures markets. On the left is a daily chart for the June Nasdaq futures contract. On the right is a 7-minute bar chart for the June S&P 500 futures contract. Futures have gaps and price data that looks like chicken tracks across your computer on a regular basis.

F i g u r e   13-1

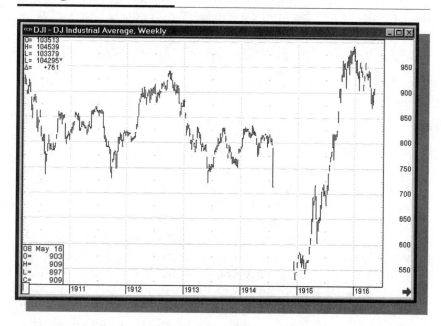

F i g u r e   13-2

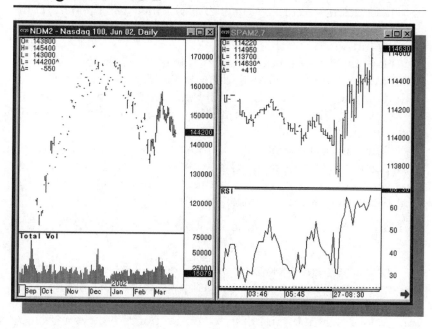

You will need to understand why futures data looks the way it does in Figure 13-2 because exchanges are preparing to introduce a whole new family of investments called Single Stock Futures (SSF). Even if you do not trade these new futures when they become available, you will nonetheless be affected by them if you trade stocks.

One of the differences between stocks and futures is selling short. Why do professionals sell short in the first place? I love this question, so let me put my portfolio manager's hat on for a moment. We sell short either because we think a stock will go down *or to reduce our risk of being wrong*. Selling short because we think a stock price will fall should require no further comment. But what the general public doesn't realize is that the second reason for selling short is to minimize the public's risk.

A common spread trade in stocks is the matched pair, or the purchase and sale of two highly correlated stocks. Correlation measures the degree to which the two stocks move together. Any stock compared to itself has a correlation of 1.00. If you compare a long position (buyer) and a short position (a short seller) in the same stock, the correlation is −1.00. A correlation of 0.00 would be the price for Ford stock versus the counter price to buy popcorn at the movies. The comparison is totally random.

If a stock has a correlation of 2.0 (which we call the Beta) compared to the Nasdaq Index, this stock will rally twice as fast as the Nasdaq Index.

Now for the example, since we have the basic idea in place. Let's say you own both UAL and AMR. Both are airline stocks, and both companies were horrifically affected by the events of September 11, 2001. Since they are in the same industry, they will have a high correlation.

Over the past 4 years, the daily variance of returns has been 0.114 percent for UAL and 0.111 percent for AMR. Their covariance has been 0.086 percent. We use a simple formula to determine the total risk or combined variance:

$$\text{Variance (UAL + AMR)} = \text{variance (UAL)} + \text{variance (AMR)} + 2 \times \text{covariance (UAL + AMR)}$$

Thus the two stocks compound the risk as they are added together, giving the portfolio a whopping daily variance of 0.398 percent. What this says is that if you own both UAL and AMR, your risk exposure is cumulative. You do not reduce your risk by owning two airline stocks instead of just one.

But look what happens if the portfolio manager buys one airline stock and sells the other short. In this case, we subtract the covariance, and the variance of the matched-pair trade falls to 0.052 percent per day. This is less than half the risk of buying one individual stock. You will not make anywhere near as much money on stocks in a matched pair, but risk-averse investors who bought into a sector specific fund will sleep a little more easily at night because the risk is also half that of just holding a long position in one stock. Therefore, this is good risk management for the portfolio, but wanting to invest in a fund specializing in the airline sector that was just bailed out of trouble by the government is not sound logic.

Selling stocks short has several huge problems and disadvantages. First, short sellers must locate stock that they can reserve to sell against. What if there is no stock available? The short seller is out of luck. You cannot sell stocks short unless you have first reserved it. You can sell stock that you do not own, but someone has to own it. That is the same as saying that you have to borrow stock, and when you do, you pay a broker loan rate in addition to the normal transaction fees.

Then there is the problem of the uptick rule. When you are trading stocks, you may not sell short on a downtick. The stock exchanges established that rule. That means that the previous trade must be at a higher price than the trade before it. In a crash, no one can sell short until the market has found the first uptick. As you can imagine, there is therefore pent-up selling pressure, and one uptick is met with heavy selling in such conditions.

Suppose there is a strong rally. There are no restrictions on stocks or on equity future indices. The sky is the limit if the market suddenly lunges upward. But futures in most other markets have both upper and lower limits.

When Single Stock Futures are launched, they will follow the same rules as other futures. There will be no need to borrow or reserve the underlying commodity, and there will be no uptick rule. As a result, the stock exchanges have opened a Pandora's box, as professionals will prefer to sell futures contracts on a stock in order to bypass all the restrictions they now face when they want to short the actual stock. The stock will be the underlying commodity, and stock prices will therefore be the cash market. In addition, when stock futures start to move and the stock itself is behind the futures market, the arbitrageurs will step in. Arbitrage is a way to make a buck by capitalizing on temporary market imbalances. However, if the professionals are all hitting the futures to avoid limitations on selling the stock short, the futures will not go up. Therefore, the stock itself must go down. The arbitrage traders will not try to buy the stock knowing they would be squashed when futures and cash both accelerate down. That is why it will now be important for stock traders to understand futures markets, even if you had nothing to do with them before.

This brings us back to Figure 13-2, which illustrates the character of the price breaks that occur in futures. On the left is a daily chart of the June Nasdaq futures contract. Equity index futures have four delivery dates each year, in March, June, September, and December. The chart on the left shows chicken tracks for much of the data, although the price bars seem to straighten out their act toward the right-hand side of the chart. There is nothing wrong with this data; it is what trading data looks like shortly after a contract rollover. About 2 weeks before the delivery date for a given contract, the exchange defines the next contract as the front month. The reason is that most of the volume traded is speculative, and, as you saw, speculators do not want to be caught holding an agreement come delivery day. Therefore, when the March contract rolled over to June, the June contract became the most active or heavily traded. Prior to the rollover, when the March contract was the front month, the June contract did trade, but it traded less often and with very light volume. As a result, the data for the June contract before the rollover looks like chicken tracks

Do you use technical analysis on these chicken tracks? No, you switch to the Cash index data. It will have a different symbol and will not be affected by rollover dates. Now is a good time to discuss continuous futures data. Technicians have ways of splicing different contracts together so that our data doesn't look so funky. However, the top analysts *do not back-adjust*. Beware of this if you use TradeStation, as it incorrectly subtracts the differences between the old and new data from the entire range of historical price data. TradeStation thinks it is preserving the integrity of the trend, but this destroys the value of the data. One technical method we will soon look at is swing analysis to project price targets from Fibonacci relationships. Data that has been back-adjusted cannot be used for price projections. Another technical method called Gann analysis requires actual price data for the life of all same-month contracts, such as December contracts only. Many vendors think they offer Gann techniques, but they do not have the data to go with these techniques. There are numerous false claims by vendors, and you need to use outside sources to learn the correct methods rather than believing everything the software distributors tell you.

The chart on the right in Figure 13-2 is a 7-minute June S&P500 contract. Equity indices trade around the clock. During the night session, the S&P500 is traded electronically through the GLOBEX system. Since North America is sleeping, the foreign traders create a thin market during the night hours. This is what a chart looks like when you display all the trading information. If you look at the time scale on the x-axis, you will notice the marks for 3:30 A.M. and 5:30 A.M. (EST). (I am located in an area using Eastern Standard Time, so I shift my charts to match instead of showing the time in Chicago, where the contract is actually traded.)

I am often asked what to do with the thin GLOBEX price data. The bottom line is this; use it. I have found that price projections that respect and acknowledge the pivots that form during the night session are more accurate than those made by charting and analyzing the trading from the day session alone. GLOBEX is indeed a factor now.

In Figure 13-3 we have a different situation, one that you will see only in futures data. The chart shows the futures market for the Nikkei 225 Stock Index traded in Chicago during our session. When Chicago is open to trade the Nikkei index, the Osaka Exchange in Japan is closed.

It's odd, but the Nikkei futures in Chicago trade in the direction in which the S&P500 is moving during the day session, as if the American markets indicate what the opening will look like in Japan. At night the S&P500 GLOBEX trading often tracks the Nikkei day session in Japan, as if the Japanese stock index is a leading indicator.. When the Nikkei futures reopen in Chicago after the regular trading session has concluded in Japan, there is nearly always a gap in prices to reflect what happened during the Nikkei day session to adjust for the price differential. It's better than caffeine to jump-start your heart in the morning. No, stick with the caffeine; far less expensive. (By the way, drink coffee, don't trade it!)

F i g u r e   13-3

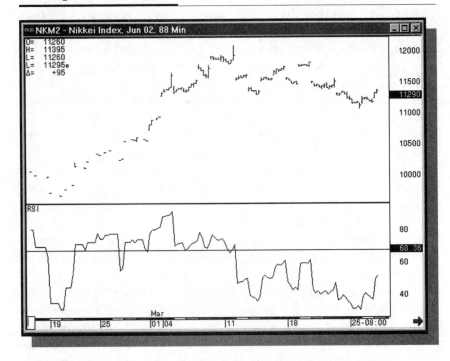

The strange character of the Nikkei futures chart leads us to a bona fide price gap in futures that arises during our regular markets. All futures markets have price limits. Most markets have price limits both above and below the prior day's market close that define the maximum trading range for the new trading session. (However, the futures markets on equity indices do not have price limits above the market—only below.) This means that you can be trapped in futures when everyone is on the same side of the market and it is forced to close. The S&P500 has graduated limit down levels. I won't go into the details of this, as they relate only to the S&P500, but in a horrific situation you can be locked into what we call a no bid market. When the market reopens the next day, the exchange defines wider limits, but you could again be trapped in a no bid market. Agriculture markets are the ones that most often experience locked limit-down or limit-up markets.

Figure 13-4 shows the daily S&P500 Cash market. We see a gap where market prices seem to jump over or below a trading range, breaking the continuity of the chart. The S&P500 Cash market is a

F i g u r e   13-4

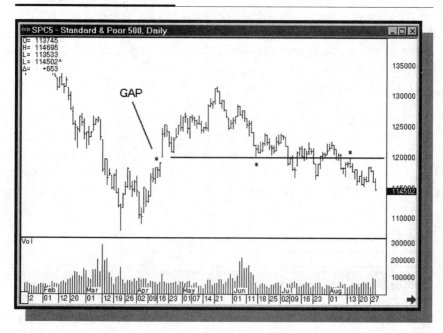

basket of the actual stocks from which the index is constructed. The Cash markets do not trade at night, but futures trade nearly the full 24 hours in the day. If futures rally all night, there will be a gap up open when the S&P500 Cash Index begins to trade the next morning.

When the market opens above the prior day's close, the price jump is called a gap up open, and this always becomes an important area of support or resistance for the market. The asterisks in Figure 13-4 show key support and resistance tests at this horizontal line. A gap is a point of recognition; the majority of traders and investors realize the direction in which the market is heading. After the gap, a strong move usually follows. In traditional books about technical analysis, you will read about running gaps and exhaustion gaps as well. In real life, differentiating such gaps doesn't do much for you. But you must have a technical reason why the market traded over that price gap. A technical reason will be a price zone of major resistance that you have found, and the result is that the market jumps right over the resistance zone. You must force yourself to identify why a gap is present. I will show you how to do this when we look at price projection techniques.

Here is your rule of thumb when you encounter a gap: Measure the change from the start of the move to the gap. The gap is often the halfway marker, so that 50 percent of the move is still ahead. You will learn other methods, but this one is the most important and the one that will most often be correct. In addition, it is not overly difficult when you are just starting. In the S&P500 chart in Figure 13-4, the gap clearly falls in the middle of the move. The price advance above the gap and the move from the price low to the gap is about equal.

In Figure 13-5 we are looking at a candlestick chart for the daily Japanese yen June 2002 futures contract. The futures market gapped up, as the cash market is open 24 hours and futures are not. This causes the catch-up scenario when futures open. However, the

F i g u r e   13-5

Cash market reversed the next day, and so futures opened below the gap that had just been created. This is a market signal called an island reversal. It is bearish in this chart and very bullish when it occurs in the reverse.

As a final thought about gaps, let me pass on some wisdom from a third-generation trader that I was given: If you have a price gap that the market has never traded within the history of the data, the market will eventually fill that gap at some point. This is true no matter how long it has been since the gap occurred and how far the market has moved away from the gap. This does not reference a gap that trading data printed in a different trending period, it specifically refers to a price the market has never printed; some day it will be filled.

CHAPTER 14

Understanding Trends and Basic Market Geometry

Figure 14-1

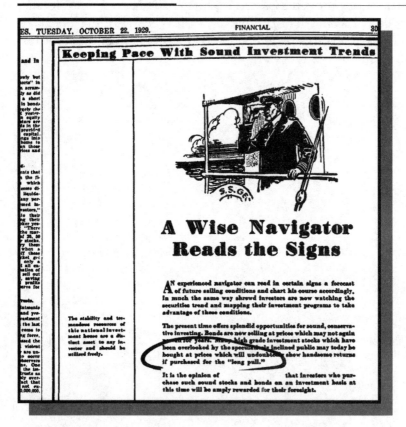

Many high grade stocks which have been overlooked by the speculatively inclined public may today be bought at prices which will undoubtedly show handsome returns if purchased for the "long pull."
—October 22, 1929. *New York Times,*
corner advertisement on page 30.

I wish I had a quarter for every time throughout the Nasdaq decline that I heard someone say, "That's OK; I'm in it for the long haul." That is what people were led to believe in 1929 when the advertisement shown in Figure 14-1 was printed in the *New York Times*. Yes, if you bought stock in a company that survived the Great Depression and World War II, the market did eventually come back. The truth is, however, that history shows that ads of this kind always appear when a bear market is growling on the horizon. An effort is made to discourage redemptions from mutual funds, as redemptions start a chain reaction that forces the fund to sell the liquid stocks it does not want to sell. This also has tax consequences that hurt everyone in the fund at that time.

The Nasdaq decline was devastating because many fund managers had never experienced a full-fledged bear market. These young managers made the mistake of designing models that used only market data from 1980 onward. Their models failed in 2000 and 2001 when the Nasdaq declined drastically, as they had programmed themselves to buy every time there was a 6 to 8 percent decline. When these models were back-tested against the DJIA from 1980 to 1999, this was shown to be the correct thing to do. But then the pattern failed to repeat, and the result was huge losses as funds stepped in too soon.

Late one night, a client asked to see every decline in the history of the DJIA. Forty faxed pages later, he had data from 1900 to 2002 with notations for every rally and bear market over that time period. Producing this was not a big problem for me, as I had the information already. That is the kind of historical review you should make, and later in this book you will see this historical data with a simple indicator. When you want to know the character of any market, go back as far as possible. It will teach you a great deal, as history does indeed repeat itself.

Let's begin a discussion of market geometry by defining market trends.

The decline in the DJIA that was seen in weekly data in 2001 is an intermediate-term trend. It is, in fact, a countertrend to the really long-term trend when the DJIA charts from 1974 on are studied.

In the bigger picture, the DJIA is developing an entirely differ-ent pattern than was formed in the Nasdaq. We discussed the rea-son for this when we discussed the importance of the strength of the U.S. dollar. Unfortunately, the Nasdaq decline was only the first shoe to drop. The DJIA will follow if the dollar weakens. Should someone ask, "What do you think about the market?" I have to respond immediately with two questions. The first is, "What mar-ket or index are you referring to?" and the second is, "In what time frame are you interested?"

When we begin to connect market price highs and lows, or to mathematically subdivide the price ranges between specific market price highs and lows, we are using market geometry. Market geom-etry can become quite complex, but the basics are easy to learn.

In the chart of the monthly U.S. 30-year T-Bond shown in Figure 14-2, three different trends are marked. Line A on the left side of the chart is a downtrend. Each price pivot high is lower than

F i g u r e   14-2

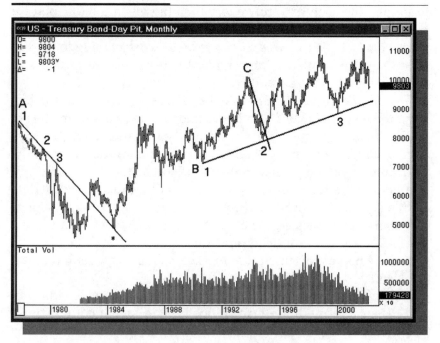

the last, and they all stay under this imaginary line that I drew connecting the price highs. The market uses this trend line as resistance prior to failing and resuming the decline. We then see that when this market was ready to reverse and start to rally, it broke above the downtrend line. As seen in this chart, after the breakout the market made one pullback to test the same line a last time. The market test is highlighted with an asterisk. Therefore, what had been market resistance for some time became market support that began the advance in earnest.

Line B shows you a rising trend line. When the price pivot lows are connected, the slope of the line is positive. Once a trend line has been touched three times, some technicians view the trend as confirmed. I do not use trend lines that just connect the dots at market highs and lows, as market geometry has greater depth than this. Whether or not a trend line becomes confirmed is of little interest to me. After we put the basic principles in place, I will show you the next step in using and creating trend lines to increase their value.

Let's take a look at line C in the same chart. Line C clearly marks a downtrend within a larger uptrend. If you are trading with 1-minute charts, you have to know what the big picture is, as it will hit you over the head eventually. But charts with very short horizons also show subdivisions of trends within a larger picture.

Trend lines, I consider are displayed in Figure 14-3. This figure shows a monthly MSFT bar chart on the top with two oscillators below. I use trend lines on indicators as well as on price data. But at this time, just focus on the trend lines drawn on prices. Trend lines should be extended well into the future, as they invariably become important market levels. This chart will show you that I do not simply connect blatantly obvious price highs and lows. Instead, I draw lines that clarify market angles that have been respected by the market as support and resistance. As an example, take the first line, which begins on the far left, and trace it across the chart. It was resistance twice, and then it defined a major bottom in 2001. Notice that the 2001 bottom has some price slippage through the trend line. However, the month that follows stays above the line, and a market signal called a key reversal forms. Market geometry is not automatic; it requires some thought. Think about spike reversals. This is a temporary condition in which the psychology of the market goes

F i g u r e   14-3

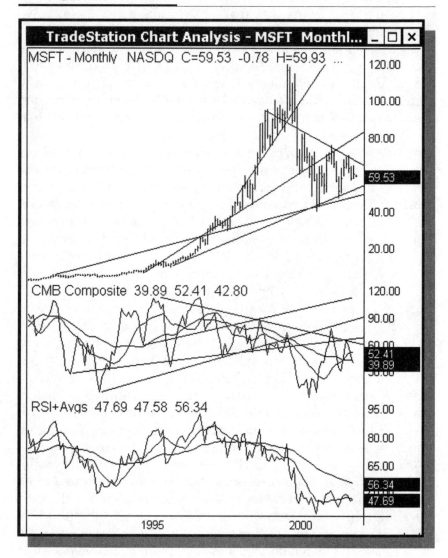

haywire. At times you will need to truncate the spikes. There is not a conventional trend line in this chart. But all the lines define key market turns.

I know that Figure 14-3 looks very confusing, as there is so much packed into the chart. But if we look at the methods independently, it will become clearer. In Figure 14-4 we are looking at the

F i g u r e   14-4

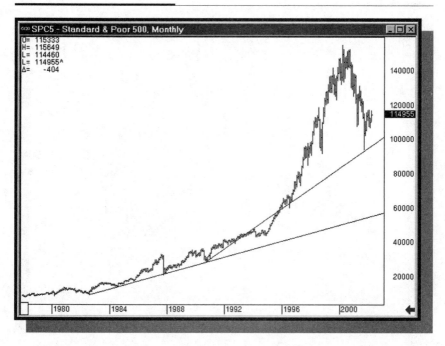

SPC5 - Standard & Poor 500, Monthly

```
O= 115333
H= 115649
L= 114460
L= 114955^
Δ=  -404
```

140000
120000
114955
100000
80000
60000
40000
20000

1980   1984   1988   1992   1996   2000

monthly Cash S&P500 Index. The trend line that begins at the far left is traditional, as it connects the price lows easily enough. But the price data goes parabolic in the 1990s, and you would not find a single trend line drawn in a traditional manner that would be of much use to you in this time horizon. So I draw a trend line from a significant low and notice that it becomes resistance prior to a significant consolidation when the market goes sideways in 1994. The market inversion where support becoming resistance or vice versa is the key. The same trend line or angle of ascent becomes important again in 1996. But the clincher is the low in 2001, which was at the same trend line extended forward in time. Therefore, I have little interest in connecting the dots at extreme price highs and lows, but instead draw trend lines that give greater importance to finding where the market's geometric angles are located.

The weekly Cash S&P500 chart in Figure 14-5 shows how important it is to pay attention when geometric angles converge. The two rising trend lines in this chart define the market level where the major decline begins in earnest. The intersection is far

F i g u r e   14-5

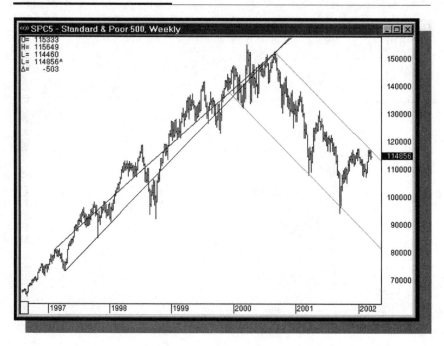

more important to us than the actual market price high, as market timing is what determines whether we have a win or a loss.

When we draw trend lines that are parallel, we call the area between them a channel. As this chapter is being written, the S&P500 is stuck under the upper trend line of a channel. This defines a high-risk area that could lead to a market failure pushing the S&P back to the lower channel line near 800. The geometric methods used to determine price projections will be discussed separately. We will also cover methods that tell us when a market is likely to break through the resistance area or to fail.

In Figure 14-6 we continue to study geometric angles in the monthly cash S&P500. Sometimes channels have secondary channels running within the data. This chart offers you a super example of why you should not continually try to fine-tune or adjust trend lines that you drew long ago in an effort to make perfect charts. The progressively lower pivot highs during the downtrend in 2000 and 2001 display failures under resistance. A failure occurs when the

F i g u r e   14-6

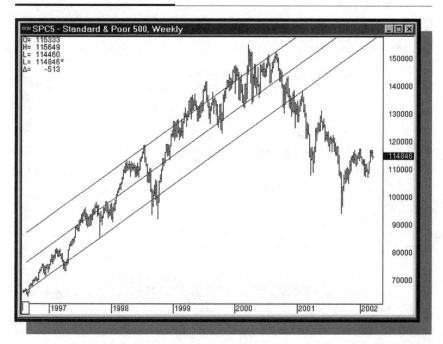

market is unable to make a touch right at the resistance line. When it fails to reach the line, it is too weak, and when it fails to retrace down to a target, it is too strong. Such failures are very revealing with regard to the strength of any market we want to study. In Figure 14-6, the price high in 2001 is the last price high in an intermediate uptrend before a downtrend resumes into the September 2001 low. Can you find the angle in this chart that marks the 2001 price high? Keep in mind that it is an angle rather than a channel line that will be parallel to the lines already drawn.

In Figure 14-7 we are looking at the monthly U.S. 30-year T-Bond chart that was shown before. Key reversals that form at spikes often define their own channels parallel to traditional trend lines that connect price lows or highs. These give early warnings and show just how critical the current levels for bonds are as this is being written. Usually a bounce occurs at these levels before a market breaks down. Therefore, rebounds off these secondary lines can be the most important moves, as they give you a world of information about

Figure 14-7

whether the market is truly weak or just fooling the masses by teasing them. Oscillators will reveal the difference for us.

The same chart demonstrates that channels can be drawn in countertrend moves as well. The channel boundaries help to define the market trend, and when they are broken, they define markets that are accelerating.

The weekly chart for Manugistics, a software company, that is shown in Figure 14-8 displays intersecting channels. Not only did the intersecting channels define high-risk market trend changes in this stock, but when we add a simple indicator below the price data, it is easy to see that the oscillator failed in 2001 and 2002 at the same resistance level near the zero line. The charts have asterisks added to help you compare the same points in time in the price data and the oscillator. We will look at oscillators later, but the one added in Figure 14-8 is a simple moving average that is plotted under the price data, rather than on top of the data. It shows how different methods add confirmation or give us greater confidence that we are right when they relay the same message. Before we

Figure 14-8

move on, do you see the large head-and-shoulders pattern in this stock's price data? The right shoulder of the bearish pattern ends directly under the bisecting channel in 2001. This stock gave lots of warning.

Market geometry requires you to train your sense of graphic design and will need hands-on application. If you would like to practice with charts that will let you compare your work with mine, please visit my Web site at http://www.aeroinvest.com.

If you select the "Books for Traders" option on the main menu near the bottom, you will find the path to the exercise charts, which have white backgrounds so that they will be easy to print. After you have worked with the blank charts, you can compare your work with the charts I'll have waiting for you at http://www.aeroinvest.com/bookanswers.htm.

You will need to enter this Web page address exactly, as there is no path from the Web site menus to the answers. The answers are for your use only. You will not be asked to sign a guest book or have to weed through pop-up windows.

Your introduction to market geometry is far from over, though. If I left you at this point, it would become confusing for you later because most books on basic technical analysis only connect major price highs and lows when identifying price trends. The reason that my use of trend lines may seem unorthodox is that I am taking into consideration far more advanced geometry that is at work in the markets to increase your probability of being right. Sometimes being overly simplistic is not helpful, as it doesn't give enough structure. So we should continue.

Market geometry is far more sophisticated than straight linear relationships resulting from simply connecting price highs and lows. The underlying premise of very simple methods of technical analysis is that all markets move up and down in an equal and symmetrical manner. However, markets have an expansion/contraction cycle that is by no means linear. In addition, we know that markets move down far more rapidly than they advance, which is a difference in acceleration. Therefore, the most elementary analysis methods work only some of the time. Methods that work a higher percentage of the time take into account the fact that there are expansion/contraction market cycles. These methods need a little more work to learn. Therefore, many people who are looking for quick and simple approaches just learn the basics and then become discouraged and decide that technical analysis itself doesn't work. What they are overlooking is the fact that there are universal laws of vibration known to the sciences that apply to market growth and decay cycles. But we'll move down that path when you have more technicals under your belt.

While we are about to add a lot of geometric lines and oscillators to your charts, the underlying premise for each should not be forced. If you are ever totally confused, take every notation and indicator off your computer screen and reconstruct the different methods from scratch. Work on developing a thorough understanding of each method by itself until it looks clear to you. In so doing, the solution to where the market is heading will suddenly present itself politely to you and say, "Here I am."

In Figure 14-9 we are looking at a daily chart for QQQ, a stock symbol designed to track the Nasdaq 100. The market geometry we are about to view uses specific angles from a single price level. If I plot points by moving 1 day forward and 1 dollar up, when I connect the dots, a line will begin to form that has a 1-to-1 ratio or rises at a 45-degree angle. The lines you see in this chart have ratios of 1:1, 1:2, 1:4, 1:8, and 1:16. I also have inverse ratios of 2:1, 4:1, etc. These growth rates are the hypotenuses for geometric triangles. The same ratios were used to build the Great Pyramid and ancient Roman and Greek architecture, and they utilize what is known as sacred geometry. We will discuss this background in more depth at another time.

The particular angles being applied here for market analysis are called Gann Lines, after W. D. Gann. You will undoubtedly stumble across something that looks similar called speed lines.

Figure 14-9

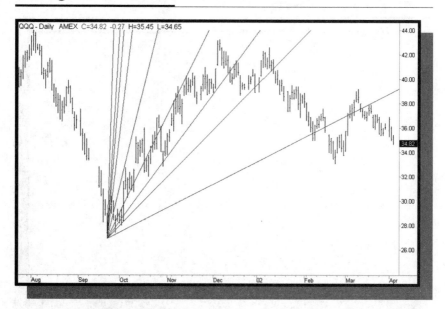

Speed lines help us track market acceleration, but I'd suggest learning about Gann lines, as this will be more profitable. Be aware, however, that Gann lines are misunderstood by most vendors. If your 45-degree line or 1:1 ratio cannot adjust to the fact that your computer does not draw charts with equal x-axis and y-axis scales, you have a vendor who does not know how to calculate Gann angles. Different vendors' features change all the time, so I cannot offer more specifics, but just because a vendor says it has this feature does not mean that the calculation is done correctly.

Figure 14-10 demonstrates the application of market geometry in a more advanced way. We are looking at the same QQQ chart as in Figure 14-9. In this case the Gann lines are projected from zero on the y-axis, and are radiating from the date on the x-axis that is directly under the pivot. The actual price low is not used. Make a close comparison between the values defining support and resistance when the zero line is used and those in Figure 14-9. Wouldn't you much rather be working with this chart? This chart technique was used by W. D. Gann, and I'll show you later how this exact method will help solve the problem that arises when a stock is first listed and we do not have any historical data to work from.

Figure 14-10

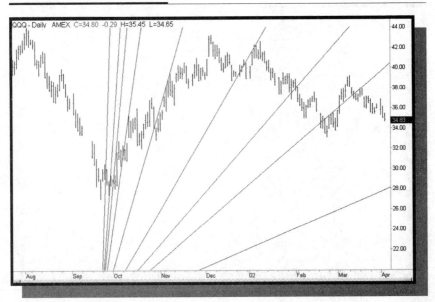

In Figure 14-11 we have applied Gann lines to the same chart taking what would seem to be the most logical approach: using the major price pivot highs and lows. Now let's look more closely at the price data from March and early April 2002. I could draw a line connecting the price lows that defines support for the downtrend. You would conventionally call it a trend line, think that the Gann lines missed it, and move on. Not so fast! Remember that I said that technical analysis is about finding the pivots that, when connected, define a relationship to the market move? Now the discipline comes into play, as we cannot move on until we have found the answer.

With a little patience, we can arrive at the notations in Figure 14-12, which show that the critical lines are radiating from *secondary price pivots*. That means that the correct pivots to use when we make a price projection may not be obvious. These lines from what may appear to be unorthodox points mark a price projection high or low that the market is respecting. If the market is making a geometric calculation and following up by showing respect to that calculation, you did not make an error when you considered other points from which to start the Gann lines. You need to look past the obvious conventions and look at the graphic results. *The market will teach you if you let it.*

F i g u r e   14-11

F i g u r e   14-12

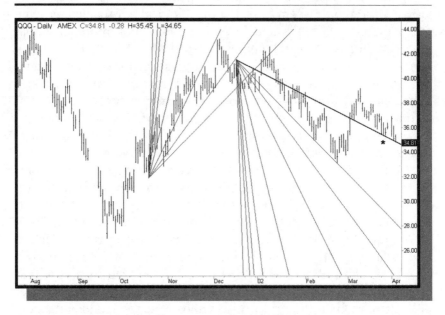

When the key angles are radiating from a price lower than the dominant price high, it means that the market is beginning to contract, and this will affect how we project support and resistance levels and also how we make price projections. The reverse will also be true when markets are in expansion cycles. But we will be able to see these pivot relationships contract and expand mathematically, so we will know exactly what phase of its growth cycle the market is in. This will become clearer when we study price projection.

Because secondary price pivots may be more important than the actual price lows and highs at the extremes, I use trend lines in the manner shown earlier in this chapter. What I am really doing is finding angles that clarify the market geometry that is at work with very simple trend tools. The sample charts introducing Gann angles will help you think outside the box and find geometric relationships that most people might never consider or discuss. If you look at Figure 14-8 again, you will see that the spikes were truncated. When this should be done and why will also be discussed in the next chapter, when we discuss price projection. I would suggest returning to some of these charts after you have read ahead, as you will see more detail as your skills grow.

CHAPTER 15

Using Market Geometry for Price Projections

So far we have been looking at market internals that help us define key trend lines and their angles of acceleration. We are now ready to look at ways to subdivide the trading ranges between price highs and lows in order to determine where the market should find support and resistance. We will then look at a method for making price projections.

This chapter will give you the method and technique, but I would suggest you also read Chapter 20 in Part 6, "Why Does Technical Analysis Work?" These two chapters together will give you a comprehensive appreciation of the number 1.618. But the technique for making price projections might have been more confusing if I had switched back and forth between how the technique worked and why it worked. So they were separated.

As a quick summary, the number 1.618 is a ratio that was discovered about 580 B.C., but it is Leonardo Fibonacci's famous number series 0, 1, 1, 2, 3, 5, 8, 13, 21, 34, 55, 89, 144, and so on to infinity that 1.618 is most closely associated with. We are now going to focus on this number's unique properties and how to apply it in a market context.

The value 1.618 is immensely important, as is its reciprocal, 0.618. It does not matter whether you multiply, divide, subtract, or add these numbers; the result will always be a Fibonacci ratio.

For example, if we multiply:

$$0.618 \times 0.618 = 0.382$$
$$0.382 \times 0.618 = 0.236$$
$$0.236 \times 0.618 = 0.146$$

If we subtract:

$$1.000 - 0.618 = 0.382$$
$$0.618 - 0.382 = 0.236$$
$$0.382 - 0.236 = 0.146$$

This is also true for:

$$1.618 \times 1.618 = 2.618$$
$$2.618 \times 1.618 = 4.236$$

and so on.

Therefore, if we use the Fibonacci ratios 61.8 percent, 50 percent, and 38.2 percent, or 0.618, 0.50, and 0.382, we will be able to calculate any other secondary Fibonacci ratios by making several projections using the primary three just listed.

Up to this point, most of my charts have been long-horizon, so let's switch to a bar chart with a very short horizon. These methods work the same way in charts with long horizons or very short horizons and can be used with any charting method, such as candlesticks, bar charts, or point-and-figure. In Figure 15-1 we have the 20-minute chart for the June Nasdaq futures contract. Many people will tell you that the way to calculate Fibonacci ratios is to take the price pivot high and the price pivot low, then subdivide the range into proportions of 0.382, 0.500, and 0.618. This is correct, but it is only the beginning.

In Figure 15-1 the first thing you will see is that I have not marked the exact price low. If you study the price lows, you will see that the two price bars marked with an asterisk at the bottom of the chart are at identical lows. Two tests of a number are more important than someone running a stop. If this had been a weekly chart, I would look at it the same way, except that the exact price low would have represented a group of traders who were trapped, having thought that a market breakdown to much lower levels would happen. *So the level that marks the price range that will be subdivided is defined as where a more intelligent low is located based on what*

the market is telling us. However, if you truncate a spike high or low, do not truncate the other extreme when defining the range. For example, in this chart I then went straight to the price high.

As described in previous chapters, if you look from right to left, you will see several bars marked with an asterisk to draw your attention to levels respected by the market. There is just one thing wrong, however: If you look at the price high that aligns near "05" on the *x*-axis (April 5, 2002), you will see that the price does not reach all the way up to the first subdivision of the range. (In all these charts, the lines are the same; which line is labeled 0.618 and which is labeled 0.382 just depends on whether I started from a price low and went to a price high or started from a price high and went to a price low when I drew the lines to subdivide the space. The ratios 0.618 and 0.382 are interchangeable; 1.00 - 0.618 is 0.382. Therefore, the distance from zero to 0.382 and from 1.00 to 0.618 is the same.

To calculate a retracement from a price low, *start your Fibonacci grid from a price low and work upward.* This is important because this way you will be able to evaluate more than just the price high as you move up the price data toward the high. If you start at the high, you have only one option for defining the price range— the price bottom. What you need to consider, as the range is drawn, is the respect shown in the past to internal pivots within the data to the calculated ratios.

Similarly, if you want to calculate retracements for a market pullback from a high, do the opposite: Start to define your range from the price high and work toward a low.

You will encounter a serious problem with most software vendors. They will draw their subdivisions at the right levels, but project them in the wrong direction, forcing the majority of people to use the method incorrectly or in a limited manner. If you encounter this, change the default setting and draw lines across the entire width of your computer screen. FutureSource ProNet will not draw the ratios at all until after the pivot points of the range have been selected. Changes to the Fibonacci ranges are extremely difficult as the calculated ratios disappear when one attempts to change the pivot points. The ratios reappear only after the new range is defined. This problem cannot be manually corrected by the trader as the software code requires a change. CQG will not permit any adjustments of their Fibonacci grid once it is drawn. This is a problem because they force traders to use an incorrect order from top or bottom when determining support versus resistance until their default is changed. Also one is forced to delete and redraw every calculation grid when a simple adjustment to one pivot point is all that is required. Third-party features can be added to CQG for an additional $100 per month. This, in my opinion, is an expensive solution for software limitations. TradeStation has this feature correctly programmed and allows flexible color changes that do not globally affect every Fibonacci set on the screen. You will prefer to have independent control for drawing more than one Fibonacci range with its own set of calculated ratios.

Returning to Figure 15-1, people who wanted to sell at the first line, or at a 38.2 percent retracement of the price decline, are out of luck, as the market did not give them an opportunity. The market failed to trade into their action zone, which is the line itself. They go away mad and say that the method doesn't work. However, let's look at this further. Do you see the price gap at the top of the chart? That is a big clue that something bigger is happening in this data.

The decline in this short time horizon is accelerating to the downside, and that is why a simple calculation to subdivide the high and low falls short. But in Figure 15-2 I used the price that follows *after the gap* as the high, as I always do, for gaps are important. Now look at the bounce up that occurs on April 5. It's dead on. Look at the price action on April 1 relative to a different retracement ratio produced from this same series. It was significant support, showing prior respect for the ratios and pivot we used after the gap.

In Figure 15-3 we need to calculate resistance after the market made the price low on April 5. Now I am using the range from the price high of the major pivot near 1420 (*y*-axis) to the price low. The market bounces up to the exact 50 percent retracement of the range and falls back to the 1380 level again. When we track all three subdividing lines from right to left, the market shows that these ratios

F i g u r e   15-2

F i g u r e   15-3

have been respected before. This is really important. Most people look only for price highs and lows and fail to study the internal levels that confirm whether they are right or not. (A price high or low does not mean only the extreme chart high or low, as demonstrated by this chart.)

But how did I know that I should use the price high on April 5 and not a lower pivot?

I knew that the price pivot near 1420 was extremely important because when I subdivided the range from the same price lows to a secondary pivot just above the gap, the resulting subdivision shows a duplicate calculation near 1420. When calculations made using different ranges fall on top of one another, you have found one of the principal building blocks of the pattern the market is forming.

To see the use of this method over longer time horizons, study Figure 15-5. Using the price low and the January 2001 price high, the range is subdivided similarly at 0.382, 0.50, and 0.618 retracement levels. A double top forms, ending the rally from the September 2001 low right at the first retracement.

F i g u r e   15-4

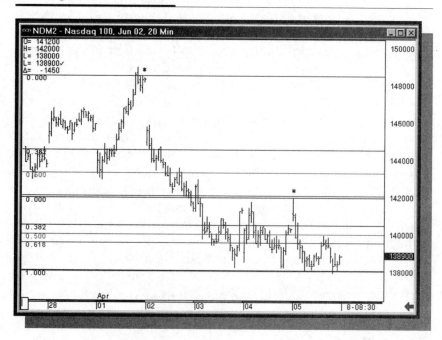

F i g u r e   15-5

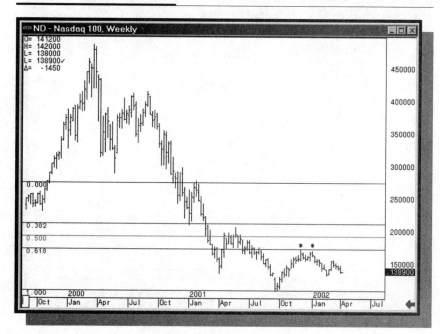

Some people ask, "But what if I use different numbers for the retracement ratios?" Go ahead and try it. Test any value you want to. After about 5 years' work, you'll realize that you are right back where you started, and that you have lost a lot of time. A universal constant of 1.618 is going to raise its head as a solution any way you look at it. That has been true since the ancient Egyptians.

If I do more than one calculation, you will again see that the January 2002 top was a double top at a brick wall of overlapping Fibonacci ratios. This is the reason you will prefer to have independent color control of each Fibonacci range set. The different colors of the set help to view the range source pivots.

If I were selling into that double top or major resistance area, I would know that I had been wrong about the market going down when the price action broke through this same zone. Now I have something to use for risk management. It is not an exact number, it is a narrow zone formed by the multiple Fibonacci ratios. In shorter-horizon charts, I have to place stops at least one full zone away. In very short-horizon trading, slippage can be calculated for a stop as

F i g u r e   15-6

the fill could be a worst-case scenario to the next zone away from the stop order. *Keep limit orders out of the zone range itself.*

Why would I want to sell into the zone that formed the market high in January 2002? Because the market was at the zone? No, I would want to sell because the market was at a major zone *and my indicators gave me permission to sell.* This is just part of the puzzle, but knowing where the market is going and knowing where you are wrong are the most critical pieces.

Let's do a price projection in Figure 15-7 to see where the Nasdaq price objective was located when the market declined from the price high at A, fell to a low at B, and then produced a countertrend rally into the price high at C. (This has nothing to do with Elliott wave A-B-Cs, if someone is wondering.)

Now we are going to use a method called Fibonacci Extensions. We will measure a move, in this case the decline from A to B, and then project price targets from a retracement price high at C. When you measure a move, you should be careful to be at right angles to the horizontal lines that mark price highs and lows. Do not cause

F i g u r e   15-7

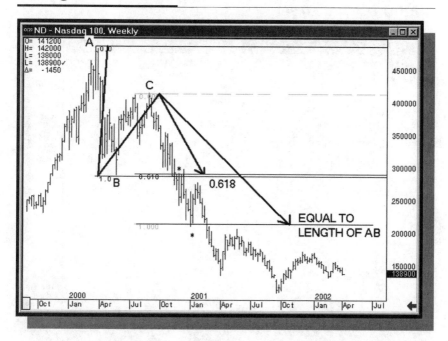

parallax errors by incorrectly measuring along the hypotenuse of
the decline. *In Figure 15-7 the swing drawn is not perpendicular so that
you can still see the price data. But the measurement of AB for the calculation is at right angles to the horizontal lines.* Relative to the length
of the move AB, project 0.618, equality (1.00), and 1.618 declines
from the high at C. I have marked the 0.618 and equality relationships on the chart. The equality relationship is realized at the
December 2000 low, telling us the market has respected the mathematical relationships used at points A, B, and C. This is important
for future calculations.

If I take the range from the price high to the April 2000 low
and subdivide it, as in Figure 15-8, it is easy to see that the market
was making a rally into the 0.618 or 61.8 percent retracement of
the range. The market was not in an expansion mode until after the
second top was made in 2000 at this 61.8 percent level.

Let's do this one more time to make sure you have it. In Figure
15-9 the distance from the price high at A to the low at B is used to
calculate the 0.618 target. The target was realized at the first low of
April 2001. It was then broken in September 2001.

F i g u r e   15-8

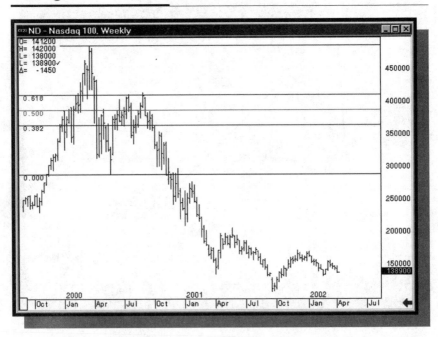

F i g u r e   15-9

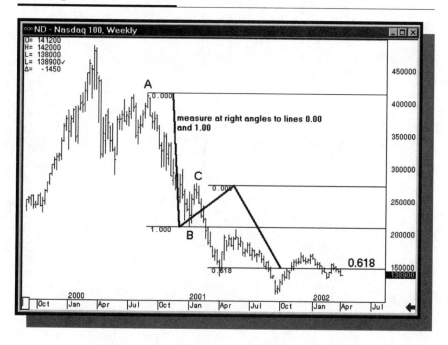

However, in Figure 15-10 I'll show you one more calculation that someone who was very advanced would make. It uses a pivot at point C, which the market never went back to after the April 2001 low. But it nails the price bottom in September 2001. You will need to spend a few years learning what has been spelled out in this chapter. The pivot point at C is an example of the kind of thing that is taught in our seminars. A trader can mathematically track every pivot from short horizon to long term. Short-horizon traders benefit as they can accurately measure precise entry and exit levels. A long-horizon trader can see early warnings when a market is stepping off course. Both benefit by minimizing position drawdown exposure.

Why did I use that particular price pivot at C? It was a harmonic interval established by internal pivots within the larger decline. An explanation of harmonic relationships will be found in Chapter 21. But you have lots to get you started, and you will need considerable hands-on time working with your computer to make these calculations rapidly. One more caution about your software;

F i g u r e   15-10

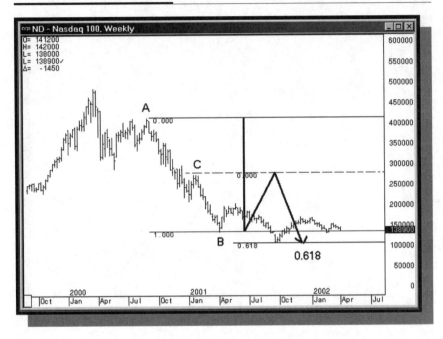

it is important to check your default settings. For example, CQG starts off with the wrong defaults. You must use 0.382, 0.500, 0.618 for retracements and 0.618, 1.00, 1.618, and 2.618 for extensions. Do not use more than these ratios if you plan to make multiple Fibonacci calculation sets. As mentioned at the start of this chapter, all Fibonacci ratios will be identified using these ratios within multiple ranges.

In the early chapters, I promised to give you a price projection from a triangle pattern. The chart in Figure 15-11 is real-time as this is being written, and the data gives the appearance of a triangle that ends at C. Remember that triangles have five legs or internal swings that coil and that the pattern must end by the time the data reaches the apex of the triangle defined by the converging outer parameter trend lines. Triangles lead to fast thrusts, and this one suggests a fast breakdown within the bear market. Calculate the length of the market move from A to B. Again, be careful to be at right angles to the horizontal lines that mark price highs and lows.

To find the price objective, project a 0.618, 1.00 relationship to

F i g u r e 15-11

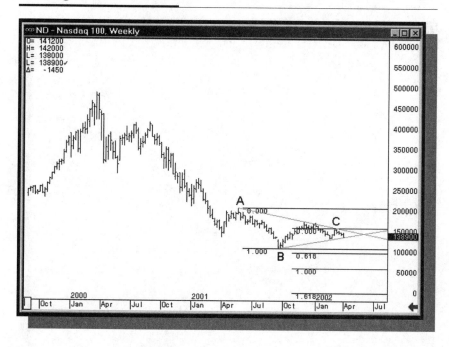

AB from C and you will have the new target. A 1.618 projection is not included, as it would be at zero, but this is the third measurement we normally define. (For those familiar with Elliott Wave Theory, use the end of wave E that is the same as C in Figure 15-11.)

If you want to identify support during a rally phase of the market, the methods are identical. Figure 15-12 is a point-and-figure chart for the September S&P500 futures contract. I mentioned when we first set up your computer that there were other ways to display data, but I didn't want to confuse you at the start. The bars of zeros and x's form only after the market has moved by a specific amount, which you define. Someday you will want to read about and experiment with this charting style, as it filters some noise out of the market data. But the technique of using Fibonacci numbers to define support and resistance levels is no different on bar charts, candlestick charts, or point-and-figure charts.

In Figure 15-13 we see the same chart later in time with a second range added. Major support is being respected at the asterisk. (The numbers on the chart are Elliott Wave interpretations, as these

F i g u r e   15-12

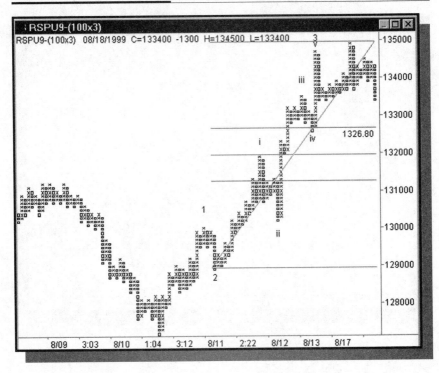

are archived trading screens.) The market bottomed at the target and then proceeded to make a new high above the price high in this chart.

You may now want to take another look at Figure 10-3, which showed a real estate chart. You now know the method applied and will have a better understanding of the chart.

Some people will tell you that Fibonacci ratios do not work. I am going to arm you with a visual that shows you why this opinion exists and why these people need to do a little more work to gain a better understanding of this method before they discard it.

In Figure 15-14, we are looking at a chart for the Dollar Index. The truth is that for this example, it does not matter what the chart shows or what time horizon it reflects. You can do this as a doodle while talking on the phone. (That's how this particular chart was created.) Take the Fibonacci tool in your software and start clicking on price ranges that the market has formed. I start with the biggest one first. In this chart, it is from the price high to a price low that

F i g u r e   15-13

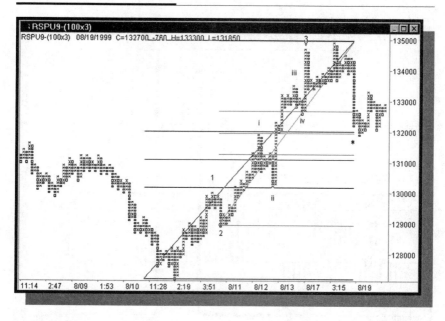

began a strong move up. Then define a range from the next key pivots. You will use one price high lower than the extreme top to one price low higher from the bottom. Then define a third range, always moving down one price pivot and up one price low, as shown. Now look where the 50 percent retracement lines fall. If they all land on top of one another, this shows that the market is moving in a linear manner and is neither contracting nor expanding. If the market is accelerating and is in an expansion cycle, the 50 percent retracement line for each compared range will be higher. (Each line will be lower in a declining market.) If the market is contracting, the 50 percent lines will reflect this also.

The people who state that Fibonacci ratios do not work are using their quote vendors' instructions and just marking the extreme price high and low. They define one range and create a single set of Fibonacci ratios, and they never suspect that maybe the problem is not that the method doesn't work, but that their application of it is too elementary. Their application will work only when the market is neither contracting nor expanding. Thus, they will be right: Fibonacci ratios work only some of the time, and do not work—for them, that is—when the market is expanding or

F i g u r e   15-14

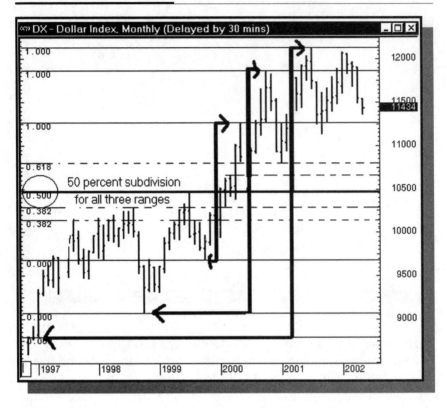

contracting, which is most of the time. Thus, you need to apply Fibonacci ratios in the ways described in this chapter.

While there is a lot more to Fibonacci ratios, you now have a solid foundation for exploring them and beginning to use them with any market. Because the methods described use multiple projections, you will be able to adjust for market expansion/contraction cycles. This is also the reason I asked you to ensure that your software was not in black and white only. Programs written for the DOS operating system do not cut it either, as the resolution is horrible, making this technique difficult to apply when you want to study price internals to identify levels for which the market has shown respect earlier. You can see why you need a good graphics card in your computer and software to match.

While Fibonacci ratios and extensions are deadly accurate, there are many other methods that you will encounter as you seek to learn more. One that is worth looking into is a method used by W. D. Gann. He subdivided the price ranges from price lows to highs, and he also used a range from zero to a price high with subdivisions of one-eighths. Take a look at Figure 15-15. This chart shows a specialized charting software package just for Gann analysis, called GannTrader. It is still Microsoft DOS-based and therefore has lots of problems because it is falling behind technologically and can cause tremendous conflicts with virus and firewall software programs operating in Windows. So I'll only mention it, but if you have the means to make the calculations, you should know that you are not wasting your time, as long as you also use the methods of Fibonacci analysis.

F i g u r e   15-15

CHAPTER 16

Ways to Detect Market Extremes Using Price, Breadth, and Sentiment

People tend to collect momentum and behavioral or sentiment indicators like baseball cards. One individual asked for my help after he had more than 170 oscillators and was proud of the fact that he knew all about each and every one of them. There was just one problem: He did not know why he couldn't make up his mind to trade. He never had enough confidence to trade, as he had so many indicators that he could find reasons to doubt any decision that he made. In this business, we call that analysis paralysis, and it can be extremely costly. Follow a game plan for researching indicators and methods so that you can weed out the ones that are just redundant.

You want to develop three noncorrelated market analysis approaches. Using two oscillators, such as a Fast Stochastics indicator with a slow MACD, provides only one market analysis approach, not two. The two studies together contribute to one market signal when used correctly. The first of the three different noncorrelated methods that I use is the RSI with a custom indicator that I call the Composite Index. Together, these two indicators and market geometry we discussed earlier from Fibonacci analysis form my first method. The second method that I use is the Elliott Wave Principle, and the third is Gann analysis. These methods may not be your preferences, but the key is to have three that are very different, and *they are noncorrelated*.

The second and third methods that I favor also have several components to create their contributing signal within my final three market signals. As an example, Elliott and Gann analysis have their own independent methods of price projection. Gann analysis alone is a very broad area of study that incorporates both time and price analysis. Each method may have several components, but I am always acutely aware that the components simply add a degree of probability to the three final signals that my favored analysis approaches give me. *You should have three noncorrelated market signals or opinions in total and no more.* Together these three different approaches provide a strong market opinion when they all agree. That way you will not develop 170 oscillators that basically do the same thing.

I have also learned from teaching that people often tweak an indicator to the point where it actually turns into something else. For example, one individual altered the RSI formula to such an extent that it looked and behaved just like a Stochastics oscillator. Just use Stochastics if that is the wave character you like momentum oscillators to look. What is most important is staying with a method so that you can intimately learn its character in various market conditions. Don't jump around exploring different methods. Make changes very slowly after you have seen the new method's performance in real-time market scenarios, not just through back-testing setups with historical data. Automating signals is a huge mistake unless you have a tremendous number of markets to track and you use the automated signals as a flag alerting you to begin your own work because certain criteria were met. I have made a tremendous effort to try and guide you to study chart internals in order to learn how a market functions and how it respects a technique. Ignoring these variations is perhaps the primary reason why "system" traders were systematically blown out of the market over the last 3 years in large numbers.

The list that follows gives methods that study market momentum, breadth, and sentiment. Someone who developed momentum analysis and then added breadth or sentiment indicators would have two noncorrelated methods, as the underlying sources of data are different. All the methods listed here strive to tell us whether the market has enough steam to plough through resistance or whether it is overextended and about to reverse and break down through support.

Acceleration

Acceleration Factor

Accumulation/Distribution Indicator
Accumulation Swing Index
Advance/Decline Ratio
Advisory Sentiment Index
ADX and ADXR
Arm's Ease of Movement
Average Balance Volume
Bollinger Bands
Bolton-Tremblay Indicator
Channel Lines
Commitment of Traders Index
Commodity Selection Index
Composite Index
Confidence Index
Cumulative Volume Index
Demand Index
Derivative Oscillator
Detrend
Detrended Price Oscillator
Directional Movement Index
High/Low Volatility Ratio
Insider Activity Ratio
Insider Buy/Sell Ratio
Keltner Channels
Large Block Ratio
Low-Priced Activity Ratio
MACD (Moving Average Convergence Divergence)
   Oscillator
Market Profile
McClellan Oscillator
McClellan Summation Index
Member Odd Lot Trading
Member Short Differential
Member Trading

Misery Index
Momentum Oscillator
Moving Average Momentum
Moving Average Oscillator
Moving Averages
Odd Lot Balance Index
Odd Lot Purchases/Sales
Odd Lot Short Ratio
Odd Lot Short Sales
Offset Moving Average
On Balance Volume
OTC Volume %
Parabolic or Stop and Reversal
Percent Industry Groups Rising/Falling
Percentage Bands
Pivot Point Channels
Plurality Index
Positive Volume Indicator
Premium Ratio on Options
Price & Volume Velocity
Public Short Sales
Put/Call Premium Ratio
Put/Call Ratio
Ratio of AMEX Volume to NYSE Volume
Ratio of Odd Lot to Specialist Short
Relative Strength Comparative
Relative Strength Index
Rate of Change—Price
Rate of Change—Volume
Sensitivity Bands
Sentiment Index
Short Interest Ratio
Specialist Short Interest Ratio

Standard Deviation

Stochastic Fast %K

Stochastic Slow %D

Stoller Bands

TRIN

Trinity Index

Up Volume % Total Volume

Upside-Downside Ratio

Upside-Downside Volume

Variable Accumulation/Distribution

Velocity

Volatility

Volume Accumulation Oscillator

Volume Oscillator

Volume Up Days/Down Days

Wilder's Swing Index

These are certainly not all the indicators and methods that measure momentum, breadth, or sentiment, but this is a healthy representative list of ways to track market extremes and participant behavior.

Here's the bottom line for all these studies. Momentum and sentiment extremes can tell us when there is a high probability that the market will reverse, but not one of the formulas or approaches in this list can tell us *how far the market will move once it changes direction*. Not one.

So why do we want to go to the trouble of learning about these various methods? Because we want to know how a market may react to the key price targets and levels of market support and resistance that we identified in the last chapter. Your price projection methods will tell you how far a market may move. Therefore, these studies and price projection methods go hand in hand. Using price projection methods alone is like seeing a train station, then having no idea whether the train will stop or go on by to the next one. We use momentum, breadth, and sentiment indicators to tell us this is not only the stop, but the end of the trip and the train will then reverse.

The indicators and methods in the preceding list represent three schools of thought.

The first approach is to study the relative opening and closing prices in some mathematical way, with the premise being that markets that are weak will close below their opening price for the period being charted and strong markets will close the period higher than where they opened. Momentum indicators as a group function in this manner. The various momentum formulas and resulting squiggles that you can add to your chart all use this underlying premise to measure market strength or weakness.

A second school of thought holds that price data alone cannot possibly tell us the whole story, no matter what kind of indicator you develop to massage and study prices. Technicians using this approach follow methods known as market breadth indicators. They rely upon formulas that study volume and market activity rather than price data alone. For example, they need to know how many NYSE stocks are advancing and declining in the same period of time. Market breadth indicators are generally followed by stock market participants. As my background has always been futures, I will introduce breadth analysis to you, but I suggest you purchase books that focus specifically on market breadth if this is a school of thought you are interested in learning more about.

Futures markets analyze both Open Interest and volume. Open Interest offers another level of transparency. For example, in futures markets, high volume alone is not necessarily a good thing. High volume that is accompanied by a declining Open Interest is a warning that money is being extracted from the market, and when this happens, analysts become more concerned about a trend reversal. On the other hand, when Open Interest is increasing along with volume, this indicates that new contracts are being agreed to, which confirms that new money is being committed. *New money must enter a market to sustain a trend.*

The third school of thought is where market behaviorists reside. These technicians develop formulas to monitor the buying and selling activity of the bearish crowd against the bullish crowd. They also analyze the activity of commercial traders versus that of the general public. The underlying premise is that the general public or retail sector is usually wrong and the smart money is usually in the hands of the people in the know, or the professional and commercial traders. These technicians also think that if a majority of market participants become overly weighted on one side of the spectrum, be it bullish or bearish, the market will find a way to do damage to the greatest number of participants. This method of analysis is called sentiment analysis, and we will take a look at a couple of approaches that are part of this school of thought as well. So let's dig in.

I come from the school of thought that was first listed: the belief that a study of price data can answer most of our market questions. Let's begin by looking at the chart of Lucent Technologies in Figure 16-1.

As this is being written, LU has just broken $9.00 and is destined to decline further. This chart is certainly from better times, but it is used to show you when prices were testing the underside of a line I added to the price data. The line that has been added is a moving average of daily closing prices. The number of daily closes being averaged, which we call the interval period, is a constant. If there are fewer daily closes in an average, the line will move more quickly and will track the actual price data more closely. Averaging together

F i g u r e   16-1

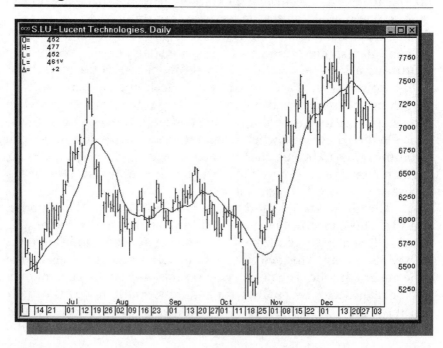

more daily closes will slow the average down, increasing the lag and smoothing effect. As each new close becomes available, the oldest price drops out of the average, making the average move forward with the price data.

Some people don't like the fact that the same weighting is given to every close when the average is calculated. When a big market day drops out of the average, as the oldest in the set, the average for the most recent period has a larger move. Therefore, these people prefer formulas that use weighted or exponential moving averages, which weight the average toward the more recent data. That way, when an old data period drops out of the average, it has less of an impact. Personally, I think you can spend years trying to find the perfect period to use and the perfect weighting and still be some distance from applying the information in a meaningful way. So I'll give you a shortcut to get you started: Stay with a simple moving average. Down the road you can tweak and test the average to your heart's content.

The period you want to use for the simple moving average will often be a Fibonacci number, the number series you learned about in the prior chapter and, I hope, will explore further in Chapter 21. The number series is 1, 1, 2, 3, 5, 8, 13, 21, 34, 55, 89, and so forth.

In Figure 16-2 we have a monthly MSFT chart with two simple moving averages. A shorter-term moving average will rise or fall more quickly than a longer-term moving average. The thinking behind using two averages is that when the slower-moving average catches up with the faster-moving average, a trend may be preparing to reverse. We watch when the distance between the averages narrow, and we pay particular attention when the averages cross. The average that tracks closer to the price data will be the faster average, or the one in which fewer periods are used to create the average. The average that lags more will have a greater number of periods used to create it. In this chart, we are using the Fibonacci periods of 8 and 21 to generate the moving averages. Why did I pick those particular averages? Because they work nicely for the chart I am viewing. There is no other reason. The price data on the left is tracking nicely. When the price data declined, the averages helped to define the trend and resistance as well. I rely on the visual appearance of the chart. If it is working, don't fix what is not broken. If prices do not respect the averages well, change the

F i g u r e   16-2

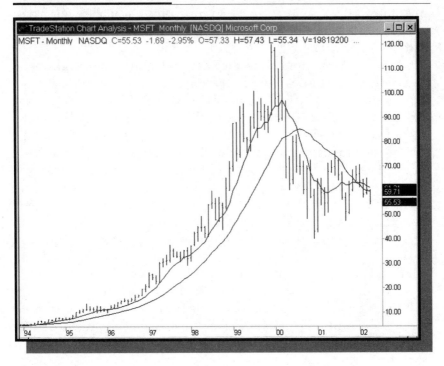

period, using a different Fibonacci number. If the data is in an uptrend, a shorter period will move the line up and a longer period will move the average down. Eventually you'll learn about back-testing and a host of other time-consuming activities. This is curve fitting, and it works until the market decides to expand or contract, breaking the pattern you found to be a perfect fit. Back-testing will tell you that a method has merit, but it is not the final step. You must always evaluate a new indicator in a real-time environment before using it to risk capital.

In the chart for LU in Figure 16-1, the average is too far away from the price action for my liking, so I would use a shorter period to create the average or add a second average with a shorter period for comparison. The bottom line about these adjustments is to work from a chart that the market is clearly respecting across the computer screen so that you can increase the probability of making sound decisions about the new data that enters the screen in real time. This is not curve fitting if you know that markets expand and contract.

Experience has taught me that this type of close observation of the data displayed within the chart window narrows the margin of error. Curve fitting means that you have determined the mean average setting, from a large historical window that works best for the data, and then make all future decisions based on that average setting. This type of curve fitting does not work, in my opinion. Just ask someone who developed a black-box trading system by only back-testing data from 1980.

You should monitor the two averages by watching the spread between them. In uptrends the faster or shorter-period average will track above the longer-period or slower average. In downtrends the spread will be negative, as the faster average will track below the longer-period average, which always lags. Many traders use what are called trailing stops and close or unwind positions if the market breaks through the average. This works well for long-horizon trending markets, but you will lose a lot of money using trailing stops if the market starts to whip back and forth. We call that being whipsawed to death. It is painful. People who only use trailing stops often do not have a price projection system that can identify precisely where a market is going or where it should not trade. Therefore, they use the average to determine trends and manage their risk. The problem is that the realized loss or damage to unrealized gains is very high by the time the stop is triggered. So learn a price projection system and keep the averages for analysis purposes. Price projection systems can also be whipsawed, but using them is much less damaging to your capital, as they dramatically reduce the cash erosion that you will experience during the whipsaw price action.

We can graph the spread between averages in a way that makes it a lot easier to read. We simply calculate the difference between the two averages and chart this difference as an oscillator. This helps us visualize when the averages have separated from each other, forming an extreme market condition. The zero line is where the averages actually cross and there is no difference. The crossover point is always important if prices have moved to test this area as resistance or support.

In Figure 16-3 we have the same monthly MSFT chart. Plotted below the data is the spread between the moving averages. The spread has been given a fancy name that I picked: Extreme xy2 Oscillator. Is this a secret formula? No, it's just the spread between two averages, but they are extremely powerful in terms of the

F i g u r e   16-3

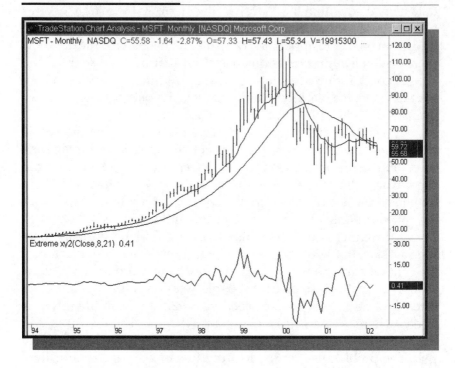

amount of information they offer us about a market. Do you see the double top in the oscillator in 1998 and 1999? This is a clear warning signal that we can easily detect. Draw a horizontal line connecting the 2001 peak and look from right to left. You will find that support became resistance at key market turns. This is not something that we would likely pick up from the averages charted on the price data alone.

I have given presentations all around the world over the years. I used to have fun with the fact that everyone wants to know the perfect formula and the perfect period to use. I would show a chart with four oscillators under the data. The more sophisticated the audience, the better, in fact, as everyone in a sophisticated audience is really tuned into indicator minutiae. It would take me about 30 minutes to highlight the different strengths and weaknesses of the four indicator setups. The response was the same, whether the audience was in Manhattan, London, Istanbul, Zurich, or Tokyo: Groups were spellbound as the comparison unfolded. They believed they were looking at different ways to setup Stochastics, a widely followed indicator, and they would carefully study the characteristics of the different methods. After the detailed review, I would take a poll to see how many people in the audience preferred each oscillator setup. Usually the majority, and sometimes as much as 80 percent, decided that the fourth setup was the best. Then I revealed the secret formula setup behind the four indicators. None of them was the formula the groups thought they were looking at. They were all different formulas that had been tweaked to look similar. That alone would surprise everyone. But the one formula that I had carefully disguised to ensure that the y-axis labels did not give anyone a clue was the fourth indicator setup. The one everyone in all major financial centers around the globe agrees upon is the one you see in Figure 16-3: the spread between two simple averages. Everyone would go ooh and ah in disbelief. We all tend to think that if something is more complex, it must be better. It isn't; it's just more complex. *The answer, therefore, is not the formula, but the user's understanding of how to read the character of that particular formula.* Therefore, don't keep jumping between oscillators or you will not be able to build a history in your own mind of how the oscillator responds for better or worse in various market conditions.

In Figure 16-4 we return to the way we first set up your computer to analyze any market or stock. Staying with MSFT, we have the monthly chart on the left and the weekly chart on the right. The averages are the same in both charts: 8- and 21-period simple averages. The spread of the averages is plotted below. When the double top formed in the monthly oscillator, we also had an oscillator peak in the weekly chart that was breaking into new highs. When an oscillator makes a new extreme high, you know that the market has enough strength to extend after a corrective retreat. Then the market will make another attempt, in this case rally.

You should sell when the weekly oscillator is at a prior high-risk extreme that the market tells you is important by looking at past performance. This sell signal occurs in 2000, when the displacement of the oscillator high challenges the old peak that occurred in July of 1999 and again near the end of 1998. I have drawn a horizontal line at the peaks to help you find the key level that is being tested and referenced. This works for any market and any time horizon. It shows you how important it is to obtain confirmation from more than one time horizon. You now grasp the

F i g u r e   16-4

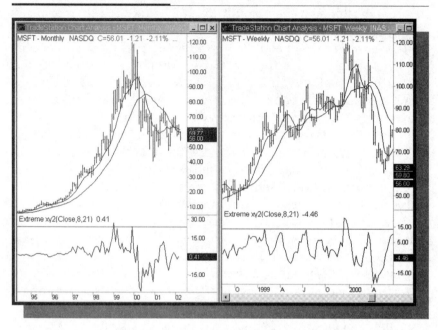

basic concepts better than most, and we haven't even looked at the most popular indicators or discussed divergence analysis, which will be used with all oscillators.

For the moment, let's stay with the same oscillator and computer screen setup. In Figure 16-5 I exchanged MSFT for Rational Software (RATL). The point is that we are again looking at just the spread between two simple moving averages using 8- and 21-periods.

In the monthly RATL chart in Figure 16-5, I have highlighted two price highs in 1996 by drawing a line above them. I have also drawn a line over the momentum peaks in the oscillator that correspond to the same time period. The second peak in the oscillator is lower than the first. Thus, the two lines, when compared, are diverging. That's a sign that the market has run out of steam, and we call this relationship between higher price peaks and corresponding lower momentum peaks *bearish divergence*. When you look at the January 2002 high in the oscillator, you will see that it also occurs at the same level at which this old divergence occurred

F i g u r e   16-5

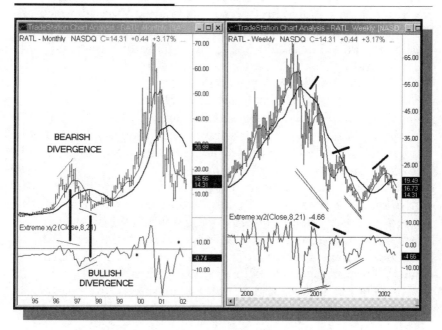

in 1996. This is more information for us to consider, and it tells us that this specific level in the indicator is extremely important.

Bullish divergence was also demonstrated in the monthly chart in 1997, when the stock made a new low and the oscillator was rolling up. I like this chart tremendously because it teaches us to look for divergences at levels other than the extreme top or bottom of the oscillator chart range. Most books that I have seen always show beautiful signals that are clearly defined at the extreme ranges of the graph. In the real world, divergence may occur in the middle of your chart range as well. The bullish divergence in the monthly chart is a perfect example. True, that would have been the bottom of the chart in 1997, but the point is to look at any divergence that occurs at any oscillator level within the entire range, as it could be meaningful. You will see this in the chart on the right.

In the weekly time horizon for RATL, I have drawn lines identifying several bullish and bearish divergences that formed between the price and the oscillator. The distance between the extremes will vary. Very wide divergence signals have a low probability. You usually have to wait until the signal forms again in a shorter time frame (such as a daily chart versus a weekly). There is no significance to my use of heavy solid lines and double thin lines in this particular chart. I was just trying to visually link matched pairs together and to keep the chart from looking too busy.

Now that you know what to look for in an oscillator, we can view two of the most widely followed oscillator formulas. In Figure 16-6, on the left is the RSI, or Relative Strength Index, and on the right is Stochastics. Both charts show weekly time frames, and both oscillators have fixed maximum ranges, as they can oscillate only between 0 and 100.

Both oscillators tell us the exact same thing, but they are visually different. Any indicator that is forced to stay within a range of zero to 100 has been normalized. This is important to know because normalized indicators will appear to lock at the extreme chart highs or lows in extreme market moves. A market that is oversold can get a whole lot more oversold before it finally turns around, and when the oscillator is locked at the top of your screen, the market can

F i g u r e   16-6

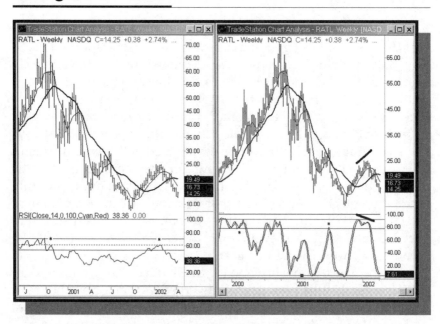

become much more overbought. All you have to do is look at the scale the oscillator travels to know whether the underlying formula is normalized or not.

The reason that normalized oscillators lock is this: A flea that always jumps half the distance between his current position and a fixed wall will never reach the wall because he moves a smaller distance every time he jumps toward the wall. That's my mathematical analogy for normalized indicators. You can't get there from here if you can move only half the distance in a single jump. Therefore, these indicators lock up when markets explode upward or downward. No price action will allow the indicator to offset the extreme position, and then when the market explodes again, the oscillator moves only back to the locked position. For this reason, I have formulas like the Composite Index, that do not lock and thus serve as reinforcement at times when conventional formulas have limited value.

The indicator on the left in Figure 16-6 is the relative strength index, or RSI. It was first introduced by Welles Wilder in an article in *Commodities* (now known as *Futures Magazine*) in June 1978. The name "Relative Strength Index" is slightly misleading, as the RSI does not compare the relative strength of two securities.

You can vary the number of time periods in the RSI calculation, but the RSI has a unique property if you leave it with a 14-period setup. Books and Web sites will tell you that the RSI usually tops above 70 or 80 and bottoms below 30 or 20. Most vendors set these lines as part of their default display. I turned the industry upside down a few years back when, in my book *Technical Analysis for the Trading Professional*, I proved that this was very wrong. Briefly, in bear markets, the markets top near 60 to 65 and bottom well below 40. In bull markets, a bottom will be seen near 40 to 45 and the indicator will travel toward 80 or 90. The key here is that the 60 to 65 zone reserved for bear markets will be exceeded fairly easily. When you are ready, you can learn more about these range guidelines in this more advanced book as a full chapter has been devoted to this topic.

The RSI is a fairly simple formula that uses an average of upward price changes and an average of downward price changes. I am in agreement with my editor that we should not give math formulas in this book. Knowing the formula does not make you a better analyst or trader. If you want the exact math formula, you will find it easily enough on the Internet. I will stick with the concepts of these different formulas unless there is a custom formula involved.

The indicator on the right is the Stochastic oscillator. This indicator shows where a market's price closed relative to its price range over a given time period. The Stochastic oscillator is displayed as two lines. The faster line is called "%K." The second and slower line is an average of the slow %K that we call "%D." The %K line is displayed as a solid line, and the %D line is sometimes displayed as a dotted line. A third moving average is sometimes calculated that slows and smoothes %K even further. In that case, %D is plotted and a slow %D is used, which is the new average. %K is then dropped from the chart itself, even though it was used in the steps to construct the indicator.

The formula was developed by Dr. George Lane. George is one of my mentors, and I have a high regard for him, as his knowledge about markets and the industry seems endless and he has helped many people at different phases in their careers. I love his explanation when I asked him how the names %K and %D were found. He said, "We tested %A, %B, %C . . ." From that answer, it seems that K and D worked best. Everything was done manually then, as computers were a rare and expensive luxury that needed complex programming skills in the early 1970s.

Stochastics is widely abused by vendors and general-purpose help texts. This is frustrating because it means that people lose a lot of money before they learn how George really uses this indicator.

Here is a perfect example of how *not* to use the Stochastic study. The source will go nameless.

The way to interpret a Stochastic Oscillator includes:

1. Buy when the Oscillator (either %K or %D) falls below a specific level (e.g., 20) and then rises above that level.
2. Sell when the Oscillator rises above a specific level (e.g., 80) and then falls below that level.

This is absolutely dead wrong. Professionals actually use the signals just described to enter their larger orders, which run the public over in the process. Why? Because Stochastics does not work this way. When the signal described here occurs, it usually happens *at the halfway point for the larger market trend that is developing*. This indicator works best when three divergences are present, and George Lane also wants to see declining volume with each divergence formation. The best rule of thumb, when you find a formula that is of particular interest to you, is to study the book written by the person who developed the formula.

The Stochastic oscillator always tracks between 0 and 100, so, like RSI, it has been normalized. Divergence analysis is the most common use of oscillators. Divergence signals give you permission to take action when a price target has been realized. Do not act on their signals alone, but keep in mind that you are using two moving averages in the formula, therefore, one oscillator will use the other as support or resistance.

What interval period should one use to set up Stochastics? The correct period will be one half of a market cycle length. Therefore, we will defer discussing the detailed setup procedure until Chapter 22, when we discuss market cycles in detail. Use 18 or 32 to begin if you trade stocks or stock indices. Do not use your vendor's default setup. When we look at the correct setup procedure, you will understand why 18 or 32 is a close start.

I could write volumes on the internal signals for these two oscillators, but the truth is that until you can easily see and identify market divergences, I would be putting the cart before the horse. So I am going to deliberately give you just enough to send you off in the right direction and then move on.

In Figure 16-7 we are looking at the weekly chart for the Vanguard Fund. Under the price data is the Stochastics indicator, which has two oscillators, and then two additional moving averages have been added on top of these two lines. You use the extra averages on the indicator the same way you would use averages on price data. This, in fact, is how George Lane sets up his trading screen. It shows that you can add indicators upon indicators to help reduce the lag problem that oscillators in general experience. Some indicators are extremely slow. Consider MACD, which is plotted under Stochastics in Figure 16-7.

MACD, which is short for Moving Average Convergence Divergence, is another indicator that just shows the relationship between moving averages. MACD is the difference between a 26-period and a 12-period exponential moving average when you use your vendor's default setup. The difference is calculated and then

F i g u r e   16-7

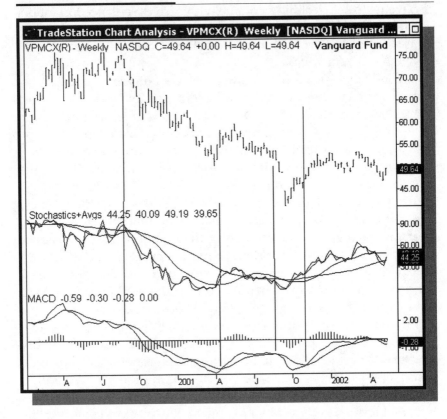

plotted in a histogram as a displacement from zero. Therefore, the data in the histogram is similar to the plotted difference between two moving averages under price as a solid line. The MACD goes a step further by using a 9-period exponential moving average of the first to form the "signal" (or "trigger") line, which is plotted on top of the MACD to show buy/sell opportunities.

MACD was developed by Gerald Appel. It is used like the other oscillators we have looked at so far. You should look for divergences between the indicator and the price data to detect oversold and overbought conditions. Three setups that you can look at are Appel's 13-26-9 combination (you will see why Appel uses 13 and not 12 in a moment), 5-24-8, and 5-34-5. Regardless of what three periods you use, this indicator lags behind trend reversals.

To help minimize this lag problem, Gerald Appel sets up two totally different MACD windows. Appel wrote the following as presentation notes,

> Since most markets decline more rapidly than they rise, it is advisable to employ a more rapid combination (shorter term moving average pairings) to track declining markets. We employ a 13-day, 26-day exponential average pairing to generate buy signals and a 19-day, 39-day pairing to generate sell signals. A 50-day moving average is employed to define trend. If the average is rising sharply, indicating a strong up trend, we would employ an even more rapid MACD pairing (6-day, 19-day) to generate buy signals and we might delay selling until negative divergences appeared, even if the signal line for the sell MACD is violated.

These comments were made during a strong bull market. A faster setup would also be paired with the original setup for timing improvements in a larger-trending bear market. Therefore, when you set up two windows with MACD, the shorter or faster indicator setup is used to detect extremes in the shorter time horizon to enter or add to existing positions within larger trends.

While one divergence in MACD may be sufficient, as this formula is slow, Stochastics is often paired with MACD, as it is a faster indicator by nature and should form two or three divergences with *repeatedly lower volume* with each divergence.

Preference among indicators is entirely personal and depends on your trading style. But a common misunderstanding that people often have is the idea that Stochastics or RSI can be used to *confirm* MACD. Do not make this error. Together these indicators form a single timing signal, but they do not confirm one another because all three studies are various averages derived from price data. *You need a noncorrelated method to obtain confirmation.* Confirmation simply means an increased probability that the expected outcome will occur. Therefore, noncorrelated comparisons such as an Elliott Wave pattern with an MACD signal offers confirmation. A momentum signal would be noncorrelated with a sentiment indicator or an indicator derived from volume.

There are lots of oscillators for you to explore. You might consider starting with the three we just covered before you venture into others. In Figure 16-8, monthly bar charts for Rational Software (RATL) are displayed on both the left and the right. That

Figure 16-8

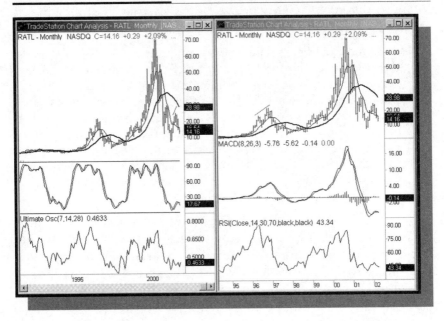

way you can see four oscillators and the character of each at the same time. The top oscillator in the left-hand chart is Stochastics, and the bottom oscillator is one that we haven't discussed called the Ultimate Oscillator. On the right, the top oscillator is MACD and the lower oscillator is the RSI. When a divergence occurs, the different formulas each signal it in their own manner. Stochastics gave three divergences, MACD gave only one, and RSI gave two. The Ultimate Oscillator and the RSI are similar in some respects, so I discard the Ultimate Oscillator because the RSI has some unique features that the other does not have. Filter out redundant signals and methods.

In Figure 16-9 we see the weekly IBM chart with Stochastics and RSI oscillators added. Moving averages are again shown directly on top of these oscillators. Look for support and resistance when the oscillator tests the averages. One signal in particular to monitor when averages are used with either price or oscillators is a test that is made right at the crossover of your two averages or when the oscillator turns right at the averages. The asterisks help to clarify these important formations.

Figure 16-9

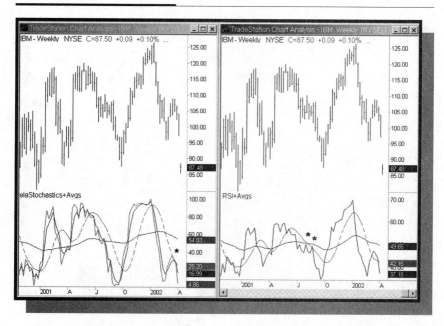

Let's move on and take a look at another use for moving averages. This is still part of the school of thought that says that prices reveal all. We are just going to go about it in a slightly different manner this time.

Both sides of Figure 16-10 show a weekly IBM bar chart. The last bar to the right might easily be overlooked. There is a huge gap down that occurred when IBM warned that its earnings were not what had previously been reported to the public. This market action allows an important comparison. Added to the price data are moving-average trading bands.

An envelope uses two averages; one is shifted upward from its mean, and the other is displaced downward. The bands from envelopes always have a fixed percentage above and below the mean value of price closes. This serves to help visualize a normal trading range. The thinking is that when traders press a market into the band extremes, there is a high risk that market reversals will occur. Envelopes can be used in any time horizon.

The bands in Figure 16-10 are a little more sophisticated than just fixed percentages. To understand the formula used to develop

F i g u r e   16-10

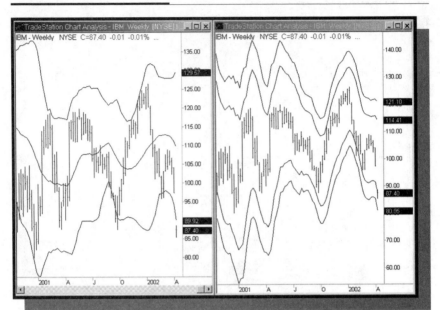

the bands on the left, you need to understand the concept of standard deviation. This is a statistical measure of volatility that, once calculated, can be added to the data's moving average. The bands in the left chart are Bollinger Bands, which are calculated in this manner. They plot standard deviations above and below a moving average. The bands automatically adjust to market volatility. These bands were developed by John Bollinger and became popular because he displayed them often on FNN, which is now known as CNBC.

One of the weaknesses of Bollinger Bands is that in strong market moves, the price data stays outside the extreme ranges for some period of time. When prices are outside the band, this suggests further market movement in the same direction as the trend. I tend to want to read bands as being maximum market displacements preceding an immediate reaction, so I favor a different formula.

What formula you use is a personal preference. I use the bands on the right to see price failures during secondary tests. In other words, touching the band once, reacting, trying to touch the band a second time, and failing to reach it becomes my market timing signal to take action. A stall also works nicely. These are the only signals I look for within the bands. The other use of bands is as you see in the right-hand chart. IBM is in an extreme situation based on prices in the current bar, and the price action has fallen past the first band and into the range of the second. The price will not bottom until there is a rebound and a test of the new lows that stays above the inside band. The price action will therefore extend, and the pattern described will help with the market timing. If you would like the formula for these bands, just copy it from my Web site http://www.aeroinvest.com. Then select *Books for Trader* near the bottom. While this is the format for any version of TradeStation or SuperCharts, you will need to work with your software vendor if changes are needed for a different system.

Both band formulas have the same character in that they narrow significantly when markets become stable and quiet. This period of band narrowing is often followed by an explosive market move.

Let's shift now to the people who believe that market breadth is the answer to market direction, as price alone is insufficient no matter what price dependent approach you favor. The indicators and methods used by market breadth analysts track what we call market internals, such as volume and the number of advancing shares versus the number of declining shares. Market breadth analysts are generally interested in stocks, and this is why nearly all of these methods employ some comparison of stock activity. An extremely popular indicator called the Advance/Decline Line is shown in Figure 16-11. This indicator is used to study momentum and acceleration. The New York Stock Exchange Composite Index is displayed above the indicator. The Advance/Decline Line is the difference between the number of stocks listed on the New York Stock Exchange that advanced in price minus the number that declined in price. Other breadth indicators that have the same underling premise are the Absolute Breadth Index, Arms Index, the McClellan Oscillator, and the Summation Index.

Market breadth indicators are used to evaluate market strength. If more stocks have advancing prices than have declining prices, this is a sign of internal market strength. The absolute value is usually smoothed by plotting an average rather than just plotting the raw value alone.

Another popular market breadth indicator is the McClellan Oscillator, developed by Sherman and Marian McClellan. In a healthy bull market, a large number of stocks are making moderate

F i g u r e   16-11

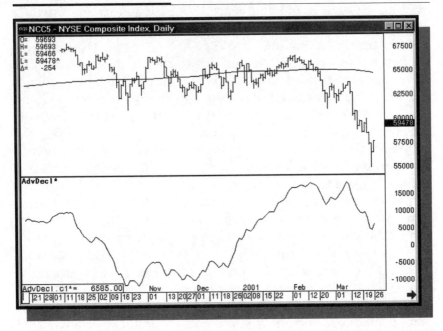

upward advances in price. A weakening bull market is character-
ized by a small number of stocks making large advances in price,
giving the false appearance that all is well. This type of divergence
is viewed as a warning signal that an end could be near. A similar
interpretation applies to market bottoms, where the market index
continues to decline while fewer stocks are declining. Extreme
readings in the McClellan Oscillator are viewed as high-risk trend
reversal pivot points.

Another widely followed indicator for breadth analysis is the
Arms Index. To calculate the Arms Index, first divide the number
of stocks that advanced in price by the number of stocks that
declined in price to determine the Advance/Decline ratio. Next,
divide the volume of advancing stocks by the volume of declining
stocks to determine the Upside/Downside ratio. Finally, divide the
Advance/Decline ratio by the Upside/Downside ratio.

If this is of interest to you, I would suggest reading the books by
Richard Arm, who is the originator of this indicator. However, all
breadth indicators experience slow market reactions at price extremes

and can remain in these extreme conditions. I would view them as analysis tools rather than market entry/exit trading signals.

Let's now take a look at the last school of thought, which contains some quite original methods favored by the market behavioral analysts within our industry. In general, market psychology involves monitoring specific market participants and interpreting their actions as an indication of what prices will do next. Obtaining the data will require a little more work on your part, but the Internet is making all our lives much easier, as charts can be viewed directly from the Web. Because some of the raw data is not easily available to the general public, few know how to read this next chart, called Commitment of Traders.

In Figure 16-12 is a Microsoft Excel chart that I made from Commitment of Traders data. This is data involving the activity of futures traders; it can be obtained from the exchange for a single week or purchased in historical files from various vendors. Every futures market has speculative buyers and sellers who never want to

F i g u r e   16-12

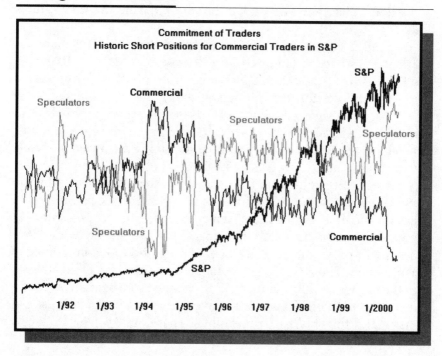

actually receive or deliver the underlying commodity. The traders, known as hedgers, who do want to complete the terms of the contract and deliver or receive the commodity have different margin requirements than speculators and must report their open positions to the exchanges as required by regulation. As a result, there is a known reported number reflecting the activities of the commercial hedgers as opposed to those of the speculators.

The thinking is that the commercial traders have been correct more often than the speculators. Therefore, the chart in Figure 16-12 shows commercial traders' and speculators' activity in S&P500 futures. In early 2000 the commercial traders held more short positions than at any other time in history. On the other hand, the speculative public held the greatest number of net long positions within a 5-year period. While the commercials were early as usual, they correctly called the bigger market move, and the speculative public lost their bet big-time. That, in a simple example, is why this information is also used by those interested in stocks.

We also watch the activity of options traders. The Put/Call Ratio (P/C Ratio) is a market sentiment indicator that shows the relationship between the number of option puts to the number of option calls that are traded on the Chicago Board Options Exchange (CBOE).

A call gives an investor the right to purchase 100 shares of stock at a predetermined price. Investors who purchase calls expect the price of the stock to rise in the coming months. Conversely, a put gives an investor the right to sell 100 shares of stock at a preset price. Because investors who purchase calls expect the market to rise and investors who purchase puts expect the market to decline. The relationship between the number of puts to the number of calls illustrates the bullish/bearish expectations of these investors.

Most of the volume in the option markets is generated by the speculative mass public. Therefore, as with the Commitment of Traders data, it is assumed that when the majority of speculators in the general public have begun to favor one side of the market, the market will prove the majority to be wrong and move in the opposite direction. The P/C Ratio is a contrarian indicator, which means that the higher the level of the P/C Ratio, the more bearish investors are on the market. Conversely, lower readings indicate high call volume and thus bullish expectations. Therefore "excessive" levels warn that the market may have a trend change as a result of overextended sentiment.

In Figure 16-13 we are looking at a chart created by www.DecisionPoint.com. The top portion displays the S&P100 Index. On the bottom is an indicator reflecting Put to Call volume. The raw data is a little too wild and needs to be smoothed. To solve this problem, we chart a simple moving average of the data rather than the raw data itself. DecisionPoint.com has used a 10-day moving average of the put/call ratio, which is very common.

Normally the Put/Call Ratio for the OEX Index is displayed as an inverse relationship to the S&P100 price data. However, inverse relationships are harder to compare. If you look at the bottom right and the *y*-axis labels in Figure 16-13, you will see that I have taken the indicator and actually flipped it upside down. As I discussed much earlier in the book, I use the tool Microsoft *Paint*, which comes free with all Microsoft operating systems. After I have flipped the indicator, all my chart labels are upside down. Normally that does not cause a problem, as I just look at the visuals. But for this book I also flipped the label on the bottom left and the months so that you could read them. If you visit DecisionPoint.com, the chart will be

F i g u r e   16-13

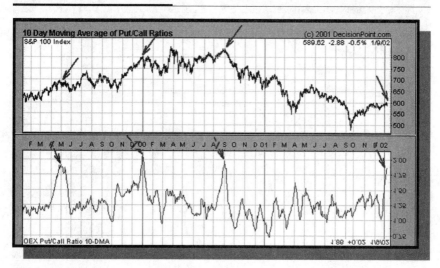

displayed in the traditional manner, with indicator spike lows marking possible price highs.

Other sentiment ratios can also be created from options trading. Figure 16-14, also from DecisionPoint.com, displays examples of the CBOE Put/Call and Equity Put/Call Ratios. These are not inverse relationships, and the indicator labels show that the chart has not been altered from the way it was first offered on the Internet site.

The concepts behind market sentiment involving options will serve you well for other sentiment indicators you may wish to explore. As an example, the Member Short Ratio measures the short-selling activity of members of the New York Stock Exchange. Members trade on the floor of the exchange, and stocks sold short from the floor are viewed as the smart money, as opposed to the Public Short Ratio. Thus, a comparison is made between the activities of different participants in the market, just as we saw in the Commitment of Traders chart. The source data may be different,

Figure 16-14

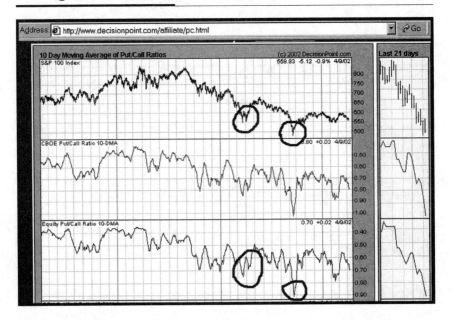

Reprinted with permission from www.DecisionPoint.com

but the concepts are the same. There is another indicator, called the VIX index, that I'll leave you to explore on your own. This is a volatility measurement; it has a short history, but it is proving useful at market bottoms in short-horizon periods.

In summary, we have been looking at three schools of thought with different philosophies about what provides the most valuable information for identifying high-risk pivot trend reversal areas in a market. The first approach studied the relative opening and closing prices in various mathematical ways, on the premise that markets that are weak will close below the opening price for the period being charted and strong markets will close the day, or interval period, higher than where they opened. A second school of thought comes from the people who believe that price data alone cannot possibly tell us the whole story, no matter how an indicator is massaged to study prices. Therefore, these analysts follow methods known as market breadth indicators. They massage and develop formulas involving volume and market activity rather than price data. Then we looked at examples from the third group, who favor analyzing the activity of commercial and institutional traders versus that of the general public. The underlying premise is that the general public or retail sector is usually wrong and the smart money is usually in the hands of the people in the know or the professionals. People favoring this approach also weigh the buying and selling activity of the bearish crowd against that of the bullish crowd, knowing that when the market participants as a whole become overly weighted on either side of the spectrum, be it bullish or bearish, the market will find a way to do damage to the greatest number of participants.

The Hottest Stock since Green Ketchup! How to "Listen" to the Media with a Technical Mindset

In 1998 the weekly newspaper *Barron's* illustrated exactly how someone should read and listen to the media: as a contrarian. In Figure 17-1 we have the market correction in the DJIA when the Pacific Rim was in turmoil and the DJIA caught the Asian Flu. The asterisk at the market top was the week where the cover of *Barron's* pictured a snorting bull with the headline "Charge." At the market bottom, marked by the second asterisk, the cover pictured a grinning bear with boxing gloves on standing before a punching bag. The headline for the bear read, "Knockout Punch?" There is a widely held opinion among analysts who track market sentiment that when the media finally put a bull, referring to the strong market on the cover, it is a market top. When they focus on a growling bear market that the majority of people feel is the end of the world, it is a bottom.

This approach never seems to fail. *Time* magazine may have the best track record in the media as a contrarian indicator, as it rarely focuses on the markets at all unless the public sentiment is overwhelmingly talking about or hiding from the equity markets. The print media are in the business of generating sales by touching upon the hot issue of the day for the potential newspaper or magazine buyer. So the media rushes in to capitalize on extreme sentiment, as this sells product.

While the print media benefits from providing a mirror image of public sentiment, television has a different problem, as it is real-time. One day when the DJIA was down nearly 600 points (it did

F i g u r e   17-1

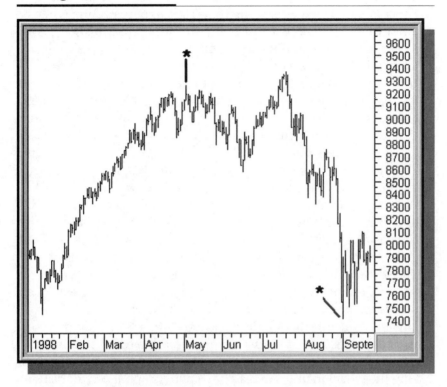

not close that low), I was listening to the television station CNBC. For some time it had been obvious that the anchors had been told by the network to find something positive to talk about. Ratings clearly decline when the station has nothing but "bad" news to report. As the only thing the public knows about markets is how to buy stocks, a decline in prices is considered bad news. So the television networks make every effort to find something positive to report, regardless of what is happening, and regardless of how silly the report may appear to people with more experience. On this particular day, it was so blatant it was comical. The quote board on my computer, which was monitoring a wide array of stocks, was glowing red from the losses. I could not have found something showing gains no matter how hard I tried. However, the CNBC anchors caught my attention when they said that they had a *big* advance to report. I thought, this is going to be good. The report went on for a considerable time about this particular stock. In fact, the anchor continued for so long that it became frustrating when he did not reveal the gains for the day that triggered this long commentary. Finally I couldn't take it anymore. I had to punch in the stock symbol to see what all the fuss was about. It was Wrigley's, and the stock was up a quarter—a mere $0.25 gain. The slapstick comic bantering and air time devoted to items like this one are the reasons many professionals much prefer Bloomberg television, which is far more informative when it comes to the markets.

Many professionals use CNBC not to monitor what is being said, but to detect a sentiment extreme from the pitch and urgency of the announcer or interviewee. A big technology stock trade that was brought to my attention came from television chatter that sounded like the best thing since sliced bread. The overwhelming enthusiasm of this asset manager was the kind of pitch that gained my attention. It was a stock I did not trade, Broadcom (BRCM). I went to see what was so great about this stock. It was trading at over $250, and it was the most beautiful short sale I had ever seen. My pool was required to exclude Nasdaq, but that restriction was changed because of this single stock, and I then sold it short on several occasions as it fell to $30. I never would have looked at it had it not been for the overwhelming enthusiasm of someone who was asking the world to buy. We read newspapers and listen to the news not for what is being reported or said, but for how it is being said. It is a great sentiment indicator.

Here's an example from a slightly different angle, but with the same idea. I was on an early train one morning making my daily run from Darien to New York City. The trip takes about an hour to Grand Central and then I would switch lines to take the subway to the World Trade Center. The day before, on a weekend, I had printed from microfiche the issues of the *New York Times* from the market crash of 1929. The printouts were the size of the actual paper, and the print font and column layouts had not changed much over the years.

I was reading my 1929 printouts between two groggy Wall Streeters that Monday morning when suddenly one of the men sitting beside me exclaimed, "Gasp! What did I miss?!" He had apparently just come back from overseas and thought the paper I was reading was the current one. Under the familiar header "The

New York Times," on the top right third, without pictures, was the headline "Stock Prices Slump in Nation-Wide Stampede to Unload; Bankers to Support Market Today." Once I explained that it was a paper from 1929, the man on the other side of me jumped in, looking as if he had seen a ghost. He said, "I am a portfolio manager. Why do you want to read these papers now?"

An historical summary cannot tell us as much as reading the actual papers of the day. It is the collective impression that forms in our mind when we scan the total presentation—advertisements, articles, business tone, scandals of the day, and so forth—that warns us when an historic market turn is approaching. What I had concluded in the early 1990s was that the speculative chatter at that time was not loud enough and that the markets would still find buyers. Why did I conclude this? Because the U.S. markets in both the 1920s and the 1990s were fueled by a cost reduction that I began to call the "T factor." In the 1920s, the economy exploded because of declining transportation costs. These lower costs changed the rules for doing business. In the 1990s, the T factor was telecommunications. The Internet changed the rules for our day by changing how we found markets, and falling telephone costs went straight to the bottom line. The advertisements and sentiment in the papers about technology stocks did not reach a sentiment until 1999. We now know what followed for technology Internet stocks and associated products.

Another warning that the speculative bubble was closer to bursting than to finding a continuation was the 1999 Super Bowl television advertisements. A dramatic change was seen, as the dot-coms bought most of the Super Bowl air time. Understanding what is hot on Madison Avenue (the advertising center of Manhattan) is a window into our culture and reflects a pulse rate that can be informative.

I might also add that CNBC redesigned its set in 1999 to allow greater coverage of the dot coms and began to report on these stocks before large monitors in a manner that was more like a play-by-play account of a sports event than like news coverage of a single sector. American media are entertainment-driven. If you have a problem with this statement, watch and read European news coverage for a single month. The BBC will give international coverage about events so that you have to objectively wonder why they were entirely absent from the American broadcast and print media.

News is itself a product to be sold, so be very objective about any media source you may expose yourself to and always do your own research on anything that may catch your investment attention.

Keep your ears and eyes wide open for changes in sentiment. Sentiment clues can be read in many different ways. The man who taught me this was my first employer in the 1980s, who reportedly first hired Mike Milken into Drexel. When we traveled by train to or from Manhattan, we were never allowed to speak, as he was engrossed in listening to the conversations around him. He was the first sentiment master I had witnessed, and he always took the time to teach us what he had learned from the tones and innuendos that he had analyzed during the commute. I am not talking about information about deals that he had overheard or the inside scoop about a firm, but just a barometric reading on the state of the economy and various market sectors. I think it is those lessons long ago that provided the roots for a market trade that was memorable.

It was a little later in my career, and I was trading for a private investor who leased two condominiums that occupied the entire penthouse floor of a high-rise building near the United Nations in New York. Security at the building, which housed numerous foreign dignitaries, was as tight as Fort Knox. I am quite confident that the key security positions for this building were filled by Secret Service agents. All the condos facing southeast had clear views down to the front driveway of the U.N. Building.

Of the two penthouse condominiums, one was dedicated entirely to the trading operation. The trading room was spectacular. It was situated in what had previously been a sunken living room with hardwood floors, at the corner of the building. Two entire walls were floor-to-ceiling glass. The trading desk was made up of two huge glass tables fitted back-to-back in the middle of the room. By day, it offered a stunning view of New York; by night, the view was breathtaking. The room was surrounded by a sparkling curtain of city lights and shimmering building silhouettes. The immense and spectacular trading desk was not cluttered with the usual cables and paper. There were nine 35-inch TV screens stacked three high, covering the full width of the room. Eight screens tracked the markets, and the center screen tracked the profit or loss of all open positions on a real-time basis. The other wall that ran the length of the room was a whiteboard where the firm's analyst kept a running tally of support/resistance levels, price projections, volatility, Fibonacci levels, and custom statistics. Now you have a feel for what this trading environment was like.

Five futures traders were employed to trade their specialties: S&P500, Bonds, Crude, Beans, and Metals. A sixth seat, at the head of the table, was reserved for the principal. I traded the S&P500 market.

Each morning when we entered the trading room, each of us was required to put a number from 1 to 10 on the whiteboard beside his or her name. This number was a personal sentiment analysis. If you felt like you were sitting on top of the world and everything was going your way; if you felt healthy, strong, and invincible, ready to take on anything that might happen that day, you would give yourself a rating of 10. On the other hand, if you had been up all night with the flu, you had just opened your mail and learned that you had been personally selected by the IRS to experience the joy of a field audit, and you wanted to kick anything living or inert that got in your way, you might give that day's attitude a rating of 1. Most of us rated ourselves between 4 and 8. A 10 was rare, and when it showed up on the board, everyone took notice of it.

One of the rare times that I gave myself a 10 rating happened to coincide with the last-ditch effort by James Baker and Tarek Aziz to prevent the Gulf War. You knew that the outcome of the meeting would lead to a ballistic market move, and that the outcome would dictate the direction. Every trader in the world faced flat lines on his or her computer screens as we waited for Baker and Aziz to emerge from their meeting at the Intercontinental Hotel in Geneva, Switzerland. We were all waiting for Secretary of State Baker's statement.

On that day, my intuition and my ability to read sentiment were like a live electric wire. Every little thing seemed to be amplified. The first jolt came after the meeting, when CNN announced that the press briefing had been rescheduled to a later time so that Secretary of State Baker could report to President Bush. That time delay alone nearly had me reaching for the phone to sell the S&P500 futures.

You don't call the boss to tell him you succeeded—that can be relayed at a public forum. You usually need to consult with the boss to define a plan of action only when you have to walk on eggshells or cover your back. While the CNN anchor babbled in Atlanta over a live picture from Geneva, you could see a reporter ask Baker a question. CNN did not broadcast the audio for this live picture, but sound wasn't needed. If you had an ounce of intuition from learning how to read sentiment clues, the answer was clear as a bell. Baker wiped his hands, left over right, right over left, and shrugged them away from his body as if he were trying to wash this whole mess off and push it away. I instantly grabbed the phone and started selling the S&P, trying to sell up to my full size without moving the market excessively. It was impossible not to move the market, as all the markets were in a deathly flat-line hush waiting to hear any news. The other traders on the desk were still waiting for Baker's press release, and they all looked at me in shock and then turned questionably to the principal of the firm, who was sitting at the head of the trading table. Somewhere in my selling frenzy, I yelled, "SELL! IT'S WAR!" The principal gave me a questioning glance. I nodded back and kept selling. About that time, the CNN camera showed Baker walking down the hall toward the press room. To me, he had the weight of the world on his shoulders, and the principal picked up on his body language. The other traders still had no sense of what was coming. About the same time, the principal looked over at the whiteboard and saw the number 10 scratched by my name. Without any further delay, he screamed, "DO IT!" We were all fully positioned by the time Baker began his now-famous "I re . . .." The markets never even let him finish the word *regret* before all hell broke loose on the screens. To my great relief, we were on the right side. The desk netted a $2 million gain within the next 30 minutes.

To this day I both listen to and watch the news—not for what is being said, but for how it is being said, to monitor the tones and unusual pitches that give clues about market sentiment that may reveal the market's next move.

PART 4

How to Handle Specific Problems

Price Targets for Stocks Just Listed and Other Challenges

HOW DO YOU CALCULATE SUPPORT OR RESISTANCE FOR A STOCK JUST LISTED WITH NO HISTORICAL DATA?

In this chapter we look at a series of questions that you will undoubtedly encounter at some time. The problem posed by this first question may appear to be insurmountable for a chartist. How does one calculate resistance or support for a stock just listed with no historical price data?

During my seminars, this question about charting an IPO that has no history will surface as a challenge. However, everyone is surprised to learn that it is possible to solve the problem by using a method that applies market geometry.

The stock charted in Figure 18-1 is Microsoft from the day it was first listed. Microsoft traded at less than a quarter dollar for the first few months. A specialized software package by the name GannTrader is used here to create precise angles from a single user-defined point. This software has fallen behind the times in terms of its operating system, as it is still DOS-driven. It has numerous compatibility issues with Microsoft Windows if you use antivirus and firewall software. The only way I have been able to run this software is in a stand-alone computer, which raises issues of data collection redundancy that become very cumbersome and expensive. However, the method of drawing precise trend lines does not require a computer and expensive software. Daily data can be plotted manually on graph paper very easily. Use 11- by 16½-inch (279-

F i g u r e   18-1

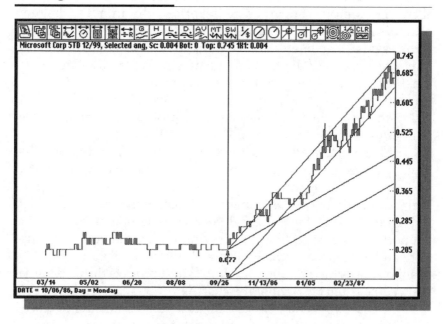

by 419-mm) paper with a 20 by 20 to the inch grid that fills a 10- by 15-inch range on the paper. One supplier of this paper is Keuffel & Esser Company, Morristown, NJ 07960.

The method involves drawing trend lines at precise angles from four chart points. In Figure 18-1 we are looking at two points from what W.D. Gann would call the secondary reaction. I will use the secondary reaction for this chart, as the price low starts a larger trend that will help you visualize the method. As soon as the price data broke above the range defined in the first 6 months, the price low would be deemed important, as is demonstrated in Figure 18-1. The Gann lines drawn here are 1×1 and 1×2 from the early October price low. You will recall from the chapters on market geometry and trend lines that this means that a change of one unit on the x axis to a rise of one unit on the y axis gives the 1×1 slope or 45° line.

To create the channel, use the exact same date and repeat the same 1×1 and 1×2 trend lines from *the zero line that is directly under the price low*. This creates an upward channel, and you can see that MSFT utilized these early trend projections.

Now let's look at how Gann techniques were used to create a channel of identical angles using the price point from the first day of trading, March 14, 1986. This is market geometry in its purest form, as it is all geometry and no market. But the angles of greatest importance beyond the first few months in Figure 18-1 are in fact the lines projected forward from the very first day.

In Figure 18-2 we are looking at a weekly chart for MSFT. Using the price low for - the first day, project or manually draw lines at the angles 1 × 1, 1 × 2, 1 × 3, and 1 × 4.

The next step is to project the same angles from the zero line directly under the first trading day to create the channel illustrated in Figure 18-3. In Figure 18-2, pay particular attention to the price highs and lows marked with an asterisk before the channel is added in Figure 18-3. Yes, the October 1987 decline stopped exactly on the support line projected from the first trading day. Then look at support and resistance with the channel added in Figure 18-3. The channel marks the price bottom in 1988 and projects the price target realized near the far right of the chart.

In Figure 18-4 you will see that these same Gann angles served MSFT chartists for 10 years, until resistance was tested as support

Figure   18-2

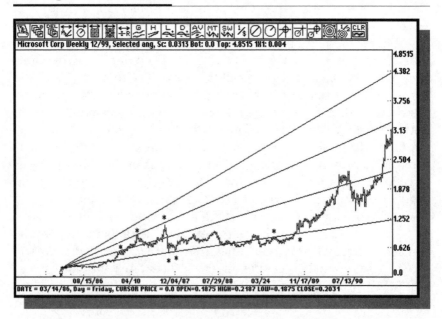

F i g u r e   18-3

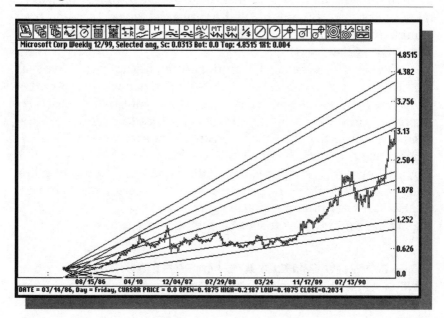

F i g u r e   18-4

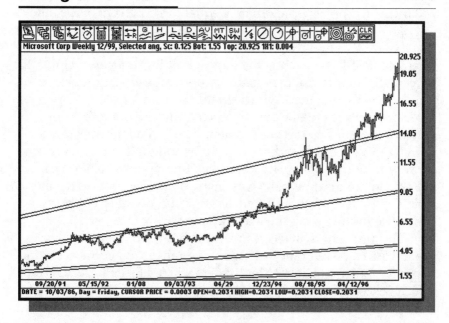

in 1996 and the market data then moved out of range. However, there are other Gann angles that are not displayed that you may want to look at on your own. In addition to 1×1, 1×2, 1×3, and 1×4, Gann also used 1×16.

New channels are created from new significant pivot points as the history of price data grows. This is why, when we first looked at trend lines, it was suggested that you extend your trend lines as far as possible into the future. This may lead to another question, however: If you use the zero line to create a channel for an IPO stock, what level other than the price low would you use for stocks with a history? The initial answer is to use the price low and the zero line under the exact date of the price pivot even if the stock is trading at $300. Gann has numerous market geometry applications, however, we can only introduce a few of his methods at this time.

HOW DO YOU CALCULATE MARKET SUPPORT WHEN THE INDEX HAS FALLEN BELOW HISTORIC PRICE LOWS?

The QQQ was launched in March 1999. Like the SPY (S&P500 Spyders) and DIA (Dow Jones Industrial Diamonds), the QQQ is an Exchange-Traded Fund (ETF) that, in this case, tracks the Nasdaq 100 Index at a price approximately equal to 2.5 percent of the index. Qs, like the Nasdaq, are heavily weighted toward technology. More than half of the underlying companies are technology specific, with Microsoft (MSFT) reflecting the largest holding at just more than 10 percent. Healthcare follows as the second largest sector represented which, when combined with technology companies, totals about three-quarters of the underlying assets. After February 2001 technical traders were faced with a problem: The Qs had fallen below their March 1999 price low, and many people thought that there was now no way to obtain new price objectives for support. As the Nasdaq 100 would not disappear the way many of the dot coms in the index did, Triple Qs traders still had to continue defining support and resistance though the issue was trading in new territory.

This problem is, in fact, similar to when a stock has fallen below the lowest Fibonacci ratio within a price range. So how do you find support in such situations? Most traders will use Fibonacci extensions, which we covered in Chapter 15 and will discuss again in a moment, but for this situation of extreme market lows, there is a better solution.

In Figures 18-5 and 18-6 we are looking at semiannual bar charts for Microsoft. The only difference between the two charts is the scale used to create the *y*-axis. Up to this point, when we have seen price data displayed, the *y*-axis scale represents the same price change, from zero up to the highest trading price of the market or stock under review. This is called *arithmetic scaling*. However, there is another way to display data. The *x*-axis scale, or time scale, remains equal, but the *y*-axis uses *logarithmic scaling*. Such a chart is often called semi-logarithmic as only the price axis is changed. When

F i g u r e   18-5

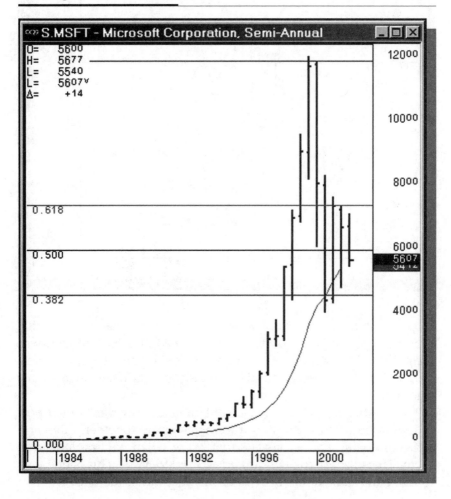

F i g u r e   18-6

Microsoft had a rally from $1.00 to $1.50, that was a substantial move. But when the stock was trading at $120, a 50-cent gain was insignificant. Therefore, on some occasions, when we have longer-horizon perspectives in mind, we study charts using logarithmic price data.

In Figure 18-6 you will see that I have identified major support in a zone where Fibonacci retracements come together. Fibonacci ratios are being applied just as they were when we first looked at them. The support zone identified is 32.60 to 33.82. This is one way to make the calculation, but I favor using another method.

Turn the chart upside down and use a log scale. (You cannot just print the chart and flip it.) You will see examples of this in Figure 18-7, where the DJIA, MSFT, and the Nasdaq 100 are all charted in an inverted manner using logarithmic scaling for the y-axis. The charts also show that I use averages and indicators with the inverted data just as I used them in previous chapters. As CQG creates a useless price scale on the right for all its inverted markets, I obtain the Fibonacci ratios that define a support zone (or, in this inverted situation, resistance) visually. Then I trace across the resistance zone to find the month and price that falls within the same zone (January 1997 in this case). Then I flip the chart right side up and find the level that corresponds to the zone so that I can actually read the real price. The exact price for MSFT using this method is 33.58. Thus, both methods described produce similar results. In May 2002, MSFT was trading near 53. This is very troublesome, as MSFT is a component of the Dow Jones Industrial Average. If MSFT trades down to 33.58, the DJIA will probably be nearer to 7350. Since the DJIA is just above 10000 as this is being written, this is a warning that we may have some serious trouble ahead. In Figure 18-7 it

F i g u r e   18-7

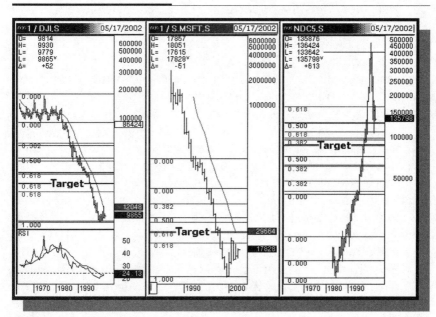

also looks as if the DJIA has the furthest to go to reach the target zone from its current position. This is not uncommon, and one index will often make a "catch-up" move to come back into line with the others. As Microsoft has 10 percent weighting within the Qs, it warns that this Exchange-Traded Fund could fall to 19. Taking the time to gain a market scenario for MSFT gives a cross-reference for other chart work we may develop from indices and ETFs.

Make a note that states, "BUY MSFT 33.60" and keep it beside the computer. If the market develops an emotional panic decline, the target is already defined. In addition, before MSFT ever reached 33.60, I would know that if it fell below 28, where another target zone was located, I would not want to own it any longer. *Always know your exit level before buying or selling short.* We use stock sectors to determine whether MSFT will fall to such an extreme. We will look at a few sectors in a moment. But be prepared, for should you be faced with a panic situation, there's no time to make any calculations. You can only react.

HOW DO YOU CALCULATE A PRICE OBJECTIVE WHEN THE STOCK OR MARKET IS TRADING ABOVE HISTORIC HIGHS?

This question offers the opportunity for a fast review of the use of Fibonacci extensions and lets us cover a way to project two market swings into the future.

We would use a Fibonacci extension if the DJIA had just exceeded the old historic price highs and we wanted to project the new price target for a big-picture outlook. Figure 18-8 shows the use of Fibonacci extensions for this purpose. The lowest price used for the projection is marked 0.00. The price high that defines the top of the range is marked 1.00. The price low marked 0.00 that is more recent and higher than the first is used to project the actual Fibonacci extensions. What we want to know is where the 0.618 relationship is located relative to the distance traveled by the market from 0.00 to 1.00. In addition to the 0.618 ratio, we also need to determine what the equality and the 1.618 projections will be relative to the measured range marked 0.00 to 1.00.

The DJIA price target will be 13838.1 at the 0.618 projection.

There's just one snag. A moment ago, we calculated that MSFT could fall to 33.60. Therefore, it seems unlikely that the DJIA will

F i g u r e   18-8

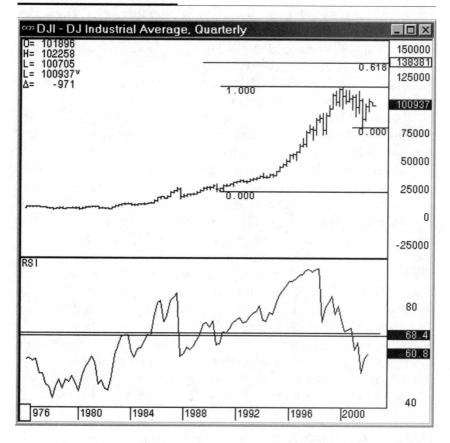

target 13838 immediately. If all market swings have a mathematical relationship, we can use this projected hypothetical objective of 13838 to work backwards. Where could such a rally begin from, if not from the lows just used to project to a new high? We like to work from confluence swing targets, knowing that Fibonacci ratios tend to congest into tight zones from different calculation points. Confluence simply means that similar projected results are derived from different internal pivot points. We saw this to be the case in Figure 18-7. *That means that 7350 is probably an important support level for the DJIA, as it is really derived from 13838, which we have not seen.* That, in fact, is how the target of 7350 was determined should MSFT fall to 33.60. The 7350 level did not require recalculating the

DJIA to reflect the change in MSFT. It was found using market geometry. So now we paint a picture in our mind that from just over 10,000 the DJIA could fall to 7350 and then rally toward 13838. If the market bottoms at 7350, the DJIA will have several Fibonacci retracement barriers to exceed. The first three barriers would be at 8630, 9092, and then 9725. If the U.S. dollar is falling, the lower zones of resistance could prove to be formidable.

But what happens if the DJIA should fall to only 7500 or pass through 7350? Every pivot that occurs can be studied to find the exact pivot highs and lows that produce a major turn in price. We may assume that the 1987 low is important for projecting a market swing because it is easily seen on our monthly charts and has historic value. But the market may show us that the key price pivot was actually higher or lower if the mathematical relationships that form in the future are not Fibonacci relationships tied to the obvious 1987 price low. What if the DJIA marginally breaks 7350? You must know the width of the Fibonacci zone. Major support is 7196–7350. The 7350 level is the top of the support zone. Breaking the lower boundary at 7196 would lead to the next target zone. They are all related mathematically in some way. How they are related will be described in Chapter 20. Chapter 20 will introduce the concept of harmonic relationships between price pivots. The more relationships within the entire price history you identify, the more accurate you can be in projecting future price movements.

HOW THE INTERNET CAN LEAD YOU
TO A POOR MARKET DECISION

The Internet can be very valuable for the individual, just as it is for small businesses in the financial industry. But it is very easy to be swayed into a poor market decision if you use the Internet for research incorrectly.

Figure 18-9 displays an Internet page found by using a search engine with the phrase "stock sectors." This Web site happens to have Dow Jones Industry Stock Sectors rather than Standard & Poor's. For my example, this will do nicely. The address is http://bigcharts.marketwatch.com/industry/bigcharts-com. The Web site has conveniently listed for us the 10 best-performing industries over the last 3 months *based on its criteria*. On the left are the sectors that are most popular with people visiting the Web site. On the right the top-

Figure 18-9

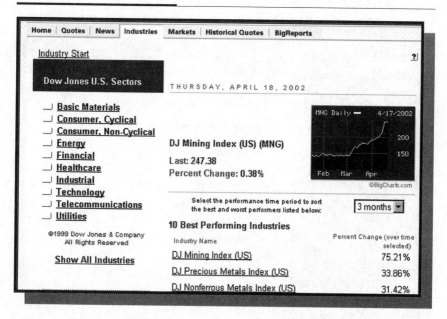

performing index is identified as the DJ Mining Index, which is reportedly up 75 percent.

We now click on that particular sector to see where it may lead.

In Figure 18-10 we now have a list of 10 stocks within this sector, with the best performers on the top. Can you detect a small problem? Notice the percentage gains. The top two stocks have large percentage gains, and then there is a significant drop-off. Most eyes will be drawn to the summary box on the left, which shows that the percentage change for the group is 56.27 percent this year. Wow! Most people will never see the distribution problem on the right, and off they will go to look at the top-performing stock in this group, Cleveland-Cliffs Inc. So we will do so as well.

Now we are looking at a chart that shows that the sky's the limit. Even if you add your own indicators to the data in Figure 18-11, you may still be enticed to buy the stock. But take a look at the top right-hand corner of the figure. *The volume traded today is only 174,100 shares.*

If the volume traded in a single day does not exceed 1 million shares, with 2 million preferable, don't waste your time. Volume

F i g u r e   18-10

www.BigCharts.com

is very important, and you can easily overlook this if you do your research from the Internet and look at price percentage movement alone.

WHAT IS THE GLOBAL INDUSTRY CLASSIFICATION STANDARD AND HOW DO YOU USE STOCK SECTORS FOR ANALYSIS?

The S&P500 index is important because it is the benchmark unit of measurement for the performance of most funds. It is also important that you have an understanding of its underlying construction and of the changes that are occurring within the financial industry, as this will help you as a stock trader or investor.

My reputation has been built upon my ability to correctly identify larger trend changes in the S&P500. The reason for my success is that I do not just analyze the stock index by itself. Doing the extra work of looking at what is developing under the surface of an index

F i g u r e 18-11

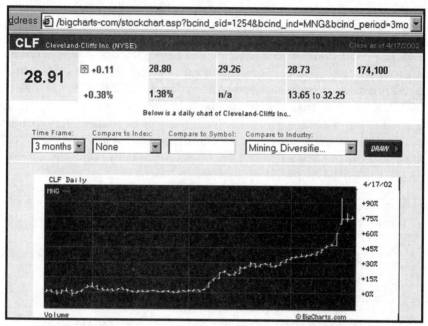

www.BigCharts.com

has proven invaluable. The S&P500 Index is composed of industry groups. These groups, in turn, are made up of sectors. For example, the Technology group is subdivided into sectors such as Electronic Semiconductors, Computer Hardware, Computer Software, and so forth. While the S&P500 does contain 500 stocks, the name is somewhat misleading, as a very small number of stocks are heavily weighted in its calculation. For example, in April of 1998, three critical groups made up 40.71 percent of the S&P500. They were Energy (9 percent of the S&P500), Technology (15.68 percent) and Financials (16.03 percent). These weightings change when the stocks in a sector have a major price change.

This information is compiled monthly and can be obtained directly from Standard & Poor's. I used to track a total of 18 sectors representing 58.58 percent of the S&P500 index, along with 12 stocks that together had a 21 percent weighting within the S&P500.

On August 2, 1999, the composition of the S&P500 sectors were changed. Standard & Poor's and Morgan Stanley Capital

International (MSCI) jointly introduced the Global Industry Classification Standard (GICS) in an effort to make global comparisons of stock groups and sectors easier. The GICS consists of 10 economic sectors that aggregate 23 industry groups, 59 industries, and 122 subindustries covering over 25,000 companies globally. A company is assigned to a single subindustry on the basis of its principal business activity as determined by Standard & Poor's and MSCI. Revenues are a significant factor in the process of defining a company's principal business activity; however, market perception is also an important criterion for classification. As a result, some of the old sectors have experienced some significant changes, as can be seen from Table 18-1.

Table 18-1

Global Industry Classification Standard:
Old versus New S&P500 Sectors and Industries

Old Sectors/Industries	New Sectors/Industries
Basic Materials	***Materials***
Agricultural Products	Aluminum
Aluminum	Commodity Chemicals
Chemicals	Construction Materials
Chemicals (Diversified)	Diversified Chemicals
Chemicals (Specialty)	Diversified Metals & Mining
Construction (Cement & Aggregates)	Fertilizers & Agricultural Chemicals
Containers & Packaging (Paper)	Forest Products
Gold & Precious Metals Mining	Gold
Iron & Steel	Industrial Gases
Metals Mining	Metal & Glass Containers
Paper & Forest Products	Paper Packaging
	Paper Products
	Precious Metals & Minerals
	Specialty Chemicals
	Steel
Capital Goods	***Industrials***
Aerospace/Defense	Aerospace & Defense
Containers (Metal & Glass)	Air Freight & Couriers
Electrical Equipment	Airlines
Engineering & Construction	Airport Services

Old Sectors/Industries	New Sectors/Industries
Capital Goods	***Industrials***
Machinery (Diversified)	Building Products
Manufacturing (Diversified)	Commercial Printing
Manufacturing (Specialized)	Construction & Engineering
Metal Fabricators	Construction & Farm Machinery
Office Equipment & Supplies	Data Processing Services
Trucks & Parts	Diversified Commercial Services
Waste Management	Electrical Components & Equipment
	Employment Services
	Environmental Services
	Heavy Electrical Equipment
	Highways & Rail-trucks
	Industrial Conglomerates
	Industrial Machinery
	Marine
	Marine Ports & Services
	Office Services & Supplies
	Railroads
	Trading Companies & Distributors
	Trucking
Communication Services	***Telecommunication Services***
Telecommunications (Cellular/Wireless)	Alternative Carriers
Telecommunications (Long Distance)	Integrated Telecommunication Services
Telephone	Wireless Telecommunication Services
Consumer Cyclicals	***Consumer Discretionary***
Auto Parts & Equipment	Advertising
Automobiles	Apparel & Accessories
Building Materials	Apparel Retail
Consumer (Jewelry, Novelties, & Gifts)	Auto Parts & Equipment
Footwear	Automobile Manufacturers
Gaming, Lottery, & Pari-mutuel Companies	Broadcasting & Cable TV
Hardware & Tools	Casinos & Gaming
Homebuilding	Catalog Retail
Household Furnishings & Appliances	Computer & Electronics Retail
Leisure Time (Products)	Consumer Electronics
Lodging-Hotels	Department Stores
Publishing	Distributors
Publishing (Newspapers)	Footwear

Table 18-1 (Continued)

Global Industry Classification Standard:
Old versus New S&P500 Sectors and Industries

Old Sectors/Industries	New Sectors/Industries
Consumer Cyclicals	***Consumer Discretionary***
Retail (Building Supplies)	General Merchandise Stores
Retail (Computers & Electronics)	Home Furnishings
Retail (Department Stores)	Home Improvement Retail
Retail (Discounters)	Homebuilding
Retail (General Merchandise)	Hotels
Retail (Home Shopping)	Household Appliances
Retail (Specialty)	Housewares & Specialties
Retail (Specialty-Apparel)	Internet Retail
Services (Advertising/Marketing)	Leisure Facilities
Services (Commercial & Consumer)	Leisure Products
Textiles (Apparel)	Motorcycle Manufacturers
Textiles (Home Furnishings)	Movies & Entertainment
Textiles (Specialty)	Photographic Products
	Publishing & Printing
	Restaurants
	Specialty Stores
	Textiles
	Tires & Rubber
Consumer Staples	***Consumer Staples***
Beverages (Alcoholic)	Agricultural Products
Beverages (Non-Alcoholic)	Brewers
Broadcasting (TV, Radio & Cable)	Distillers & Vintners
Distributors (Food & Health)	Drug Retail
Entertainment	Food Distributors
Foods	Food Retail
Household Products (Non-Durables)	Household Products
Housewares	Meat Poultry & Fish
Personal Care	Packaged Foods
Restaurants	Personal Products
Retail (Drug Stores)	Soft Drinks
Retail (Food Chains)	Tobacco
Services (Employment)	
Services (Facilities & Environmental)	
Specialty Printing	
Tobacco	

Old Sectors/Industries	New Sectors/Industries
Energy	***Energy***
Oil & Gas (Drilling & Equipment)	Integrated Oil & Gas
Oil & Gas (Exploration & Production)	Oil & Gas Drilling
Oil & Gas (Refining & Marketing)	Oil & Gas Equipment & Services
Oil (Domestic Integrated)	Oil & Gas Exploration & Production
Oil (International Integrated)	Oil & Gas Refining & Marketing
Financial	***Financials***
Banks (Major Regional)	Banks
Banks (Money Center)	Consumer Finance
Banks (Regional)	Diversified Financial Services
Consumer Finance	Insurance Brokers
Financial (Diversified)	Life & Health Insurance
Insurance Brokers	Multi-Line Insurance
Insurance (Life & Health)	Multi-Sector Holdings
Insurance (Multi-Line)	Property & Casualty Insurance
Insurance (Property-Casualty)	Real Estate Investment Trusts
Investment Banking & Brokerage	Real Estate Management & Development
Investment Management	Reinsurance
Savings & Loans	
Health Care	***Health Care***
Biotechnology	Biotechnology
Health Care (Diversified)	Health Care Distributors & Services
Health Care (Drugs—Generic & Other)	Health Care Equipment
Health Care (Drugs—Major Pharmaceuticals)	Health Care Facilities
Health Care (Hospital Management)	Health Care Supplies
Health Care (Long-Term Care)	Managed Health Care
Health Care (Managed Care)	Pharmaceuticals
Health Care (Medical Products & Supplies)	
Health Care (Specialized Services)	
Technology	***Information Technology***
Communication Equipment	Application Software
Computers (Hardware)	Computer Hardware
Computers (Networking)	Computer Storage & Peripherals
Computers (Peripherals)	Electronic Equipment & Instruments
Computers (Software & Services)	Internet Software& Services
Electronics (Component Distributors)	IT Consulting & Services
Electronics (Defense)	Networking Equipment

Table 18-1 (Continued)

Global Industry Classification Standard:
Old versus New S&P500 Sectors and Industries

Old Sectors/Industries	New Sectors/Industries
Technology	*Information Technology*
Electronics (Instrumentation)	Office Electronics
Electronics (Semiconductors)	Semiconductor Equipment
Equipment (Semiconductor)	Semiconductors
Photography/Imaging	Systems Software
Services (Computer Systems)	Telecommunications Equipment
Services (Data Processing)	
Transportation	
Air Freight	
Airlines	
Railroads	
Shipping	
Truckers	
Utilities	*Utilities*
Electric Companies	Electric Utilities
Natural Gas	Gas Utilities
Power Producers (Independent)	Multi-Utilities
Water Utilities	Water Utilities

Some sectors have been significantly affected by these changes. As an example, Figure 18-12 shows a chart prepared by Standard & Poor's to help us visualize the differences between the new sector and the old. By Standard & Poor's calculation, the new sector Application Software has only a 0.39 correlation with the old sector, Computers (Software and Services). That means that it does not correlate to the old index.

Mutual fund investors who favor sector-weighted funds should be aware that many Internet sites have not adopted the new S&P sectors. It is very possible that the people managing some of these Web sites are unaware of the changes, as many of them are not in the finance industry. The risk is that someone will decide to enter a sector-specific fund on the basis of Internet research that does not correlate to the new sector definitions. Funds will want to be com-

F i g u r e   18-12

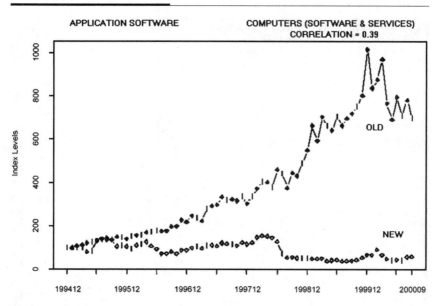

pared to the new sectors for performance purposes, however their fund names could be similar to those of the old sectors.

One way for you to do your own sector research is to subscribe to a vendor that supplies sector data. Bloomberg and Reuters both have data on S&P500 sectors that comes directly from Standard & Poor's. Other vendors were cut off when Standard & Poor's restructured their groups. However, a few data vendors have reconstructed the indices from the underlying stocks. Omega Dial Data, an end-of-day data supplier will be compatible with SuperCharts, a stripped-down version that is similar to TradeStation. However, TradeStation does not allow third-party data any more, though you can transfer any formula you create from TradeStation into SuperCharts. You can even pick up older versions of TradeStation (4.0 as example) for stand-alone applications on eBay. (Be sure the security block is included.)

Let me give you charts of five of the current sectors with monthly time frames (Figures 18-13 to 18-17) so that you will have something to compare your data with when you are ready to start your own research. Using indicators and Fibonacci price grids as described earlier, the potential future path for these sectors has been drawn to the right of the current data. Can you explain why

F i g u r e   18-13

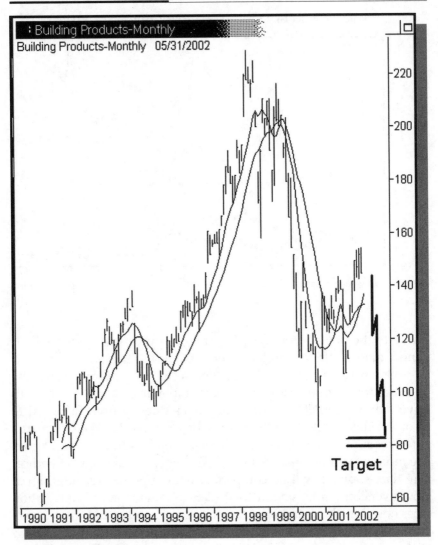

S&P500 Building Products Sector

these sectors were selected? What index do they represent—
Nasdaq 100, DJIA, or S&P500? Do any of them have a relationship
to interest rates? Why do the projected paths end at these target
zones? If the projected path is proven to be correct, you then need
to look at the new indicator positions and calculate new Fibonacci
targets for the trend reversal. Note that the price paths drawn do
not reflect time objectives relative to the x-axis. Another considera-

F i g u r e   18-14

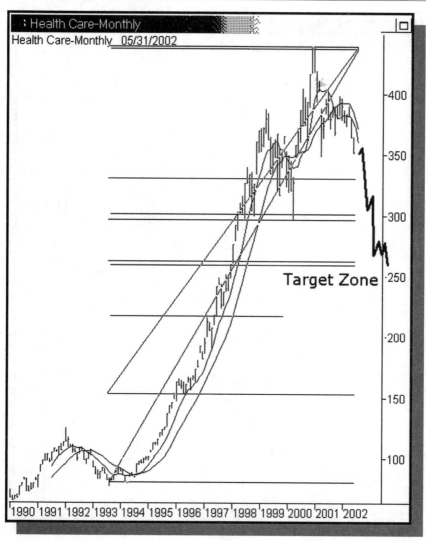

S&P500 Health Care Sector

tion is the fact the Nasdaq 100 is rebalanced annually by the exchange. At the end of 2001, the technology sector weighting dropped from 71 percent to less than 60 percent. While this shift should not be too surprising to many given the freefall in the technology group, the increasing weighting of nontech sectors, including health care and consumer goods, is unknown to many and is very relevant when it comes to tracking the Nasdaq or Qs.

F i g u r e   18-15

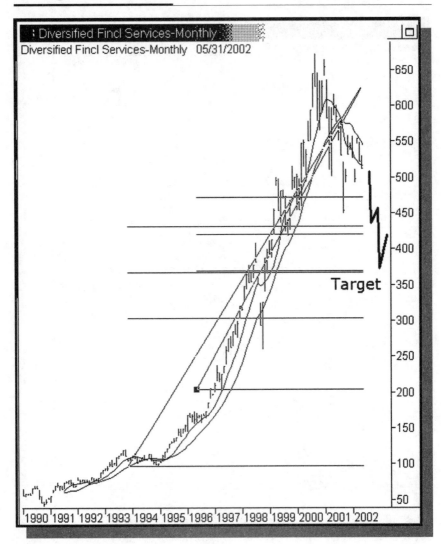

S&P500 Diversified Financial Services Sector

F i g u r e   18-16

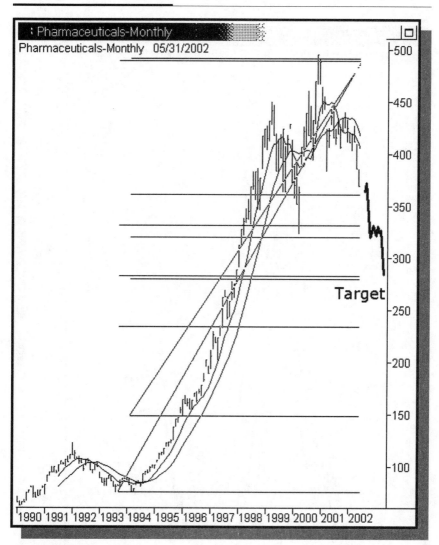

S&P500 Pharmaceuticals Sector

F i g u r e   **18-17**

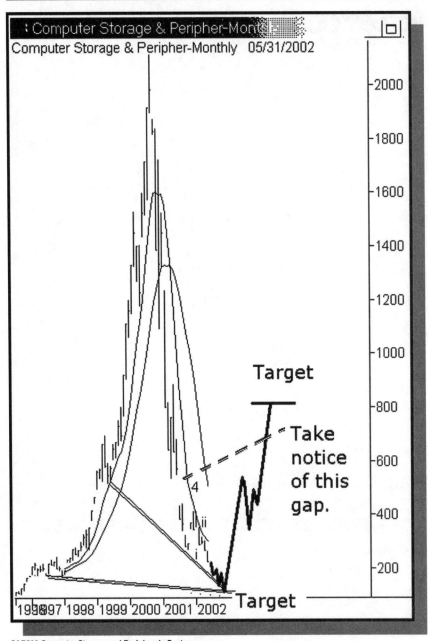

S&P500 Computer Storage and Peripherals Sector

PART 5

Lessons from Global Market Shock Waves

CHAPTER 19

Lessons from Global Market Shock Waves

THE AMERICAS CATCH THE ASIAN FLU IN 1998

The "Asian Tiger" nations are located along the eastern Pacific Rim: Taiwan, Japan, Hong Kong, Indonesia, Thailand, Malaysia, and, more recently, mainland China. In the mid 1990s, the economies of these nations were expanding dramatically, and they were flooding the Western nations with an unending stream of low-priced goods.

Then, suddenly, something happened. One by one the Asian Tigers seemed to implode. Their currencies dropped precipitously in the foreign exchange market. Positive economic growth slipped into recession, and then slumped into deep depression. The resulting affliction, which spread to Europe and the Americas, was called the "Asian flu."

When we caught the Asian flu in 1998, Asia's crisis had all the ingredients of a financial panic that was firmly rooted in the Asian public sector. Yet the North American media proclaimed that we were caught off guard. Once again a global event that originated overseas was thought to be a total surprise, as New Yorkers and the general public in the United States still tend to think that the world tracks our equity markets. In earlier chapters, chart examples were given showing why a sense of what is happening overseas is always important. The truth is that the Asian markets were incredibly overextended and were ripe for an avalanche. What happened, and what did we learn?

The factors leading up to the Asian flu are important because the currency markets dictate the health of nearly all the other markets around the world. This is one area where having some understanding behind your charts is a real benefit. A currency crisis tends to catch those whose focus is on stocks alone off guard in a devastating way. For this reason, some of the history behind the Asian flu will add to your concern the next time our charts tell us that a major event is on the near horizon.

Asian banks are large debtors to foreign banks, and a large part of the debt is very short term. Despite the so-called sound fundamentals in Asia during 1997—such as budget surpluses, high savings rates, low inflation, and export-oriented industries—foreign creditors began to withdraw money from Asia because of growing concerns about currency overvaluation, bank scandals, and weak real estate markets. (This is a sentiment warning similar to insider selling!) When Thailand devalued the Thai Baht, these concerns multiplied. Suddenly, international banks became wary of extending new loans in Asia as the old loans fell due. The banks were becoming a bit worried about Asia's long-term prospects, although these still looked rather good, but they were much more worried about what the other investors were doing. Each investor understood that Thailand, Indonesia, and Korea would be pushed into outright default if enough creditors pulled the plug on new loans. In the end, each creditor started to rush for the doors precisely because the other creditors were doing the same thing, triggering a stampede.

The key central banks, led by the Federal Reserve, might have extended some credit lines to their Asian counterparts without great public fanfare and without adding to the market's anxieties. But there was a big misstep: When the International Monetary Fund (IMF) arrived in Thailand in July 1997, it proclaimed that everything was wrong and that immediate surgery was needed. I like *Time* magazine's cartoon profile of the IMF, garbed as Superman, sweeping low over the earth and extinguishing financial blazes, but in this case the IMF missed the mark: It brought a torch to an oil spill.

The IMF ignited the oil spill and created a public panic when it recommended as the solution immediate bank closures, high interest rates, and severe budget cuts. Suddenly the IMF, through its own actions, had proclaimed to the global markets that the situation in Asia was catastrophic, akin to that in Argentina, Bulgaria, and Mexico. To make things even worse, the same message was repeated in Indonesia in November 1997 and in Korea in December. By then the panic had spread to virtually all of East Asia.

In Indonesia, Korea, and Thailand, stock and currency markets plummeted after the IMF came onto the scene, despite the $100 *billion* in bailout loans to these countries. One of the lessons we must always remember is that in a crisis, when banks start to clamp down on making loans, there are liquidity problems. In an all-out market crash, it doesn't matter whether you called the decline correctly from your charts and sold the market short timely if, near the bottom, you find that there is no one left to pay the gain owed to you. Gains always come out of someone's pocket.

One major firm I traded for in New York had the best minds of the firm analyze what its strategy should be if a devastating earthquake brought the financial district of Tokyo to a halt. If a major global center suddenly ceased to exist, what was the best portfolio strategy for the firm? (It never entered our minds that the catastrophic event would happen in New York City.) It was decided that global liquidity issues would be the first priority. That means that in such a major shock wave, the banks would not be able to open, as they would not have the physical cash reserves to do business when people ran for cash. Therefore, our strategy would be to convert all positions into cash at the first hint of trouble. Shock waves have a similarity in that the first few seconds are chaos and the market direction is predictable. This has nothing to do with market trends; it has everything to do with professionals executing predefined plans to move assets under a protective umbrella. We buy short-term Treasuries, fully backed by the ability of the American government to tax the people, so that there is no risk of default. We also buy gold. We sell just about everything else. In those few brief seconds, as others try to figure out what is happening, professionals go into an autopilot execution plan without the need for a second's thought.

The Asian crisis was not a sudden event that happened in seconds, but like most crisis situations it involved bank liquidity. It was an evolving crisis because of the IMF's insistence on closing "weak" banks. The result was that local banks stopped making loans and started to call in their existing loans in order to build up their frail cash reserves so that they would not be viewed as weak. As a result, while Asian governments could borrow funds, the countries' economies were crashing because businesses could not find the funds they needed to bridge short-term cash flow differentials. As a result, businesses were failing in large numbers.

The IMF, however, is not a World Bank superhero. It is us. *We the people* and our elected government are the IMF, and this time we messed up big time. The IMF is the instrument by which the U.S. Treasury intervenes in developing countries. When the United States took the initiative in bailing out Mexico in 1994 and Korea in 1997, it turned to the IMF as the institution that could provide the cover, the staff, and the bucks to do the job.

Clout within the IMF is controlled by voting rights, which are determined or weighted by financial contribution (the so-called quota), so that the United States, the European Union, and Japan combined have a comfortable majority. Moreover, the quota allocations are designed to preserve the voting clout of the developed countries. For example, India and China have fewer votes than the Netherlands. China does not welcome the constant hovering of the IMF, and for this very reason the Asian crisis moved to the brink of a new precipice. Here is why.

In 1996 the nine developing East Asian countries sold 40 percent of their exports among themselves. When that source of export demand dried up as a result of the deepening crisis and currency devaluations, these countries were under increasing pressure to sell to the only remaining buyers—Western developed countries, especially the United States. We are the world's dumping ground for surpluses. Europe is less so until the price becomes very low; then they too begin to buy. The worse the Asian crisis became, *the more the Asian countries had to produce* to pay their staggering loans if they were not to default. Our own exports dried up because Asia could not pay. Farmers who were counting on high exports lost their markets. Companies across numerous sectors, from medical equipment to Nike shoes, watched their fastest-growing markets dry up and shut down. When a country has to devaluate its currency, everything costs it more. But prices of the products it produces drop, and so it has to produce more of them. As a result, the glut of products that began to flow into the United States from Asia planted the seeds that would topple the technology market. We had the Asian flu in 1998, and people wonder why markets topped in 1999. Few make this connection, as people do not think about globalization, but the Nasdaq decline could have been triggered in

1998. Here is how we narrowly missed an early free fall across all equity indices.

We came to the brink of a total global crisis when there was talk by China that it would devaluate its own currency. Was this a result of economic conditions or a warning to the IMF to stay out of its hair? Probably both, but it was an effective way to send a message to the U.S. Treasury and American politicians through the IMF to back off and go home.

Since 1973, exchange rates for most industrialized countries have floated, or fluctuated according to the supply of and demand for different currencies in international markets. This is not true for China. China's currency is fixed, and so it did not fall in value during the Asian crisis. In addition, China's currency is not convertible, meaning that it cannot be exchanged for U.S. dollars or European currencies. If you want to convert China's renminbi into dollars, the exchange has to be associated with a trade flow, either an import or an export. The critical link that the American public did not understand is the fact that the cost of goods in China is a delicate part of the equation among the Asian Tiger nations.

Under a fixed-exchange-rate system, only a decision by a country's government or monetary authority can alter the official value of the currency. Devaluation is a deliberate downward adjustment in the official exchange rate, reducing the currency's value. During the peak of the Asian crisis, China's government threatened the IMF with a devaluation of its currency.

A devaluation of China's renminbi would have produced *a further drop in the value of other Asian currencies* and led to a potential default on European and American investments and loans in China. China played its trump card: Either the IMF would back down or China would break the last cord keeping the Asian crisis from collapsing every stock market and economy around the world. A deep depression throughout the Pacific Rim would have ended companies' efforts to raise production in order to keep their heads above water. They would not be able to pay their government loans when overproduction efforts failed. As a result, global trade would come to a screeching halt, and Europe and the United States would rapidly fall into deep recessions. China's economy rests on a "bubble" of speculation, largely fueled by excessive American bank lending for risky, low-return investments. America sees China as a growth market, so American companies, in particular those with export development expectations, would have been hammered in a devaluation on several front lines.

While the risk of checkmate was averted when the IMF backed off, the problem was only sidestepped. The risk of a global currency crisis has not been eliminated. We know from our charts that a currency crisis would have ripple effects on Commodities, Interest Rates, and Stocks. One of the key signals that the world is losing faith in the strongest currencies is a growing upward trend in gold. The advice I am offering, and the lesson we should learn from the Asian flu in 1998 and the Nasdaq top in 1999, is to never turn our backs on a currency crisis. What happened to the Nasdaq in 2000 and 2001 will happen to the DJIA if a major currency crisis were to emerge. What you may also find of interest is that advanced chart work suggests gold may see a rally throughout 2002 and continue until July of 2003. There is potential for the strongest part of the gold rally to occur in 2003. As a result of this chart work we must all monitor currencies and gold closely as charts are warning us the newspapers will be covering a major event of some sort. January 10, 2003, could be important for the financial markets.

THE "DOT GONES": RESEARCHING OPPORTUNITIES AFTER A MARKET IMPLODES

The dot coms are dot gones primarily because they forgot the lessons of the late 1980s. History does indeed repeat itself, and the ingredients that fuel a bubble and lead it to burst are similar. In this segment, I will detail these similarities for you.

Business and financial markets are riddled with the bursting of speculative bubbles. For background information, I recommend reading *Extraordinary Popular Delusions and the Madness of Crowds* by Charles MacKay for references to some of the more spectacular bubbles in history. It was written in 1841 and can be found through any of the bookstores on the Internet with a financial market focus, like TradersPress.com. You will learn about the South Sea Bubble, the Tulip Bulb Mania, and a host of other periods in history when public greed has run amok. For a history of the 1929 crash, I suggest that you do *not* dive into the books that are currently in print, as they are academic in nature. It is people and sentiment that make for a speculative bubble, and the book that best documents the stories, the meetings, the emotions, and the successes and failures behind the 1929 crash is called *The Day the Bubble Burst: A Social History of the Wall Street Crash of 1929*. It was written by Gordon Thomas and Max Morgan-Witts and was published by Doubleday & Company. It is out of print, but I know that it can be found, as a little store in Boston helped me find my copy.

While I am listing books, may I also suggest that you pick up a copy of Peter L. Bernstein's *Against the Gods: The Remarkable Story of Risk*, published by Wiley.

The point is that the crashes, bubbles, and acceptance of risk that have occurred throughout history have already been eloquently documented. What has not been addressed by historians of these events is what comes next after a bubble bursts. What do the survivors do after a crash? Are there opportunities? How do you find them? Should you buy stocks that continue to exist in name but that trade as nearly penny stocks after the crash? (No. Look for industries that can move into the void the collapse of these stocks created and companies that can develop the ruins left behind. For example, the Internet infrastructure remains, although the dot coms have vanished. *The Internet will be developed by software companies.*) There are many such questions, but it seems as if everyone focuses on the drama of the day and provides little guidance for the future. In fact, many doomsayers believe that there is no future. I do not agree with that philosophy at all.

In the history of the DJIA, there have been many contractions that have been called crashes. These are not necessarily deep percentage declines, but if it forms rapidly, a market correction is given the label "crash." We easily forget, or want to forget, these contraction periods, and it requires a pictorial review to refresh our memory or to give us a wider view of history that we may not have experienced. For this reason, I have prepared a series of charts, shown as Figures 19-1 to 19-11, with a simple 14-period RSI under the weekly DJIA data from 1900. The series shows us that the technical methods of today would have worked well for all these historical declines. Clearly technicals do not care what stock substitutions are made within the underlying DJIA.

The charts need little comment from me, as in the prior chapters you learned how to read the notations. Key divergences and support/resistance levels have been marked to help guide you. Interestingly, the Great Crash of 1929 could have been technically traced from top to bottom and back through the market reversal with just a simple RSI indicator and the skills you have been developing to this point.

Crashes have happened in the past, and crashes will happen again. The 1929 crash was certainly the most devastating, but even then—after much pain and a war that ended the Depression—the financial phoenix did finally rise again. Every single one of these crashes offered opportunities for someone who was smart enough to survive, and then gutsy enough and brave enough to step in. But you will have that courage only if you have an understanding of how to assess the risk versus the opportunity.

Now let's take a look at the historic declines in the Dow Jones Industrial Average.

Figure 19-1

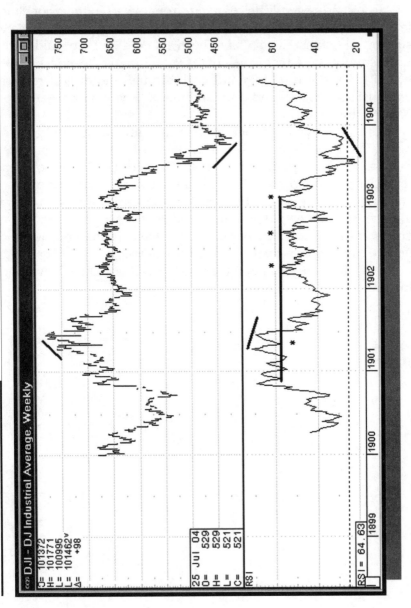

Dow Jones Industrial Average 1900–1904

224

Figure 19-2

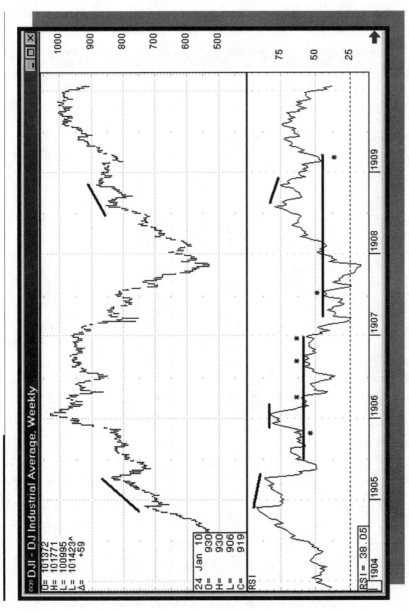

Dow Jones Industrial Average 1904–1909

Figure 19-3

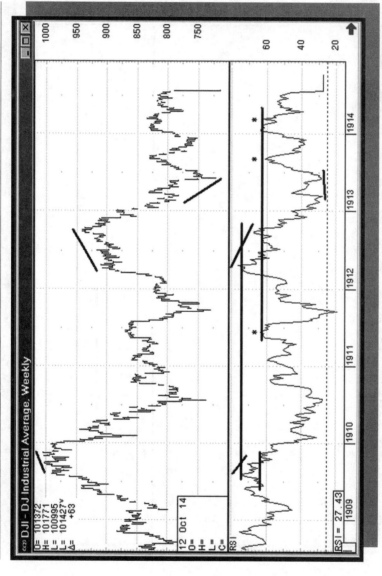

Dow Jones Industrial Average 1908–1914

Figure 19-4

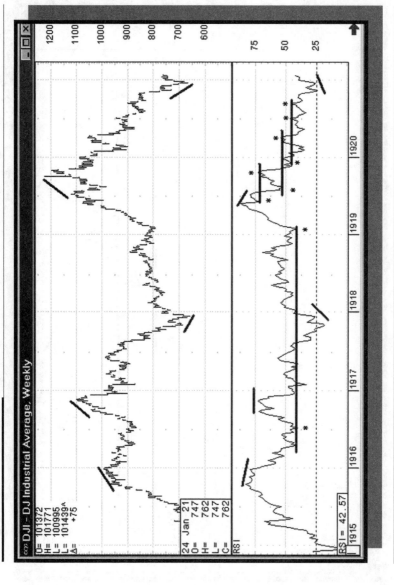

Dow Jones Industrial Average 1915–1920

227

Figure 19-5

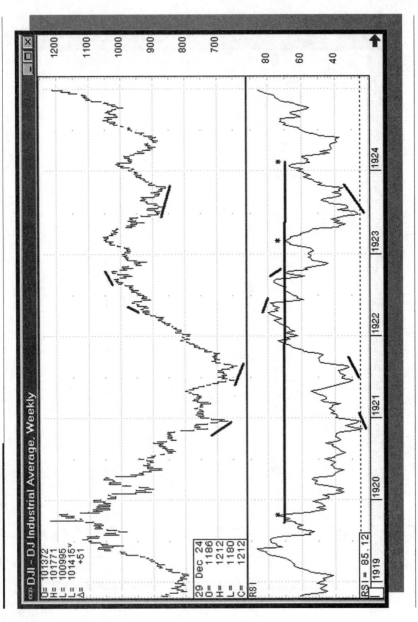

Dow Jones Industrial Average 1919–1924

228

Figure 19-6

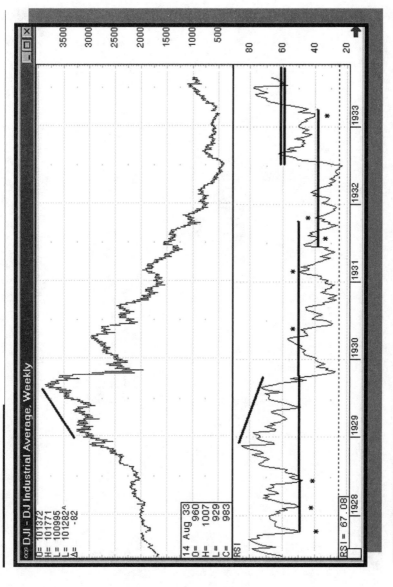

Dow Jones Industrial Average 1927–1933

Figure 19-7

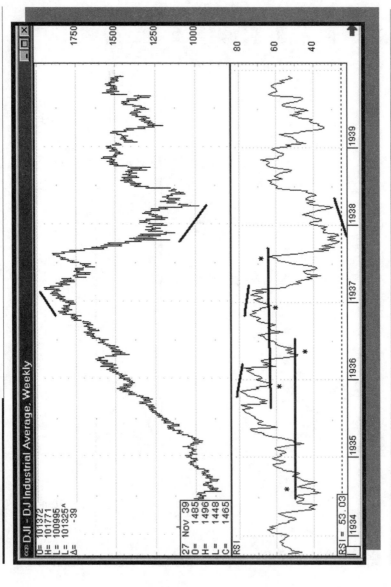

Dow Jones Industrial Average 1934–1939

Figure 19-8

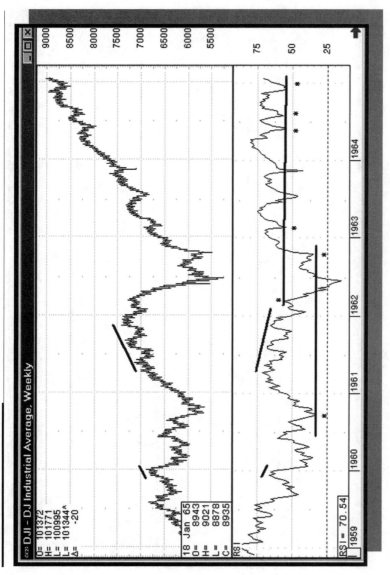

Dow Jones Industrial Average 1959–1964

Figure 19-9

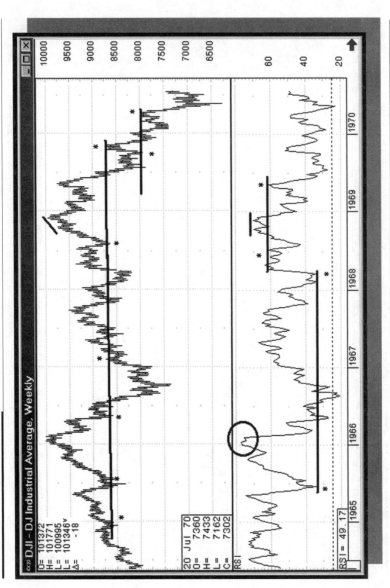

Dow Jones Industrial Average 1964–1970

Figure 19-10

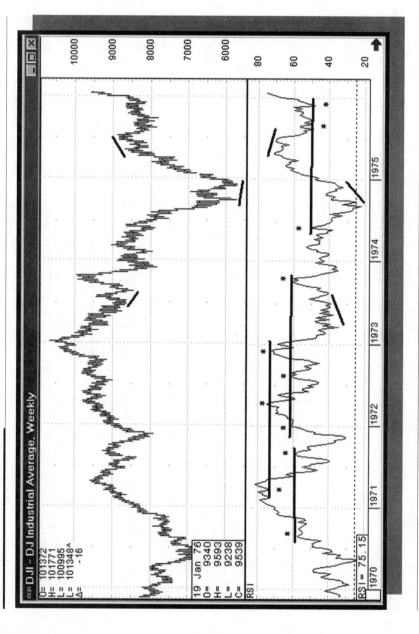

Dow Jones Industrial Average 1970–1975

Figure 19-11

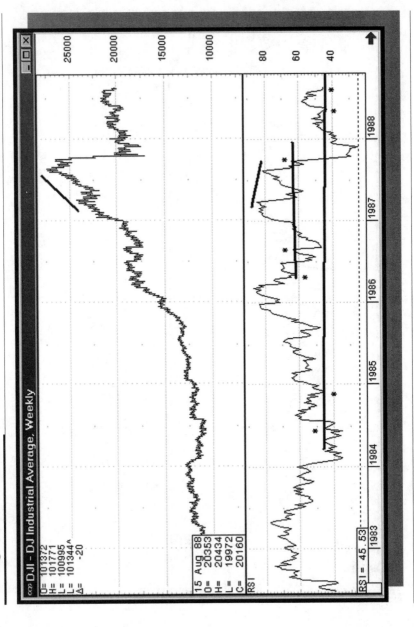

Dow Jones Industrial Average 1982–1988

Let me detail the patterns that form a common thread linking these major speculative events. The demise in technology could have been foretold if we had learned the lessons presented to us in the 1980s. Early in my career I was very fortunate to learn from individuals viewed to be central figures of that decade. To make a long story short, I was the brand manager of Kodak's Professional Color Films, when a late connecting flight rerouted my business trip for Kodak, and it rerouted my entire career. The man who I met on that unscheduled flight led to my first job on Wall Street. He reportedly had hired Michael Milken into Drexel Burnham & Lambert.

Milken earned $500 million in 1988 alone. He was known then as the Junk Bond King, although "junk" was always more formally referred to as "high-yield" or "non-investment-grade" bonds. All bonds are benchmarked to Treasury Bonds, and then Corporate and Municipal Bonds are rated according to risk. The top four ratings are AAA, AA, A, and BBB. Then there are BB, B, and CCC. Investment-grade means having a rating above a BB. The truth is that only 5 percent of the high-yield bonds were associated with hostile corporate takeovers. Of the rest, some funded friendly mergers, allowing companies to adapt to global markets. Others provided the financial means for enterprising smaller businesses to grow, helping to rebuild American business after a bear market.

History shows that people who accumulate great wealth are frequently attacked by the culture from which they sprang. Our modern-day Milken is Bill Gates, and some upstart visionary who is now in his or her business infancy will someday become the next generation's Milken or Gates.

Milken was toppled when the government charged him with 98 criminal counts of stock fraud and racketeering. Many people who were close to the situation believe that Milken was toppled by a former junk bond king who had been dethroned and later became a government witness. The government now has Gates in its crosshairs, and he is battling to keep the Microsoft empire that he founded intact. The principal supporters of the government are once again those firms that were dethroned. Whether you view these men as scapegoats or crooks, there is no denying that they and others like them changed and revolutionized business in America.

So why are the corporate takeover years of the 1980s and the growth of the dot coms in the late 1990s similar? And if they are similar, what lessons did we forget so quickly?

There are three periods in American financial history that I will use to make my comparison. In each it can be said that financial control shifted away from the powerful institutions and into the hands of smaller, enterprising businesses.

The first example was the birth of the original Bank of America in California in the early 1900s. The visionary here was a man named Giannini. (The Bank of America that exists today is an entirely different entity, as I documented in my first book.) Giannini believed that the power of the small individual depositor could challenge the Wall Street power institutions and the almighty J. P. Morgan. This was a period in history when there were no 15- or 30-year mortgages, no consumer loans, and no payment plans. The early 1900s, as you can see from Figure 19-1, were experiencing a horrific bear market. *This is the first key ingredient, as bear markets shift public sentiment away from the status quo to a desire and need for change.* People were very anti–big bank and anti–Wall Street. So Giannini found his opportunity in a period of discontent.

The Bank of America became an American institution after the the Great San Francisco Earthquake, when Giannini had the guts to extend loans for rebuilding when no bank in the East would take the risk.

Giannini surmised that *future growth potential* was a better measure of risk than historical earnings or balance sheets. In this regard, the Milken years and the dot com explosion were similar to Giannini's vision, as in all three periods the emphasis was on people's future income potential rather than their historical earnings.

Giannini provided the financial backing for Disneyland, the first subdivisions, and a host of institutions that we take for granted and that now dot our landscape, such as supermarkets. All of these were risky projects to finance when there had been no prior history of success or failure. Milken constructed the financial means by which a host of corporations found backers for their enterprises when they were in their infancy or on the brink of expansion. Today, some of these enterprises are megaliths as Federal Express, MCI, and Warner Communications, which was absorbed into Time (now AOL Time Warner) at a value of $13 to $14 billion. When Milken stepped in, Warner Communications was considered to be on the verge of bankruptcy. AOL Time Warner has now come full circle as it struggles in 2002, as are telephone and wireless companies.

It can be said that Milken was no different from Giannini. Milken also saw an opportunity in close juxtaposition to a bear market when large lending institutions turned their backs on smaller businesses. The bear market of the early 1970s led banks to avoid the risk of investing in American companies by moving more than a trillion dollars into other countries. Their primary focus was on Latin America. That meant that American businesses, still hurting from the market decline and economic slump, had nowhere to turn for financial assistance to help them rebuild. That is why high-yield bonds exploded on the scene when they did and why they were viewed as the means to rebuild America's future earnings potential. The banks did not have the guts to make these loans, and instead tossed away a trillion dollars, along with the future potential that comes with investing at home.

Milken once used the Singer Company as an example. Banks would have willingly given Singer a loan or bought its bonds in the mid-1970s because in its 100-year history the company had never missed a dividend payment. The due diligence would have focused on Singer's ability to sell sewing machines and fabric in the future, based on prior sales trends at that time. But Singer lost millions when women went into the workforce and lost interest in sewing and their attempts to diversify failed. The historical balance sheets could not have foreseen the change in the social climate. Milken made it clear that the potential of what he considered some of the most important industries of his time was still off in the distant future: There was not a single investment-grade company in the medical diagnostics, toxic waste disposal, or cellular telephone industries. But he was also quick to point out that Wall Street and banks once called Henry Ford's Model T a "junk" investment as well.

So this is the first real stepping-stone toward a speculative bubble: *Potential earnings in the future come to be viewed as less risky than measurements of past performance.* When Giannini offered low-interest-rate loans to rebuild San Francisco, he was betting on future earnings to pay off the loans. Milken believed that a country had to invest in its own human resources in order to grow. The dot coms were valued in the same way, as they had no real earnings; it was their future potential alone that led to billions flowing into the new industry and that caught the speculative interest of the general public. The public, however, is always the last group to follow the cash flow trail, as you will see.

The general public does not jump onto the speculative band-wagon until the major banks that once refused to lend to smaller businesses suddenly find themselves losing out. It is only when major banks make a change in their risk assessment and begin bet-ting on the future high-growth potential of a company that the public begins to take notice.

During Milken's era, when a dollar flowing into Latin America from major banking centers flowed right back out the back door again, the bank loans to these countries soon became nonproductive losses. Banks were then in the position of having to find income, with a limited number of investment vehicles from which to choose. High-yield bonds became the vehicle for making earnings and were suddenly viewed as having only moderate risk for the larger institutions. The second step toward the speculative bubble was therefore in place, as banks jumped on board to make money from the newly defined method of risk assessment.

The third and final step that fuels a speculative bubble is the media telling the general public that they are missing out. The media bombard the public with constant coverage of the big money flowing into the new trend from reputable lending institu-tions. People see advertisements for these companies, and they see their neighbors benefiting from the growth of smaller businesses. Shortly thereafter, a new speculative bubble hits its full stride. We saw this in the 1980s, it was repeated again in the late 1990s, and we will see it again in the future: When *banks begin to focus on future income rather than past returns, a new bubble will be born.* In 2002 we are experiencing the contraction phase of the cycle. Banks and investors are once again risk adverse. The return to GAAP account-ing and anti-Wall Street sentiment will tighten and restrict loans to small business ventures. However, small business will most likely lead us out of our most recent recession as it has done in the past. Therefore, charting of small-cap stocks will be informative and start a new cycle when venture capital sees an opportunity where the big banks will only see great risk.

Here is the big question that should always be asked after a market bubble bursts: "What is the void remaining?" With the death of junk bonds after the Milken years, cable was in place with-out a function. Telecommunications and the birth of the Internet swooped in to use the infrastructure that was lying on the ground in the aftermath of the fallen junk bond king.

With the demise of the dot coms, what is the void that they have left behind? The Internet is not going to go away. You should not invest in the firms that imploded and are trading at a small fraction of their value in their heyday. Instead, you should invest in the companies *that can capitalize on their demise* and fill and develop the void they left behind. So who will fill this void? It will most likely be software companies and companies that are directly associated with software. The infrastructure is in place, and someone is going to use it and develop it. Follow the money trail as it has been the key in the past. Microsoft is holding $60 billion in cash. This is a cash reserve the savvy investor and trader should monitor. Will Microsoft survive? Most likely. What companies does Microsoft have contracts with, and what companies is it backing by providing development capital? If software should grow, peripherals for security, data backup, and megastorage might also be a consideration. Keep in mind that the cable lines for accessing the Net have been overproduced and were part of the Asian dumping, so don't go into the old sectors that formed the original speculative bubble.

The trend change can already be seen where we no longer buy software, but rather lease it through the Internet. In the next cycle, revenue flows from software will far exceed computer hardware. Computer hardware will be given away like booze in a casino as hardware will provide the means to generate repeating revenue streams from leased services. Old-money companies like Caterpillar and John Deere rely on inventory management systems controlled by software packages written by companies we have little experience with, such as Rational and Manugistics. (I'm not making investment recommendations. Do your own research.) Kodak will take your digital images delivered through the Internet and make prints that you can view in a conventional manner. Why? Because it is losing market share in conventional distribution outlets to the Internet and has to find a way to recapture lost sales to digital imaging. Therefore, to hold market share, it, too, has tapped the Net. Today we buy everything from furniture to shoes through the Internet—I even found an antique bathtub and plumbing for my new home through the Net. My trading software is leased and is available only through the Internet. Medicine, real estate, and used car sales are affected by Internet accessibility. The trend is growing rapidly and that means an opportunity will once again grow from a market bubble burst.

Once you have identified a company and you know the sector it is in, the rest is done through technical analysis. It is all technical momentum and sentiment once you know the company's name. Watch the daily trading volume. When volume for a single day starts to exceed that of the largest caps in the DJIA, such as XOM on the same comparative day, you know that institutions have begun to take a keen interest. Always have an exit plan to manage your risk before you take a position. But it is clear that when a speculative bubble bursts, there are always a few smart survivors who will reevaluate and find the opportunities that have been left behind.

SEPTEMBER 11, 2001

The number of ways I have tried to avoid putting any reference to September 11 in this chapter can no longer be counted. But it would be blatantly obvious if it were not included, as it is the shock wave of our lifetime. Rather than tearing us down, it brought America together, and ended a time when we took so much for granted. When New York sent two huge beams of light into the night skies where the Towers once stood, I realized that the Towers represented hope and pride, and that they still stand within each of us, brighter, higher, and stronger than before.

The markets were closed on September 14 when I answered the phone near a computer. I was physically sick and in an emotional daze, like many others. While I was on the phone, I glanced up at the computers and saw that our markets had been stopped in a time capsule. As I ended the phone call, tears once again poured down my face.

The markets were closed, so there was no new data to push off the screens the horrific 2- and 3-minute data bars that recounted the painful story. The tidal wave was violent, as the bond and equity markets tried to whip back to premarket open attack levels when it was thought that this just could not be happening. Then the markets explosively reversed their direction a third time when we knew an act of war was unfolding. This was the third major shock wave I had experienced, and in each case the violent market moves in the first few critical seconds had been similar. But the first time I experienced such a shock wave, I was trapped in the sharp reversing tidal wave, as I had never seen intraday data on such an event. So in the hope that others who become front-line traders might benefit from seeing how a shock wave rolls though the markets, I began to capture the screens that were frozen in time. I just took random captures, as I could not think straight, and so I missed several key markets, such as oil and currency cross-rates. The captured charts are displayed in Figures 19-12 to 19-30.

I am unable to discuss the charts. The best I could do was to make a brief comment here or there on the charts themselves. I still find tears pouring down just from preparing these charts for publication, and it has been 6 months since the attack. But these few charts speak a thousand words for those who come after us about how the shock wave passed through major currencies, fixed income, gold, and stocks around the world. The professionalism in the gold market pit was courageous, as the traders stayed and executed orders until the building began to fall. Thank God they made it out safely. Shock waves will occur again in the markets some day in the future. I only pray the cause is nature's fury and not mankind's stupidity.

Figure 19-12

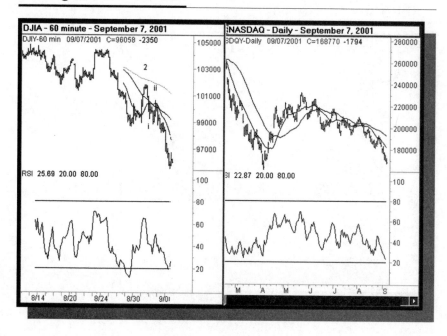

F i g u r e   19-13

F i g u r e   19-14

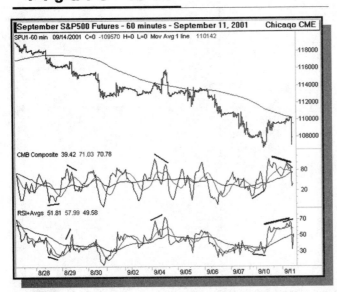

F i g u r e   19-15

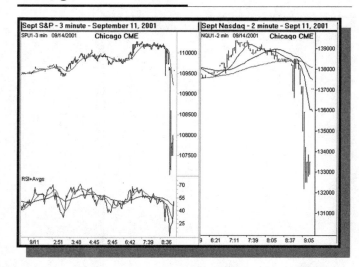

F i g u r e   19-16

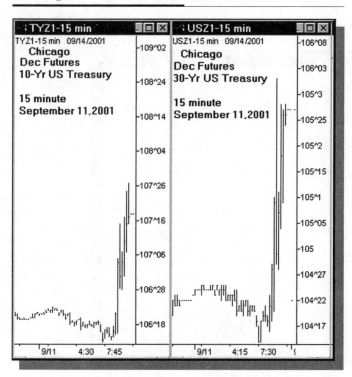

F i g u r e   19-17

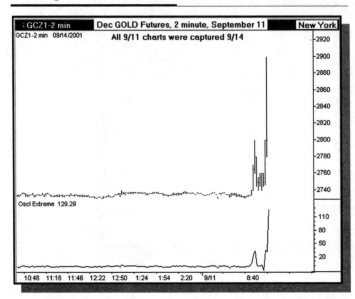

F i g u r e   19-18

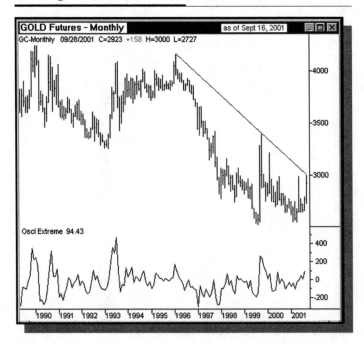

F i g u r e   19-19

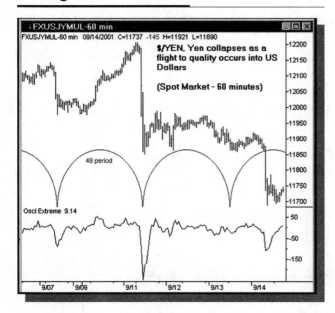

F i g u r e   19-20

F i g u r e   19-21

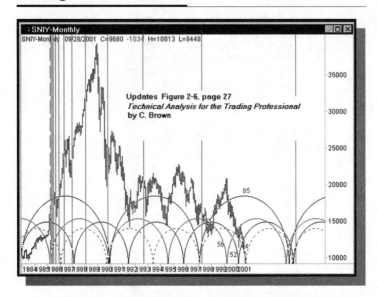

Updates Figure 2-6, page 27
Technical Analysis for the Trading Professional
by C. Brown

F i g u r e   19-22

LONDON FTSE Stock Index
60 minute, Sept 14, 2001

F i g u r e   19-23

F i g u r e   19-24

F i g u r e   19-25

F i g u r e   19-26

F i g u r e   19-27

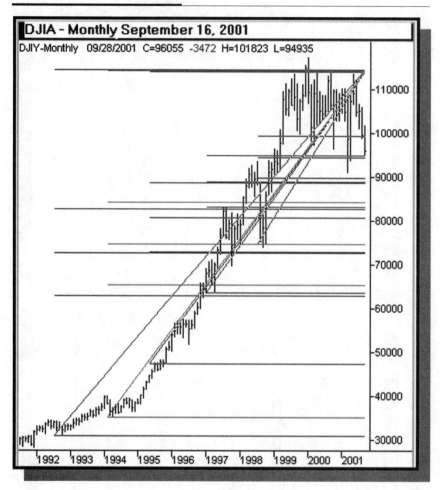

DJIA - Monthly September 16, 2001

DJIY-Monthly 09/28/2001 C=96055 -3472 H=101823 L=94935

Figure 19-28

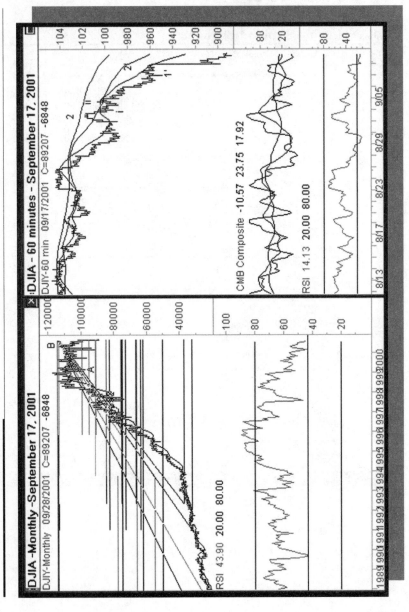

250

Figure 19-29

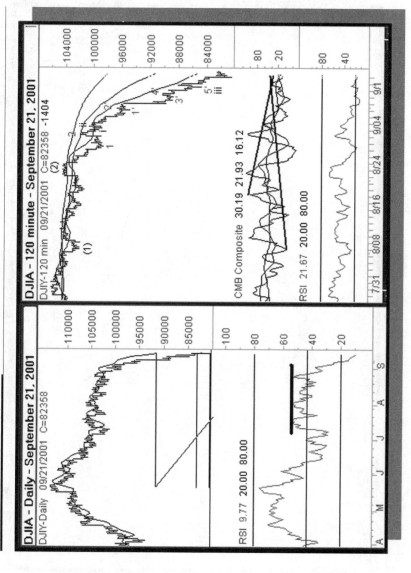

251

Figure 19-30

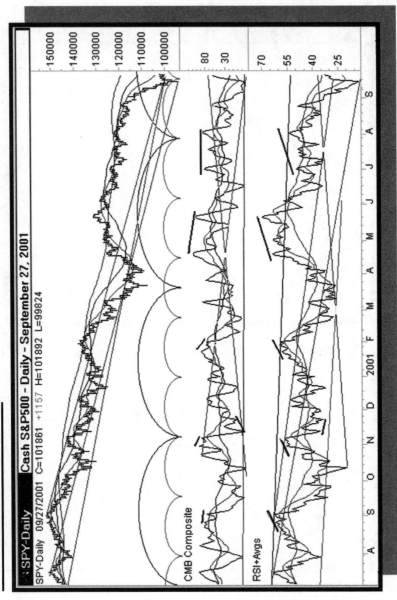

SPY-Daily | Cash S&P500 - Daily - September 27, 2001

SPY-Daily 09/27/2001 C=101861 +1157 H=101892 L=99824

CMB Composite

RSI+Avgs

PART 6

Why Does Technical Analysis Work?

CHAPTER 20

What Do Seashells, Hurricanes, and the Dow Jones Industrial Average All Have in Common?

Figure 20-1

The universal constant of 1.618, or Phi, was a ratio known to the ancient Greeks as the Golden Section. The Renaissance artists knew it as the Divine Proportion. It has been known to mankind since 580 B.C., when Pythagoras stepped into a blacksmith's shop and reportedly heard two hammers striking an anvil in perfect harmony. When the hammers were swung by different people, the perfect harmony remained intact. It was from the ratios between the hammer weights that this one man, so far ahead of his time, surmised that harmonic frequencies and mathematic relationships connected all things, including the heavenly bodies.

While the ratio itself was known in 580 B.C., it was only through the son of a Pisan merchant, born in 1175 A.D., that we learned of its unique mathematical properties. Leonardo da Pisa became the mathematician we know as Leonardo Fibonacci. His father served as a customs officer in North Africa. As a result, Leonardo was schooled in Barbary (Algeria) and later in Egypt, Syria, Greece, Sicily, and Provence.

In 1200 he returned to Pisa, Italy, and used the knowledge he had gained on his travels to write *Liber Abaci*, or *Book of Calculations*, in which he introduced to the Latin-speaking world the decimal number system. The first chapter of his book begins:

> These are the nine figures of the Indians: 9 8 7 6 5 4 3 2 1. With these nine figures, and with this sign *0* which in Arabic is called zephirum, any number can be written, as will be demonstrated.

In the book he showed practical applications of the numbers to demonstrate their usefulness for merchants and businessmen. Because the practical examples showed that using this system was significantly easier than using Roman numerals, the system caught on quickly. It was Fibonacci who saved us from hearing, "We begin tonight's report with the DJIA closing at MCMXCVIII." (That would be a decline to 1998!)

Fibonacci is best known for a simple series of numbers, introduced in *Liber Abaci* and later named the Fibonacci number in his honor.

The series begins with 0 and 1. After that, use this simple rule: *Add the last two numbers to get the next.*

1, 2, 3, 5, 8, 13, 21, 34, 55, 89, 144, 233, 377, 610, 987, . . .

The series came from Fibonacci's answer to a puzzle constructed by Emperor Frederick II in a mathematical tournament at Pisa. Such competitions were common in his day, and the problem presented was this:

> Beginning with a single pair of rabbits, if every month each *productive* pair bears a new pair, which becomes productive when they are 1 month old, how many rabbits will there be after *n* months?

Thus, it was the solution to a puzzle about rabbits that Fibonacci published in his book and that in retrospect became one of the most important number series we know. The golden section or divine proportion is closely related to the Fibonacci series. This value is obtained by taking the ratio of successive terms in the Fibonacci series. As the successive terms are compared, they draw closer and closer to the same value for each comparison, giving the solution of 1.618, as we see in Figure 20-2.

If you sum the squares of any series of Fibonacci numbers, they will equal the last Fibonacci number used in the series times the next Fibonacci number. This property results in the Fibonacci spiral, which is seen in everything from butterfly wings, seashells, hurricanes, galaxies, and even markets.

Ancient architecture such as the Great Pyramid of Giza and the Greek Parthenon applies the golden ratio, 1.618. Leonardo da Vinci clearly knew of the Fibonacci ratios because his notebooks and works are filled with exact Fibonacci proportions from his sculpture, art, city designs, and scientific studies. The Fibonacci ratios are found throughout art and sculpture. The Egyptian two-dimensional representation of the human body uses precise Fibonacci ratios for every strictly proportioned measurement. Our own bodies and those of living creatures of the sea and air are proportioned in numerous ways with the Fibonacci ratios 0.618 and 0.382. Figure 20-3 shows *some* of the Fibonacci relationships within the Swallowtail Butterfly. It is the internal proportions of life itself that show us that the golden ratio 1.618 is the mathematical key that binds us all.

F i g u r e   20-2

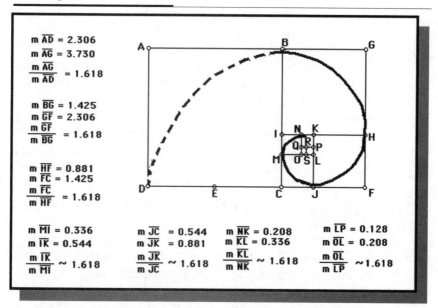

$$m \overline{AD} = 2.306$$
$$m \overline{AG} = 3.730$$
$$\frac{m \overline{AG}}{m \overline{AD}} = 1.618$$

$$m \overline{BG} = 1.425$$
$$m \overline{GF} = 2.306$$
$$\frac{m \overline{GF}}{m \overline{BG}} = 1.618$$

$$m \overline{HF} = 0.881$$
$$m \overline{FC} = 1.425$$
$$\frac{m \overline{FC}}{m \overline{HF}} = 1.618$$

$$m \overline{MI} = 0.336$$
$$m \overline{IK} = 0.544$$
$$\frac{m \overline{IK}}{m \overline{MI}} \sim 1.618$$

$$m \overline{JC} = 0.544$$
$$m \overline{JK} = 0.881$$
$$\frac{m \overline{JK}}{m \overline{JC}} \sim 1.618$$

$$m \overline{NK} = 0.208$$
$$m \overline{KL} = 0.336$$
$$\frac{m \overline{KL}}{m \overline{NK}} \sim 1.618$$

$$m \overline{LP} = 0.128$$
$$m \overline{OL} = 0.208$$
$$\frac{m \overline{OL}}{m \overline{LP}} \sim 1.618$$

F i g u r e   20-3

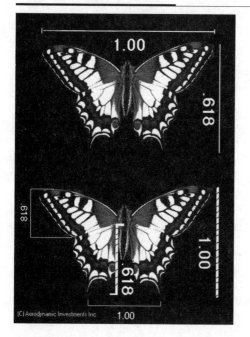

But Fibonacci relationships are not found only in art, architecture, and nature. Several of the great classical musicians constructed their symphonies around the number 0.618. Consider Beethoven's Fifth Symphony, a segment of the score of which is displayed in Figure 20-4. The motto is repeated three times. When you divide the number of musical bars or measures between the second and third appearances of the motto by the number of bars between the first and second appearances, the result is 0.618. When Pythagoras first discovered this proportion of sacred geometry, he believed that all things were connected by means of mathematical harmonic vibration. Science, music, and astronomy were inseparable as subjects of study until the 1800s. Then Einstein's Theory about energy and matter returned us to these early principles with a new understanding.

Table 20-1 may give you a whole new perspective on how we may all be connected. The number that becomes the mean distance within our solar system is Phi, 1.618. Pythagoras was right in 580 B.C. when he suspected that the ratio he heard from the sound of two hammers might be the vibration ratio that connects the heavens and all living creatures. We will look at this harmonic concept more closely in the next chapter.

F i g u r e   20-4

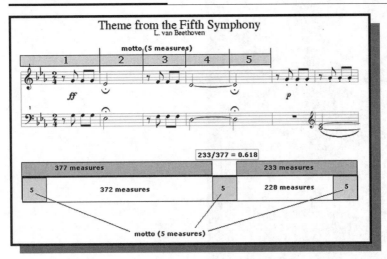

Table 20-1

The Relative Mean Distance of All Planets and the Largest Asteroid Is 1.618

Planet	Mean Distance in Millions of Kilometers (per NASA)	Relative Mean Distance (Mercury = 1)
Mercury	57.91	1.00000
Venus	108.21	1.86859
Earth	149.60	1.38250
Mars	227.92	1.52353
Ceres (largest asteroid)	413.79	1.81552
Jupiter	778.57	1.88154
Saturn	1433.53	1.84123
Uranus	2872.46	2.00377
Neptune	4495.06	1.56488
Pluto	5869.66	1.30580
Total		**16.18736**
Average		**1.61874**
Phi		1.61803
Variance		(0.00043)

We have looked at many areas of technical analysis, but the truth is that we have only scratched the surface. As a member of the review board for our industry's journal, published by the Market Technicians Association, I can confidently say that there is an exciting growth phase underway in many areas of technical analysis. With the growing acceptance of charting methods, many people are stepping forward to share research that they have been silently doing behind closed doors for years. The growing openness is itself fueling the industry's push beyond current boundaries toward new applications and understanding.

This book uses only linear mathematics in demonstrating technical analysis, but some day, to better evaluate the natural expansion and contraction cycles in the markets, you will be learning about fractal geometry as well. This is a newer field of mathematics whose computer-generated solutions are visually beautiful and duplicate the complex patterns found in nature, such as those that make up clouds, trees, mountain ranges, shorelines, and weather patterns, among other examples. Fractal geometry began as a fuzzy cloud of hypothetical theorems describing chaos theory. Most of us had no idea how to apply these concepts to our day-to-day market needs—we just wanted to know when to buy or sell the market. Fractal geometry has continued to evolve, and now it has tangible applications with real benefits. For example, fractals create intelligent imagery from space, where a small portion of information is like a DNA coded string. Once the small signal is received on Earth, it can be expanded to reveal all the information contained in the small thread, like a seed that is allowed to bloom. One set example I was shown by a company in Atlanta was a small data set that contained a few pixels from an unidentifiable eye. That was all you could see. But from this small piece of information, the computer was able to solve for all the missing data sets. What resulted was a complete tropical parrot in minute detail, from the tip of his beak to the rich colors of each individual tailfeather, right down to the claws. The data had such detail that you could zoom through five different levels of magnification.

More than ever before, we are coming to understand that the patterns in nature are created from mathematical formulae. I spend much of my time when I'm not actively trading on the frontiers of research in this area. This new field of mathematics allows us to develop a new and deeper understanding of expansion and contraction or growth and decay cycles. This, in turn, leads to new analytic methods that can be applied to the financial and commodity markets, which are subject to the same forces. If your indicators form a divergence at a time that is out of phase with the market's growth and decay cycle, the market will ignore the indicators and plough right through them. We have always been aware that looking at signals in one indicator or one time horizon was insufficient. Using multiple time frames helps to filter out those isolated signals that are out of phase or out of sync, whether the trader is aware of the higher math that is being applied or not. The difference now,

F i g u r e   20-5

however, is that we are beginning to understand more fully why technical analysis works.

The Fibonacci price projection methods that we covered in Chapter 15 are an application of the universal constant that occurs in *anything* that contains a growth and decay or expansion and contraction cycle. Fortunately, it is not necessary to go through a lot of high-level math to show you how this new field of mathematics is changing our understanding and application of charting techniques. Take a look at the three computer-generated solutions to a fractal equation that appear in Figures 20-5 to 20-7. (I am not using the Mandelbrot formulas, for those with knowledge in this field.) You will see that the computer solutions are visually stunning works of art. (They can be seen in full color on my Web site.) Yes, the imagery is very cool. But what is the common graphic element in all three computer solutions?

F i g u r e   20-6

F i g u r e   20-7

The common graphic element is the logarithmic Fibonacci spiral. You applied the Fibonacci ratio 1.618 and its reciprocal 0.618 when you obtained price objectives for support or resistance and when you used price swings to project new price extensions. The ratio 1.618 is called Phi and is a universal constant. It is the program for all life from DNA to hurricanes (Figure 20-8).

If the Fibonacci spiral is the common mathematical model for all expansion and contraction cycles in our universe, what significance does it have for the markets? Markets are the products of people's expectations and disappointments. Markets must abide by the same universal laws of growth and decay. The charts in Figures 20-9 and 20-10 translate this theory into practical application for analyzing market data. The same spiral is shown at work in the price data

F i g u r e   20-8

Hurricane Floyd

of the Dow Jones Industrial Average. Figure 20-9 shows the market high in 1929, the crash that followed, and the recovery phase in the early 1930s and 1940s. There are also secondary spirals at work that would map the price pivots in the data that are not defined by this grand-scale spiral. But the Fibonacci spiral alone will not fully explain these charts as you will soon discover in Chapter 21.

Figure 20-10 shows more recent data: the expansion cycle that has been unfolding since 1974, with plateaus from which the DJIA launches each new leg up. The chart in Figure 20-10 was captured in August of 1998. At that time the DJIA had only just reached this curious area of resistance. We now know that as of May 2002, the DJIA has not been able to exceed this area of resistance. If you imagine yourself standing on the floor of a great coliseum with the seats expanding ever upward around you with slightly more leg room in each successive row, you will have the right three-dimensional visual image when you study the growth cycle for the DJIA that is developing in these charts. I now apply this charting technique to intraday data to project not only price but coinciding time objectives from the same three-dimensional graphic.

The DJIA will eventually break through this larger spiral boundary that has defined resistance for a couple of years. However, the volatility swings in the markets of the future will make the swings of today seem tame. But this is all part of the universal order of things; it will not be changed by rules, price limits, legislation, or fundamentals. Apparent destruction will always be followed by growth into an ever-widening dimension of the larger spiral as long as there are markets.

We think in two linear dimensions, as this is manageable for us in the context of our day-to-day analysis and the features of our existing software. But the computers and market analysis of today will look old-fashioned once three-dimensional modeling becomes commonplace. The application of fractal geometry in three dimensions will define price projections with greater accuracy by adjusting them to the universal laws of expansion and contraction cycles. When we first began to look at the use of Fibonacci ratios to identify price projections, we began dabbling in a topic so big that a serious study of it could consume a lifetime.

F i g u r e   20-9

F i g u r e   20-10

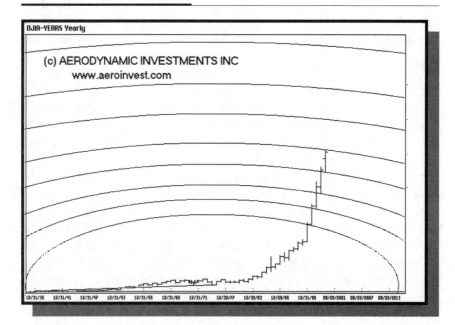

CHAPTER 21

A Universal Higher Order and How All Things Are Indeed Connected

The last chapter provided more background on the Fibonacci ratio, 1.618, and its reciprocal, 0.618. We saw how this ratio occurs in various ways in nature, astronomy, and music. Now we will look at harmonic vibrations that connect market pivot points. If you are not curious about anything more than knowing where to buy and sell, you may want to skip this chapter. But before long you will come up against the same questions that many of us have pondered. Why do markets sometimes ignore perfect technical signals in a single chart but at other times respect the same setup? Why do markets develop repeating mirrored patterns down through the various time horizons? Why does the market turn at the exact price projections derived from by two noncorrelated methods? In fact, why does technical analysis work at all?

Answering these questions will make us better traders because they will give us a depth of understanding about the methods we use to judge the markets. The bottom-line conclusion from the work I am continuing to explore can be summarized in the following way. Fibonacci ratios are only one piece of a larger puzzle. The larger puzzle is the fact that *markets expand and contract in accordance with harmonic vibrations that are indeed measurable.* And the reason Fibonacci ratios are contained within this larger puzzle is the same as the reason that all ancient and present-day people, cultures, and continents have the Fibonacci ratios 0.382, 0.500, and 0.618 contained within the construction of their various musical scales. It is only through a study of harmonic principles and the mathematical construction of musical scales that one begins to understand how to better predict the price of a specific market pivot point and the date at which it will occur. The realization that peaks and troughs in market data are mathematical vibrations has led to various practical applications. The most important is knowing when to take action on a specific market signal and when to let it pass because *you know the market will do likewise.*

Vibrations are harmonious when there is a direct mathematical relationship between the frequencies at which the two aggregates are vibrating. Two strings with a harmonic relationship will be *sympathetic* to each other. This relationship causes an action/reaction called *sympathetic vibrations*. Vibrations that are mathematically dissimilar are said to be in *dissonance*. To our ear, dissonant vibrations are just plain noise, and extreme dissonance causes physical pain. Markets ignore technical signals that develop at dissonant nodal points, as they are out of phase or key with the developing expansion or contraction cycle of greater importance.

There are times when markets should not be traded. That does not mean when there is a bear market. Rather, the market should be avoided when it is in a transition phase, shifting key or preparing to move from a contraction cycle to an expansion cycle or vice versa. We can see mathematically when these periods of transition occur, as the minute details from short intraday data and daily data produce mathematical noise. The short-horizon market internals defined by the small pivot points become very difficult to connect to one another mathematically. When this happens, it warns the smart trader that a change is in the wind. In such an environment, stops are easily run and technical signals that normally form across multiple time horizons to confirm one another cannot be found. Often a weekly chart will be directly opposed to a daily chart, and short-horizon chart signals will conflict yet again. When a string is being tuned, the result will sound like noise until suddenly there is a new harmonic relationship with the vibrations near it. When the market is retuning, no one wins. The smart trader who has been in the business a long time knows that there are three positions: long, short, and out of the market holding cash. Trading and investing is a race without a finish line, and you have to know when to step into the race. If you went head-to-head against a single market all the time, you would lose. The market has time on its side, and we do not. But markets that move up or down with pivot points that show mathematical cohesion are extremely profitable.

When we visually look at price data, there are times when a symmetrical balance and rhythm develop. The choppy nature of the data at the start of a rally is often duplicated near the rally's conclusion, giving symmetry to the overall appearance of the price progression. You will recall that when a gap forms in a market, it can often be used as a marker that defines one-half of the market's current trend. This is using market symmetry, and the best chartists always make an effort to study the balance, symmetry, and proportional rhythms that constantly occur within the price data.

Without ever knowing about the Laws of Harmonic Vibration, a technician can still stumble upon the right harmonic frequencies by using methods that filter out signals that are simply noise and have a low probability. Without your knowledge, you have already been steered in this direction. Beginning in the first few chapters, I guided you to set up your computer so that you are viewing two charts at all times, displaying data from time periods that have a ratio of 1 to 4. This ratio lets us filter the isolated technical signals that occur in dissonance within single charts and allows us to act on signals that define a unison or harmony when they appear in two time periods concurrently. There are reasons behind many of the techniques or methods recommended in earlier chapters that could not have been discussed at that time without breaking the flow of the explanation. But if you are curious, I will share with you now why harmonics and market movement are intertwined.

The research path I traveled was previously followed in the 1920s by a man who is still respected by analysts and traders today for what he accomplished. His name was W. D. Gann. Gann not only studied markets but developed theories about the Laws of Vibration. In a sense he was a modern-day Pythagorean, as he too believed that all things were connected by mathematical relationships. The principles underlying his various methods were harmonic in nature. It is no accident that the ancient Egyptian calculator he resurrected for modern-day market analysis was called the Harmonic Wheel or Square of Nine. His methods are known by few traders, as he deliberately wrote everything in code in order to disguise his work from those who did not want to fully devote their time to a serious study of the markets. His son, like so many offspring of original thinkers, took a faster route and summarized his father's work by using percentages for all projections. He did a great disservice by doing so, as the majority of books about Gann analysis written today follow the son's approach and not W. D. Gann's original methods.

Gann's original approach provides amazingly accurate price and time projections when the methods are utilized correctly. The methods that Gann's son produced are good estimates, but in today's volatile markets being accurate to within a 16/32nds in bonds, for example, is not good enough when risk management is a concern. W. D. Gann's methods in today's markets are accurate to within three ticks for major spike conditions in bonds. Thus, the original methods need to be fully documented, and that is the book I am under great pressure to write by my colleagues. Maybe that will be the fourth and final book as my business exit plan.

During my research, when I was trying to learn more about W. D. Gann I asked, "Why would a trader in the 1920s with a documented track record of 83 percent winning futures trades suddenly shut down his business and travel halfway around the world to examine the Great Pyramid of Giza in person?" W. D. Gann reportedly compounded a fortune in excess of $50 million by using the ancient Egyptian calculator that was once used to forecast the price of rice. Furthermore, he kept his fortune by knowing to retreat from the market prior to the 1929 crash. Yet this ancient tool, which is used daily in my office with his methods, remains accurate for markets in the twenty-first century.

You are now familiar with basic methods of market price projection using Fibonacci ratios. The methods you have been given are introductory in nature but very effective. When Fibonacci and Gann price projections overlap one another, however, it is market magic. Markets stop directly on the confluence target with precision, as if they had hit a brick wall. Intraday, daily, and weekly trading time horizons yield the same results. We knew this, but we were unable to say why this was true, as no one knew why the Gann wheel worked. We only knew how to apply the method. The wheel itself had not been mathematically decoded in some 2000 years. However, I suspect that Gann decoded the wheel and did not talk about it. You will understand why I draw this conclusion in a few moments.

Some Gann targets are clearly Fibonacci ratios, *but not all Gann price projections from the ancient wheel are Fibonacci numbers.*

Gann analysis will lead you through the fields of sacred geometry, music harmonics, physics, chemistry, art, astronomy, and the ancient Wonders of the World. What is interesting is that when I began to unlock the riddle of the wheel, I did not know that it was an unsolved puzzle and I was unaware that Gann had followed the same route. It was only after I presented the decoded Square of Nine and Gann's Hexagon wheels before my professional colleagues at our industry's Silver Anniversary Convention that I learned of Gann's travels and how long this puzzle had been unsolved.

Gann's wheel is a harmonic-frequency calculator, and this has enabled us to plot harmonic charts that define resistance points within real-time market scenarios in both long and intraday chart work. Figure 21-1 shows the harmonic vibrations rippling through the monthly S&P500 Index from the 1987 market low. There are two harmonic scales in different keys at work in this chart. Where the harmonic intervals of the two scales coincide, a bolder line forms, just as we saw when two Fibonacci levels intersected in our conventional charts. The difference, however, is that the Fibonacci ratios are only some of the arcs that form in a total harmonic series. When you look closely, these charts reveal not only time but acceleration intervals as well.

F i g u r e   21-1

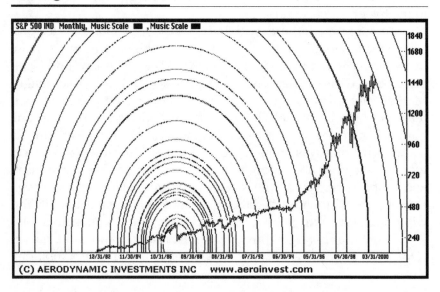

To understand how harmonic charts developed requires some background. Most scholars agree there are five ancient musical systems: Pythagorean Intonation (Greek), Iszfahan (Persian), Arabic, Semi-intonation, and Chinese. When musical scales are created, the cycles per second or frequency interval between each pair of notes is measured in units called cents. (Interestingly, cents and financial cents have the identical symbol.)

The ancient Pythagorean diatonic scale contains three notes with 382.4, 499.9, and 618.2 intervals within the series. We know that these are the Fibonacci ratios 0.382, 0.50, and 0.618. Thirty-two musical scales were mathematically studied, and it was found that they all had three notes that would fall on the Fibonacci ratios.

To make a very long story short, all musical scales are developed from a prime number raised to an exponential number. For example, the Pythagorean scale is a mathematical series using 3 as the base. The first note is 3^0, and anything raised to the power of zero equals 1. Then 3^1 is followed by 3^2, the next in the series is 3^3, and so forth. But these ratios have to be rearranged or sorted to create the scale that our ears hear as a series of rising or descending tones. The pitch letter names are followed in parentheses by the exponential associated with the note in the Pythagorean diatonic natural minor scale: A (3^0), B (3^2), C (3^{-3}), D (3^{-1}), E (3^1), F (3^{-4}), G (3^{-1}). You can see that the order of the exponentials have been significantly changed from the first sequence. The next note begins the series again one *octave* higher. It was this step, in which the results were sorted so that the intervals between notes would be correct, that unlocked and decoded much of Gann's wheel.

Classical music such as that of Mozart and Beethoven requires that instruments within an orchestra be tuned similarly. The scale that we are most familiar in Europe and the Americas is called Equal Temperament and was first developed by a Swiss mathematician named Leonard Euler. The Pythagorean scale has a quirk called the Pythagorean Comma: If instruments play an ascending scale of Perfect Fifths through seven octaves, they will not be able to return to the first note they played after they descend the scale. Therefore, we now use a musical system of tuning that is based on a 12-tone scale whose "steps" or degrees have logarithmically equal intervals between them to resolve this problem.

Mathematically, what we did was destroy the perfect harmonic ratios so that we could keep the instruments in an orchestra together.

In Equal Temperament (*temperament* literally means "manner of tuning"), the only notes that still have perfect harmonic ratios are those that start each new octave. To offer a few examples for readers with a musical background, the musical interval called a Minor 3rd should have a theoretical ratio of 1.20, but the modern scale is 0.892 percent flat. A Perfect Fourth should have a ratio of 1.333, but modern temperament has to accept an error of 0.125 percent sharp. A flat falls short of the perfect ratio, and a sharp exceeds the ideal ratio. Every interval in a modern scale is flat or sharp except the octave, which has both a theoretical and an actual ratio of 2.00.

Gann knew this, and it will help you to visualize how multiples of 12 form "octaves" in the following manner:

$$2(12/12) = 2^1 = \text{the ratio 2:1 = 1 "octave"}$$
$$2(24/12) = 2^2 = \text{the ratio 4:1 = 2 "octaves"}$$
$$2(36/12) = 2^3 = \text{the ratio 8:1 = 3 "octaves"}$$

Gann defined market projections for resistance and support by using the ratios 1:1, 2:1, 4:1, 8:1, 1:2, 1:4, and 1:8, which have perfect theoretical harmonic ratios. He also used the ratios 1:3, 1:16, 3:1, and 16:1. Gann traders are very familiar with these specific ratios. But, perhaps to your surprise, so are you. We applied them when I was introducing trend lines and market geometry.

In Figure 21-2 we have a weekly Merrill Lynch chart showing the use of Gann lines. In addition, two market pivot points marked A and B have been added to show where Gann and Fibonacci price objectives identified the exact same target levels. The harmonic ratios that duplicate Gann's angles are more than coincidental.

W. D. Gann probably shut down his business to travel to Egypt in the early 1920s to solve or decode the last rows, called the Cardinal Cross, in order to complete his deeper understanding of the tools he used daily to trade the markets. I understand this motivation, as I too became obsessive-compulsive about cracking the code of this mystical wheel, displayed in Figure 21-3. But after the task was completed, there remained a truly astounding connection between Gann's wheel and the Great Pyramid of Giza: *The same margin of error that is present in the center rows of the ancient calculator is also present in the Great Pyramid.*

The area of the south triangle of the Great Pyramid is 0.61938. The area of the east triangle is 0.619744. Then the measurements,

Figure 21-2

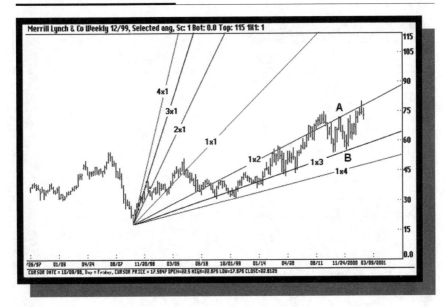

which are recorded to six decimal places, take a curious turn. Take these dimensions and try solving for the altitude of the Great Pyramid using the Pythagorean Theorem, $a^2 + b^2 = c^2$. You cannot do it.

Since the area of a triangle equals the base times the altitude divided by 2, solving for altitude gives the south triangle an altitude of 0.786424 and the east triangle an altitude of 0.787096. But the triangle's altitude does not match the altitude given by the apothem's right triangle. The actual altitude is different. The actual altitude of the south triangle equals 0.782375, and that of the east triangle measures 0.782933.

When I engaged the services of an engineering firm to identify my error, their findings using MathCAD software verified the discrepancy (see Figure 21-4). Then the computer produced the startling solution that also decoded the final rows and columns along the 90° axis within Gann's harmonic wheel to unlock the entire puzzle. W. D. Gann had duplicated an ancient Egyptian calculator that calculates harmonic frequencies within the markets to identify price objectives in the future from existing pivot price lows and highs.

F i g u r e   21-3

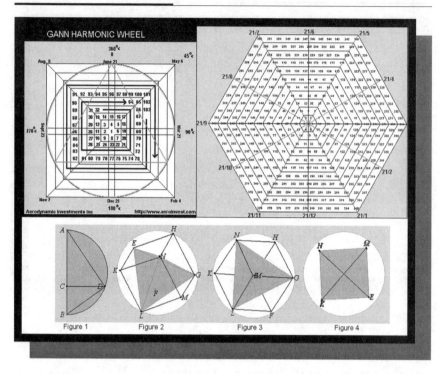

Understanding that markets oscillate with harmonic relationships alters the way some technical methods are used. Fibonacci projections, for example, take on a new dimension of accuracy when the price levels used to start the retracement or extension swing are those obtained from a Gann wheel. In Figure 21-5 you will see Fibonacci projections applied as described in prior chapters, but with the difference that I then project extensions from harmonic price targets rather than just from extreme price lows or highs. This demonstrates that technical analysis can be applied with only a basic understanding, but that there is also another dimension being developed that changes the way some methods are applied for those who are motivated enough to dig much deeper.

The knowledge that Gann's wheel defines harmonic relationships has applications that reach far beyond the analysis of pivot points within global markets. When a sequential table is constructed from the prime notes in a scale and then extended to extremes well

F i g u r e   21-4

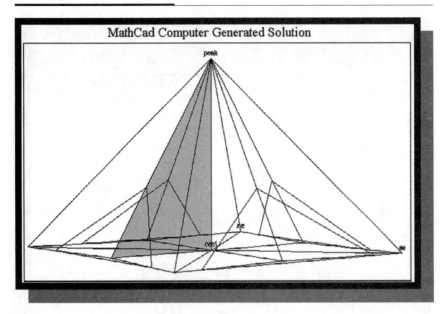

MathCad Computer Generated Solution

beyond the human audible range, the result is a harmonic conversion table of sorts between sequential octaves. If you then sort all measurable frequencies known to us using this same conversion table, you will find that the ancient Greeks and Egyptians were right to think that all things were connected through harmonic *sympathetic vibrations*. As you look down the conversion table in Figure 21-6, you can see that there is indeed a universal higher order. There is a harmonic relationship connecting the slowest waves within our brain to the highest frequencies of the spectrum. The sorted tables also raise the question of whether time itself might be just a higher octave within this harmonic series connecting us all.

If you are interested in the story behind the decoded Gann wheel and would like to learn more about harmonics in the markets, please ask for the 2-hour video I donated to the Market Technicians Association at http://www.mta.org. All proceeds go to the MTA Educational Foundation to help rebuild our industry's primary library, which was lost when the World Trade Center was destroyed. While you are welcome to explore the visuals and content of the original presentation in detail on my Web site (just click on

F i g u r e   21-5

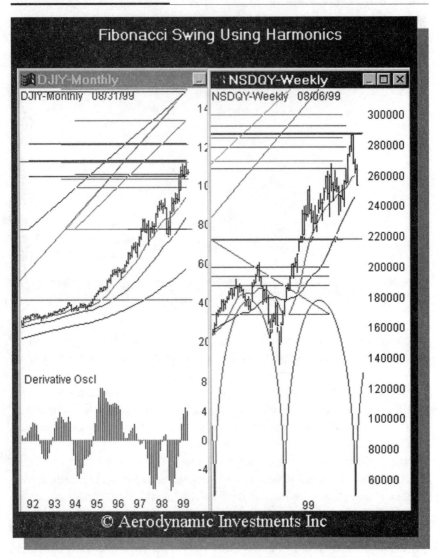

Great Market Technicians of the 21st Century: Galileo, Fibonacci, and Beethoven at www.aeroinvest.com), it would be impossible to connect the flow of the material without the audio description. The material on my Web site provides a way to study the graphics in sharp detail at your own pace after seeing the video.

F i g u r e   21-6

Note	C	D	E	F	G	A	B
Delta	.50	.562	.625	.666	.75	.833	.937
Brain	1.00	1.125	1.25	1.333	1.50	1.666	1.875
Waves	2.00	2.25	2.50	2.666	3.00	3.333	3.75
Theta wave	4.00	4.50.	5.00	5.333	6.00	6.666	7.50
Alpha wave	8.00	9.00	10.00	10.666	12.00	13.333	15.00
Beta wave	16.00	18.00	20.00	21.333	24.00	26.666	30.00
ELF	32.00	36.00	40.00	42.666	48.00	53.333	60.00
Radio	64.00	72.00	80.00	85.333	96.00	106.666	120.00
Waves	128.00	144.00	160.00	170.666	192.00	213.333	240.00
ELF	256.00	288.00	320.00	341.333	384.00	426.666	480.00
ELF	512.00	576.00	640.00	682.666	768.00	853.333	960.00
VLF	1024.00	1152.00	1280.00	1365.33	1536.00	1706.66	1920.00
Radio	2048.00	2304.00	2560.00	2730.66	3072.00	3413.33	3840.00
Waves	4096.00	4608.00	5120.00	5461.33	6144.00	6826.66	7680.00
VLF	8192.00	9216.00	10240.0	10922.6	12288.0	13653.3	15360.0
VLF	16384.0	18432.0	20480.0	21843.3	24576.0	27306.6	30720.0
VLF	32786.0	36864.0	40960.0	43686.6	49152.0	54611.3	61440.0
VLF	65536.0	73728.0	81920.0	87373.3	98304.0	109222.6	122880
VLF	131K	147K	164K	175K	197K	218K	246K
VLF	262K	295K	328K	349K	393K	437K	492K
AM radio	524K	590K	655K	699K	786K	874K	983K
AM radio	1048K	1180K	1311K	1398K	1573K	1748K	1966K
HF radio	2097K	2359K	2621K	2796K	3146K	3495K	3932K
HF radio	4194K	4719K	5243K	5592K	6291K	6990K	7864K
VHF radio	8388K	9437K	10486K	11184K	12583K	13980K	15729K
VHF radio	16777K	18874K	20972K	22367K	25166K	27961K	31457K
VHF radio	33M	38M	42M	48M	50M	56M	63M
FM TV	66M	Four	Octaves	Ultra	High	Radio	Freq.
Radar	1056M	Eight	Octaves	Micro	Wave	Radio	Freq.
IR Rays	128000	Four	Octaves	Infra	Red	Waves	9000
Visible							
UV Rays	4000	Five	Octaves	Ultra	Violet	Rays	141 Ang.

PART 7

Market Cycles and Long-Term Cycles of Importance

Market Cycles and Long-Term Cycles of Importance

A Russian by the name of Nikolai Dmytriyevich Kondratieff (1892–1930?) who worked in the Agricultural Academy and Business Research Institute in Moscow was given the daunting task of finding a means of disrupting business in capitalist economies. He focused his work on the major economies of the time: the United States, Great Britain, Germany, and France. He first considered wholesale prices and then looked at interest rates, wages, and foreign trade. He adjusted production figures to allow for population change and used a 9-year moving average (a technical analysis application) to remove statistical "noise." What he discovered is a long wave cycle that today we call the Kondratieff Economic Cycle. It showed that capitalist economies follow a cycle of 50 to 60 years with an average periodicity of about 54 years, and that nothing anyone could do was going to change this. This cycle is shown most clearly by the behavior of prices and inflation, and hence interest rates, which rise and fall over time. The maximum inflation occurs at the peak and the minimum at the trough.

Kondratieff's superiors could not accept the idea there was an inherent self-correcting mechanism perpetuating capitalism, so for his efforts he was banished to the Gulag, where he was condemned to solitary confinement. He became mentally ill and died from his cruel sentence.

Kondratieff's work would have been lost if a German translation had not been printed outside Russia in 1926. But it did not gain attention until it was published in English in 1935 and it was found that his work confirmed what was known about wholesale prices during the nineteenth century.

Three years earlier in the United Kingdom, Lord Beveridge had studied wheat prices back to the 1500s and reputedly was able to extend the work back to 1260. He too discovered many cycles and published his findings in 1921 and 1923. One of the cycles Lord Beveridge identified also occurred every 50 to 60 years *with an average periodicity of 54 years.*

You may have noticed that the length of the cycle that Kondratieff and Lord Beveridge identified is close to the Fibonacci number 55. The top perimeter of the Kondratieff Wave, 60, is also the periodicity of the Chinese calendar. This is interesting, but 60 itself is not a Fibonacci interval—or so it may seem at first glance.

The Fibonacci series 0, 1, 1, 2, 3, 5, 8 . . . can also be written $F[x]$. Starting with 0, $F[0] = 0$, $F[1] = 1$, $F[2] = 1$, $F[3] = 2$, $F[4] = 3$, and $F[5] = 5$. The series displays a variety of patterns, including several interesting cycles. For example, the sequence begins with the numbers 0, 1, 1, 2, 3, 5, and these same numbers appear *in the same order* as the final digits that repeat every 60 values.

$$F[60] = 1,548,008,755,920$$
$$F[61] = 2,504,730,781,961$$
$$F[62] = 4,052,739,537,881$$
$$F[63] = 6,557,470,319,842$$

and so on.

The same pattern holds for

$$F[120] = 5,358,359,254,990,966,640,871,840$$
$$F[121] = 8,670,007,398,507,948,658,051,921$$
$$F[122] = 14,028,366,653,498,915,298,923,761$$

and so on.

If we now divide the Fibonacci number 55 by 3, a common harmonic interval, the number 18.3 results. This is in fact the next longest economic wave. It was discovered by Simon Kuznets, an American economist. He based his analysis on real estate in America and identified a cycle of 18 years. Kuznets was awarded the Nobel Prize for his work, and the wave was subsequently named after him. There are many economic peaks and troughs that are attributed to the effects of this cycle.

Now let's consider the result when we divide the Fibonacci number 55 by 3 and then divide by 2 (the second most common harmonic interval). The result is 9.15. A French economist by the name of Clement Juglar studied the rise and fall in interest rates and prices in the 1860s. He is credited with finding the boom-to-bust period of 9 years that is now called the Juglar cycle in his honor. Juglar identified four phases in each cycle: prosperity, crisis, liquidation, and recession.

In his book *Cycles: Mysterious Forces That Trigger Events*, Edward R. Dewey tells the story of a group of investors on Wall Street in 1912 who had heard that Rothschild had a secret series of curves that he used to forecast price movements. The group hired a mathematician to break the secret Rothschild formula. The group then adopted an investment strategy that tracked a 41-month stock cycle, and was successful. Whether this story is myth or fact, the periodicity alone is interesting. In 1923 Joseph Kitchin published in the Harvard University Press the article "Review of Economic Statistics." In this article he describes a 41-month cycle that he found from the study of American and British statistics from 1890 to 1922. During this period, an independent study was being conducted by another Harvard professor, W. L. Crurn, who found a 40-month cycle in commercial paper rates in New York. This cycle is said to be about 4 years in duration and is named the Kitchin cycle.

Looking at the periodicities of these four main cycles—Kondratieff (54 years), Kuznets (18 years), Juglar (9 years) and Kitchin (4 years)—one might consider them to be harmonic. A Kondratieff wave could consist of three Kuznets waves, and one Kuznets wave could be defined by two Juglar waves that are composed of two or three lower-degree Kitchin waves. Should the sequence be in phase toward a cycle low, the coincidental impact would be the Great Crash of 1929 and the following Great Depression. So the additive nature of cycles becomes of tremendous importance. *The long-term cycles that one should be aware of that influence the markets like an ocean tide clock are the periods of 35.5, 8.88, 5.92, and 4.44 years.*

The best way to use traditional cycle analysis is to observe when the market's trend coincides with the lows of multiple cycles with different periods. When multiple cycles cluster together in phase, the price movement can accelerate to lower price objectives. However, the cycles you see are composites of numerous other cycles, some of which you may not have detected. Thus, trading on cycle placement alone is strongly advised against. Let's establish a background for using multiple cycles.

A single cycle can be thought of as a wave that produces undulating positive and negative displacement or influence on prices at regular intervals. In reality the cycle will not be perfectly symmetrical, so we focus on the cycle lows, which we see as sharp spikes down in price data, to find a frequency that seems to have a repeating pattern. Cycles with long and short periods are present in markets, and these composite cycles are created by combining waves with various periodicities to find their additive net energy. At any given time some cycles will be rising as other cycles fall. To create the composite, the various waves are added together.

In Figure 22-1 we are looking at a price grid without the price data. Drawn on the grid is a representative construction of two

F i g u r e   22-1

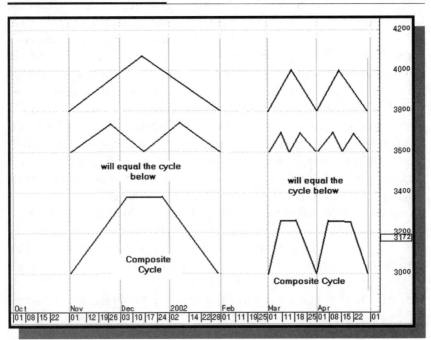

composite trading cycles. These hypothetical composite cycles are contained within the chart for General Electric. If we use a tool that looks like an arc or half circle under the price data, we can expand or contract the repeating interval lows in our half circle until we see a fit between price lows and arc lows in our cycle finder tool. Some software draws horizontal lines, which in my view are harder to use. *Keep in mind that you want to bisect price lows.* However, one cycle is insufficient because we want to develop an understanding of the composite trading cycles influencing this stock. So we add cycles with a longer period and find that they too have price lows that correspond to those of the first cycle identified. The two cycles in Figures 22-2 and 22-3 do not account for the rally into the price high. Therefore a third and longer-term

F i g u r e   22-2

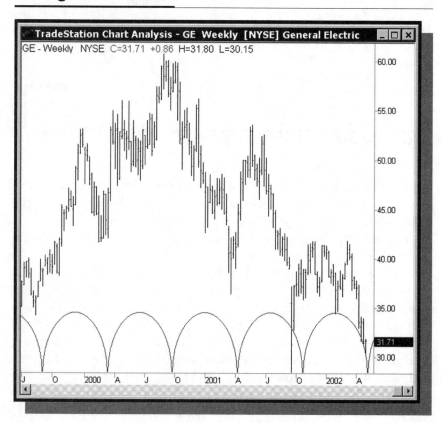

F i g u r e   22-3

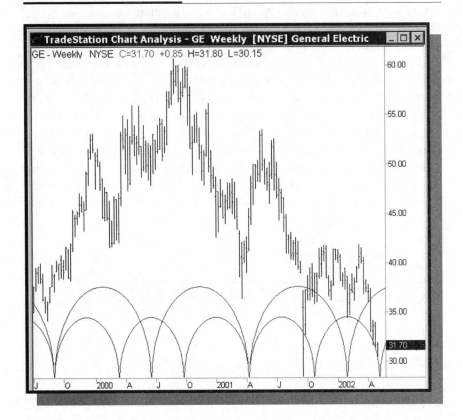

cycle must be located. In fact, there is a price low of great importance just out of view in Figures 22-2 and 22-3. In Figure 22-4 the
September 1998 price low helps us see the very long-horizon cycle
that is entering the picture. This sort of chart work is better seen in
monthly or longer bar charts.

Be aware that single fixed-period cycles can invert. This
means that a cycle that has displayed a series of regular, consistent
price lows suddenly inverts and becomes a price high. Be very
careful with the use of a single cycle. When you study the chart
closely, it will appear that GE topped at a point that is out of phase
with a dominant cycle. That is the real world of cycles, and that is
the reason that multiple cycle clusters are the best way to apply
them. It is the additive properties of cycles that are of greatest inter-

Figure   22-4

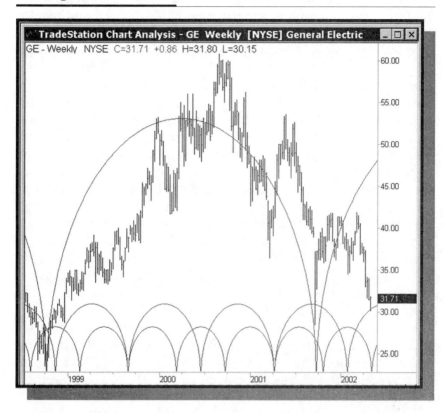

GE - Weekly NYSE C=31.71 +0.86 H=31.80 L=30.15

est. For example, three cycles with different periods that come into phase with lows at similar times might warn that a lower price projection than the one that was first calculated when the cycles were out of phase will be realized.

We use a single fixed-period cycle to set up momentum indicators. In the early chapters I suggested that when setting up Stochastics, you use an interval of 16 or 18. I suggested that because I knew it would be much closer than the default value your software vendor was likely to use. But why a period of 16 or 18? Using a cycle finder tool, determine a cycle that fits the price lows in the market you wish to chart. Most readers will be trading stocks or North American equity indices. Many financial stock indices in the United States display price lows at an interval or frequency of 32 or 34 in various time horizons, as market data has fractal properties. The way we set up a momentum indicator is to divide an identified dominant cycle length by 2 and use the result as the setup period for our indicator. So setting Stochastics near 16 before we looked at cycles in more detail was an educated guesstimate. "Stochastics happens to be fairly forgiving when you know to use half a cycle period," explains George Lane. RSI, however, will use a 14-period setup because we are reading the indicator for trend signals, which is not the way in which a majority of people will use this oscillator formula. You will read about Fibonacci cycles, where the interval is not a fixed period, but instead the period increases with each cycle projection based on the Fibonacci series. As for fixed-interval cycles, look for tight clusters of Fibonacci cycles to increase their value. In a previous chapter the Nikkei chart in Figure 19-21 uses Fibonacci cycles, in addition to the fixed-interval cycles. The same chart is found in my book *Technical Analysis for the Trading Professional*, in Figure 2-6 on page 27. The cycle periods have not been adjusted. When you study the Nikkei chart, the Fibonacci cycles are the vertical lines that bisect the data from the chart top to the bottom of the chart. You will notice that each cycle has a slightly longer period relative to its relationship with the one preceding it. The same cycles have been monitored for over five years. This means the cycles clustered together in Figure 19-21 will be extremely important.

Most people discuss cycles using fixed intervals. Another method you can explore on your own is the use of the Fibonacci series to determine the areas where a market may become magnetized and gravitate toward a low or high. Market geometry has other options, and cycles that are portrayed as circles can elongate and become elliptic in character. When the markets form a parabolic rise, the acceleration geometries will parallel an ellipse pattern and can be drawn on the price data itself. When a market fits into a channel defined by an ellipse, it is said to be in a blow-off rally. In Figure 22-5 we see the Nasdaq plotted as a line on close chart. Two ellipses originating from different price lows with different eccentricities or acceleration curves were then drawn to channel the data. Prior to the market top, I recall thinking, "This market is surely going to top before these two elliptic curves come together and cross." The price high in such an event cannot be determined, as the general public is out of control. But the smart money sits on the sidelines when the slope of the ellipse becomes vertical along with prices, waiting to jump in when the bubble bursts. Where the two elliptic curves cross is a cycle termination target that is viewed as a cluster. The Nasdaq, as you see, pressed to the convergence of these two elliptic cycles to an extreme. A market that is in a parabolic rise has only one way to end its cycle. The Nasdaq has retraced *all of the parabolic rise,* which is a normal resolution for an elliptic trend.

Market technicians are barraged with suggestions that there are social and business cycles—trying to find correlations in such wild comparisons as women's skirt lengths in North America versus the DJIA. While it appears that the DJIA is in an uptrend when higher women's hemlines are in fashion, I'd put very limited weight on such comparisons. However, there are cycles that are worthy of your attention. W. D. Gann was very aware that seasonal solstice and equinox dates frequently define price highs or lows for

F i g u r e   22-5

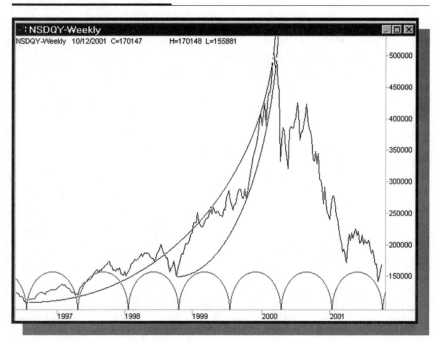

numerous markets. He also paid attention to lunar and solar eclipses, which, as I am learning firsthand, have made some rather astounding market calls for longer-term trend reversals. Agriculture traders are of course attuned to seasonal weather cycles, and massive screens showing weather patterns and conditions across the United States are displayed right on the exchange floor itself.

While cycle analysis is indeed fascinating, we do not want to invest or trade on the basis of cycle analysis alone. But through the careful review of major and minor cycles that cluster together, we may see signals that might have been overlooked in our other technical methods.

PART 8

Putting It All Together with Risk Exposure in Mind

CHAPTER 23

A Broker Has Just Recommended that You Buy a Stock. What Do You Do Next?

Your broker has just called you, all excited. He has found a stock whose fundamentals have changed for the better, and the market has been moving the symbol. Your friend recently visited this place and said that he had had a lot of fun and that it had been crowded for that time of year. You are aware that new advertisements are being placed all over your area. In fact, as you were waiting for your train this morning to take you to work, you noticed the triple billboard beckoning you to come visit Trump Casino and Resorts. Based on your broker's recommendation, the recent trending gains in the stock, and your friend's enthusiasm for the casino, you decide to buy a few shares. Product familiarity is worth a small gamble. Right?

Wrong. Thank your broker and tell him you'll get back to him after you have done your own analysis.

So where do we begin? Let's start by comparing the monthly and weekly charts with a simple 14-period RSI. Right from the start I see a common error that we need to set straight. An extremely common error made by the general public is to buy stocks trading for less than $5. This broker is getting all excited because in 2 weeks the stock has moved from $2.00 to $3.50, for a 75 percent price gain. There are so many problems with this logic that I hardly know where to begin. Brokers are not traders.

> Rule 1: Look for a stock with a win to loss ratio of no less than 3:1. In other words, you may risk $1 to make $3. For Trump Casino to make 3:1, it has to advance 300 percent. The

only thing that isn't against this stock is that the old high was $35, so at least the stock has been to the target level before and a rally is retracing this old range. But if the stock you are looking at has to advance 300 percent into new price highs where it has never traded, you would be better off visiting the casino's craps table, backing three come-out points with full odds, then rolling the dice to see what happens next. Trading is not craps.

Rule 2: The risk to reward ratio of 1:3 has a catch: The risk portion of this ratio should not exceed 3 percent of your total capital allocated for trading or investing. There is something called element-of-ruin, which means that you need to have staying power and longevity in order to play this game. Many in our industry believe Ralph Vince introduced something called the Optimum f, a way to calculate how much should be risked on any single trade. Oddly enough, this concept originally comes from Dr. Edward O. Thorpe, who wrote *The Mathematics of Gambling*, which described how many units to bet based on the current card count in blackjack. If you bet more than 3 percent of your capital on one trading idea, you will be blown out of the market because *you cannot win against time*. In the case of Trump Casino, when it hit $3.50, it fell the very next day to $2.40. In this price range the stock is too volatile, as the percentage swings in your capital would be horrific. A stock that trades at $3.50 one day and falls to $2.40 the next day has a large drawdown. (Drawdown was discussed in Chapter 1.) So even if this stock runs back to $35, you don't want any part of the advance until Rules 1 and 2 can be satisfied along with your chart criteria. The final straw is the average daily volume traded is insufficient. Go back to your broker and tell him you are not interested.

Your broker is persistent and calls you back on a different day with another stock for your consideration. He has done a lot of work and he knows that you do your own analysis now. This time he suggests you look at a stock for your opinion. The stock is trading near $34, which at first glance appears to be the ideal price level to define a double top. But don't drop this stock on first glance just because there is a potential price pattern. Do not use price patterns alone and fail to check your indicators. We covered price patterns because they add to our technical signals. However, patterns alone are not shortcuts to a final decision.

In Figure 23-1 we are looking at a chart of CMC, or Commercial Metals, which is traded on the New York Stock Exchange. On the left is the monthly chart, and on the right is a weekly view. The first thing I see is the breakout in the RSI above the old highs reserved for bear markets. (Bear market rallies top in the range 60–65. Ranges are discussed in detail in my book *Technical Analysis for the Trading Professional*.) The monthly chart RSI is at 72.93 and is not diverging with price or showing that it has reached a level that was a former high-risk indicator peak. On a monthly basis, this stock has more room on the upside. Now let's look at the weekly chart enlarged in Figure 23-2.

Interestingly, the stock in a weekly time horizon also shows that the RSI is breaking out above the old range reserved for bear markets. It is now over 72 and is not challenging former momentum

F i g u r e   23-1

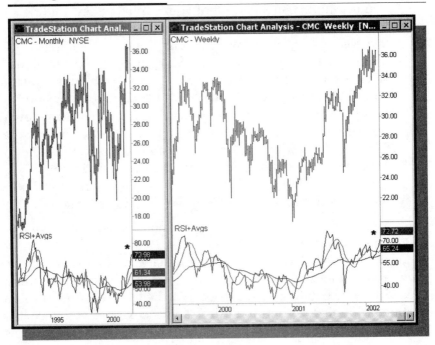

highs. There is more room on the upside in this time horizon as well. But I also see something else in this chart that you may have overlooked.

The price level where a double top once formed in 1999 and 2000 has now become a price support level in 2002. The asterisks highlight these price levels when you look from right to left through

F i g u r e   23-2

the chart. I like that a lot. So I agree that this stock has the potential to advance. The next step is to determine a level to which it should not fall so that we can calculate our risk and know when we should bail out if we are wrong.

Using Fibonacci retracements in Figure 23-3, we find that there is a support zone that coincides with the highs in June through

F i g u r e   23-3

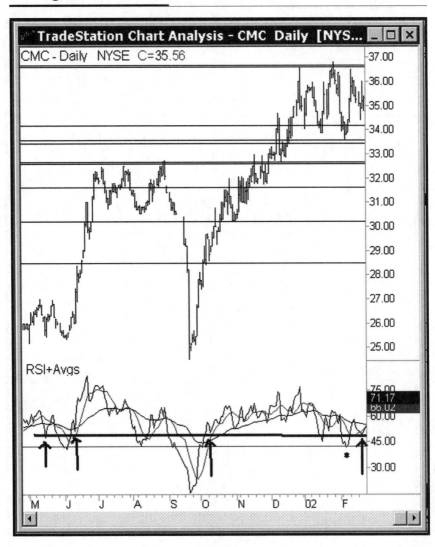

August of 2001. In December of 2001 a brief pullback shows us this former zone of resistance did indeed become support. The Fibonacci calculation is correct as the market showed respect to this area. There is also a support zone that the market recently tested in February of 2002 that is near $33.50 that is higher than the major zone just referred to. Good! We have a double zone for protection if we buy. So if the stock is bought now at current levels, it should not trade below $32.50, which is the zone that corresponds to the old highs in 2001 prior to August. OK, the risk is defined. Now we need to look at the reward side of the equation.

The daily chart in Figure 23-3 shows that the RSI has been using one specific level in the past to start numerous rallies. The heavy black arrows will make sure you do not miss them. The RSI is currently just above this zone now giving us a higher probability because the market has shown respect for this level in the RSI in the past. Also notice the test at 45 in the RSI. I am beginning to like this stock a lot for a short-term trade. So now we need to figure out where this stock could go. We need a price target to complete our risk/win ratio.

In Figure 23-4 we can make a Fibonacci extension calculation. From the low made in September 2001 up to the recent high, we can project from the recent pullback an equality or 1.00 move and a 1.618 move. The heavy solid line shows the level the swing projection is being made from; it is the same level at which resistance in 1999 became support in 2002. The price objectives are roughly 46 and 51.

If we buy near $36 and know we are wrong at $32.50, we have a loss of about $3.50. (It is "about" because stops are not always filled at the exact level at which we enter them.) If we are right and we realize the first objective at $46, we will have a $10.00 win. That means if we are wrong we risk $3.50 per share. If we are correct we gain $10 a share. The risk to reward ratio is just shy of our 1:3 guideline. How might we reduce the risk further? Do not bet the full 3 percent of our capital normally allocated to a single position. OK, this is a buy in the context of these charts in Figure 23-4, but *do not act* on this. It is an example only and not a recommendation. By the time this book has passed through the publication process, which takes up to 8 months, we will see if this real-time scenario was correct or not. If the targets are realized, indicators tell us a very deep pullback may then follow, and we will have to evaluate from scratch whether we should buy the stock again or not. The

F i g u r e   23-4

process we just reviewed of reading indicators and signals, calculating support and resistance zones, then defining specific risk to
reward targets, is the logic tree we repeat for every trade.

As you become more sophisticated, the indicators will guide
you with a depth of understanding that comes from hours of
study. You will also have several ways to calculate the risk and
reward price projections that contribute to your longevity in the
markets. But you have enough on your plate now to get you started,
and this simple example shows how you might put these technical
analysis methods together for your own purposes.

The 27 Million Dollar Lunch

Do you recall the story I shared with you about the time when I was trading during the Gulf War from a penthouse suite near the United Nations Building? Well, that story has an ending that's worth repeating. Chapter 1 began with a strong emphasis on risk management being paramount, and this is the last message I would like to impress upon you before we depart.

No matter how hard we work to excel in our ability to use technical analysis, there is a line that we must never cross. We know where that fine line is drawn, and we cross it when our judgment clouds over and the discipline that we worked so hard to develop begins to fade. The feeling that you are invincible is a sensation that creeps up your back slowly after a string of successes. Then it sits on your shoulder and whispers in your ear, saying, "You can do no wrong." Should you ever hear that small voice, pull the power cord from your monitor and leave the markets for 3 weeks. DO IT! This story may come to mind and save you from a similar fate if you cross that line.

Ego is perhaps the only rational explanation I can give for one particularly expensive lunch on Wall Street. In fact, this astonishing lunch was not for a crowd of people, or even for an extravagant couple—just for one man. One individual trader. A trader who entered a single bond order, established *no stops*, then left the building for lunch. That lunch ended up costing $27 million . . . without the tip!

This memorable lunch occurred in the summer of 1991. You have already met the diner in an earlier chapter. He owned the double penthouse suite with the awesome glass trading room overlooking the Manhattan skyline and the United Nations Building where I once worked early in my career. That day the principal of the firm entered a private order, unbeknownst to our main trading desk. This was common. However, this time he entered an order *to double his original bond position every two ticks that the market moved against him.* Then he established no stops . . . and walked out of the building for lunch!

Sure enough, the Federal Reserve elected to use this very day and lunch hour to intervene in the markets. A fast market was soon underway against him, and the brokers who had been given this order executed his instructions to the letter! POOF! He was blown out of the markets in his private account. In minutes he owed the Chicago Board of Trade $27 million. This started a chain reaction of events, as the desk was notified that his private account now had insufficient funds to cover his trade. All positions for the trading firm had to be closed immediately. The business accounts were frozen by the time the principal returned from lunch . . . 90 minutes and $27 million later.

The situation the next day was even more shocking than the events that forced the business to shut down. There was a mad scramble. Vendors and creditors were busily stripping the offices. They were ripping out the computer screens, walking away with the furniture, literally stripping the entire penthouse floor. There was a panic unfolding as creditors worked to get hold of any asset they could lay their hands on. They were like vultures stripping a carcass. Somewhere in the scramble the grand glass trading desk had been cracked, and scars marked the walls where the large computer screens had been rushed out of the room. A lone secretary was left standing guard, trying to fight off the onslaught of vultures from raiding the files and business records. She lost. The grand hardwood floors of the sunken trading room were covered with dead wires and cables from the once highly productive nerve center of a high-powered finance center. It was a case of riches to rags. Everything was gone in just 24 hours. Yet as this onslaught was taking place high above the rush of people and taxis flowing by unaware on the streets of Manhattan, the market in Chicago reversed. The same trade only 24 hours later *would have been right*. But it no longer mattered. What had happened could not be undone. The trader had been blown out of the market, and as when a fist is pulled from a pail of water, the void was already filled.

I recall shaking and showing signs of shock—not because I had lost my job, which was bad enough, but because I had witnessed the destructive power of the markets firsthand. My shock was the sudden realization and acceptance that *this could happen to anyone if his or her ego was in complete domination and control.*

The firm's principal was aggressive and dominating, and had a temperament so explosive that the broker who took the fatal order would not have dared to ignore his instructions. He was verbally, mentally, and sometimes even physically abusive. His every trade would be translated into a personal victory or great defeat and was a reflection of his own self-worth and self-esteem. When our ego is in control, we attach our very soul to a win or loss. Losses become devastating, crushing blows. He had to conquer everyone who ventured into his personal battlefield—the market— or die in the attempt. In the end he opted for the latter, and his business vanished, along with all those it supported.

In several Asian languages, *ego* literally translates into "the limited self" or "the small self." This also implies that we need to learn much more than just the mechanics of how to read a chart and the tools that guide us. Markets will teach us more about ourselves than any other endeavor or challenge we may elect to take head on. *The key is detachment.* The more we detach from ourselves, the more effective we become as traders. That's hard to do, but it is true.

The cartoon character Pogo summed it up perfectly: "We have met the enemy, and they is us." We become our own judge, jury, and executioner. The best way to keep our ego in check is to maintain a beginner's mindset. I may have years more experience than you, but I am still a student. It is only through continual preparation to the best of our ability that we can bring to the market all the courage, confidence, concentration, hope, motivation, and excitement that comes from being a successful market participant. But we must never lose the balancing edge of our respect for and slight fear of the power behind the markets.

I will never forget the lessons I learned when the grand pent-house suite was ransacked and scarred. No single trader or investor can move the markets. Thus, you need to recognize the signs of self-sabotage and ego. If you make a statement like, "I don't care what the indicators say—it's going down," that is when the market is destined to rally. I have been guilty of the same thing. As soon as I start to skip over numerous models because there is no doubt in my mind about what is going to happen, the market runs me over. Overconfidence and ego seem to go hand in hand. An open mind, a calm mind, is willing to consider other points of view before draw-ing any ironclad conclusions.

The truth is that this is what *Technical Analysis* is *All About*. We learn about ourselves, one another, and what makes our culture fit together with others that suddenly are not so distant and isolated from our own. We are indeed all connected, and the markets prove it to us every day.

The Growth of Technical Analysis in Universities and Colleges

One of the signs that technical analysis is gaining acceptance is the number of colleges and universities that are offering accredited courses. The number of new schools seeking the guidance of the Market Technicians Association (MTA) to assist them with the development of academic programs is continuing to increase. The MTA is the organization that defines our professional code of ethics and promotes the development and application of technicals for market analysis. While the MTA was founded only in 1993, it has provided the seed for the International Federation of Technical Analysts (IFTA), whose board members include several of the founders of the MTA. So the two organizations are closely linked.

Through the efforts of these organizations, a three-tier program has emerged that leads to a Chartered Market Technician (CMT) designation in the United States or a Diploma in Technical Analysis (DITA) from the international organization. I am a designated CMT, which involves either three examinations or two examinations and the option of writing an original research paper, which must be accepted for publication in the *MTA Journal*. If you have an interest in earning a CMT or DITA designation, the best place to start is by contacting the MTA in the United States or the IFTA for international candidates.

While the number of schools continues to grow to more than 30 now, this list will provide you with an idea of the acceptance and appeal that has begun to surface.

TECHNICAL ANALYSIS ACADEMIC PROGRAMS

Baruch College
Bentley College
Fort Lewis College
Fordham University in New York (Graduate School of
Business Administration)
Georgia Tech
Golden Gate University
Illinois Institute of Technology
Iona College
New York Institute of Finance
Oregon Graduate Institute
Rutgers University
University of Richmond
University of Wisconsin

COMING SOON—CURRICULUM UNDER DEVELOPMENT

Massachusetts Institute of Technology
Wharton School of Business

Some readers of this book may be in the academic environment
and have a personal interest in developing their own programs.
You may also have an interest in contacting a professional organization and becoming part of the sharing of ideas and guidance that
occurs when people with similar interests come together. This list
will provide you with Internet addresses and names for some of
the growing number of international and North American societies
that have emerged since the Market Technicians Association was
founded in New York City.

TECHNICAL ANALYSIS ORGANIZATIONS

United States: Market Technicians Association
http://www.mta.org

International: International Federation of Technical
Analysts (IFTA), http://www.ifta.org

Australia: Australian Technical Analysts Association
http://www.ataa.com.au

Canada: Canadian Society of Technical Analysts
http://www.csta.org

Germany: German Technical Analysis Society
http://www.vtad.net

Hong Kong: Technical Analysis Society (Hong Kong) Ltd.
http://www.tashk.com.hk

Italy: SAIT, the Italian Society in IFTA
http://www.siat.org

Japan: Nippon Technical Analysts Association
http://www.ntaa.gr.jp

New Zealand: Society of Technical Analysts of New Zealand
Incorporated, http://www.stanz.co.nz

Switzerland: Swiss Association of Market Technicians
http://www.ifta.org/SAMT/default.htm

U.K.: Society of Technical Analysts in the UK.
http://www.sta-uk.org

INDEX

ABOUT THE AUTHOR

Connie Brown, CMT (Chartered Market Technician), is president of Aerodynamic Investments Inc. Ms. Brown has been an active institutional trader in the financial markets for over 15 years.

Ms. Brown is on the *Market Technicians Association (MTA) Journal* review board, the industry's professional publication for technical analysts. Her second book, *Technical Analysis for the Trading Professional*, was selected by the MTA as required reading to prepare for the third and final examination that awards professionals the industry's Chartered Market Technician accreditation.

Ms. Brown continues to actively trade managing a QEP hedge fund, and advises numerous financial institutions and banks in Europe, Asia, and the United States.